# The Novels of Harriet Beecher Stowe

# The
# Novels of
# Harriet Beecher Stowe

### 〰 *Alice C. Crozier* 〰

New York · Oxford University Press · 1969

*To my mother and father*

# Preface

Uncle Tom was killed by Simon Legree because he would not inform on his escaped fellow slaves, Cassy and Emmeline. Tom does not deny that he knows where they are; he does refuse to betray them, knowing that Legree will kill him. The reason that Tom is today regarded as a symbol of the cowardly, boot-licking slave is that he forgives Legree: " 'Mas'r, if you was sick, or in trouble, or dying, and I could save ye, I'd *give* ye my heart's blood; and, if taking every drop of blood in this poor old body would save your precious soul, I'd give 'em freely, as the Lord gave his for me.' " The "self-sacrificing love" which to Harriet Beecher Stowe was the most lofty Christian virtue and with which she so generously endowed her hero, Uncle Tom, is often regarded today as neurotic or deceitful or both.

Uncle Tom's detractors might well approve of his action; what puts them off is his talk. The two cannot be separated, however, without losing sight of his motive, which is the key to what Mrs. Stowe calls his "martyrdom." Tom dies, as Mrs. Stowe believed Christ died, sustained by God and moved to bear his pain that others might live. Tom is motivated by Christian love. He exists for no other purpose than to demonstrate to the reader that such love is powerful enough to reconcile the bitter members of a society on the verge of civil war. This is the message of the novel. Today, few people would find that message believable (Mrs.

Stowe herself rejected it four years later in *Dred*), but, ironically, we still use her melodramatic and evangelical language, not as professing believers but rather as secular critics who seek to convey a sense of importance or urgency by using such words as damnation, salvation, guilt and redemption. One thing we need to be aware of, and rereading Mrs. Stowe's work reminds us, is what such language and such feeling once meant.

There is another source of interest for the reader with a taste for literary history. Mrs. Stowe was a contemporary of the great mid-century authors. Born in 1811, she was eight years younger than Emerson, seven years younger than Hawthorne, six years older than Thoreau and eight years older than Whitman and Melville. Our fascination with the work of these men, who were so unusual in their time, has made us quite accustomed to the figure of the American artist unread and misunderstood in his own time. Not only would this be notably true of Hawthorne and Melville, and somewhat also of Whitman and Thoreau, especially given Whitman's hope of reaching a proletarian audience, but it would be true too of such major figures later in the century as Emily Dickinson or Henry James; even Mark Twain was seen by Van Wyck Brooks as "alienated," and to a degree the argument still persuades. In contrast, then, to such people who were writing at the same time as she was, Mrs. Stowe's work leads us to examine what was popular, what did sell and was admired by critics and readers of the day. This book points out two main features of Mrs. Stowe's work that can be taken to typify what was generally expected and accepted in the fiction of her time. The first is that her novels are historical novels, in the tradition of Scott. The second and more important factor is the paramount importance of Byron. It was Byron, not Wordsworth, who mattered to Mrs. Stowe's contemporaries, and the reasons are extremely significant. We have tended to underestimate Byron's preeminence among nineteenth-century readers, specifically including the general or mass audience of the time, and the result has been a distortion of our understanding of the period. Because Mrs. Stowe was not a great original literary genius, because she often wrote carelessly and uncritically responded to the fashions of her day, she reflects those fashions clearly. This is not to say that Mrs. Stowe's fame rested on the literary opinions of the readers of *Godey's Lady's Book*. She was respected by a majority of educated critics and readers. She wrote in what we might call the mainstream of American fiction in the first half of the nineteenth century.

And then, with one stroke, she permanently discredited herself by her celebrated article, "The True Story of Lady Byron's Life." It was rash to make the revelations she made in that article, and in the book that followed it the next year, but Mrs. Stowe hoped to assist one in undeserved disgrace, Lady Byron, and also to help in the work of divine justice before which the magnificent poet's sins must eventually be confessed. It is not an exaggeration to say that, since she made that confession on Lord Byron's behalf, she has not, except by a handful of critics, been taken seriously as a writer. The article was written in the summer of 1869. It is time Mrs. Stowe's work was reconsidered.

Students of the late Perry Miller will recognize at once my very large debt to his books, his lectures, and even his conversation. Nobody who studied with Miller for seven years as I did could fail to be not only instructed by his learning but also inspired by his expectations of what the study of American literature could accomplish. I am very much indebted too to Professor Kenneth B. Murdock, who was also my teacher at Harvard. Dr. Barbara M. Solomon of Radcliffe invited me to read the letters and papers in the Beecher-Stowe Collection and generously discussed them with me. For quotations from the material in the Beecher-Stowe Collection I acknowledge the permission of Mr. David B. Stowe and of the Schlesinger Library, Radcliffe College. I am grateful to the American Association of University Women for a fellowship at an early stage of my work. The Research Council of Rutgers University provided a grant for typing of the manuscript. My especial thanks are due to Miss Delight Ansley for preparing the index. Mrs. June Trax assisted me by prompt and accurate typing of the manuscript. I am glad here formally to record my thanks to my husband, Robert E. Crozier, for his critical reading of all versions of the manuscript. My most rigorous and patient teachers have been my parents, to whom the book is dedicated.

A. C. C.

New Brunswick, N. J.
July 1969

# Contents

Table of Contents

*The Novels of Harriet Beecher Stowe*

# CHAPTER 1

# Uncle Tom's Cabin; *or,*
## *History in the Making*

*F*or most people today, any mention of *Uncle Tom's Cabin* brings to mind a sensational, highly sentimental polemic against the enormities of Southern slavery, which in its day moved millions to tears of pity or outrage by a melodramatic tale of such crude intensity that it has become a part of the folklore of the Western world. We may think of the book as a fantastic even fanatic representation of Southern life, memorable more for its emotional oversimplification of the complexities of the slave system than for artistry or for insight. The tremendous sales of the novel at the time, its contemporary reputation among critics both English and American, and its allegedly explosive political influence seem to us to be due to the inflammable state of the public mind in this country only nine years before the outbreak of the Civil War. It would be an error to disown these recollections. Even today *Uncle Tom's Cabin* carries great emotional force and continues to affect our consciences and our regional pride.

In seeking to understand Mrs. Stowe's achievement as a novelist and a polemicist, we need sufficient historical imagination to restrain the modern reader's impatience with the extravagance of some of the language of Victorian sentimentality. We should also, however, be aware that the effectiveness of the novel does not now and never did chiefly derive from fantasy or from exaggerated emotion. A contemporary reader would have been more tolerant of various turns of incident and phrase which may strike the mid-twentieth-century reader as incredible or clumsy. Nonetheless, we cannot assume that the impact of *Uncle Tom's Cabin* was due to the gullibility or maudlin taste of its early readers. What seemed significant to them was, on the contrary, the novel's apparent accuracy, the impression it conveyed of an authentic piece of reporting.

This was the issue over which debate immediately began in 1852, and even during the serial publication, when Southern audiences angrily attacked Mrs. Stowe's scenes of Southern life as gross misrepresentation. They said, essentially, that conditions in the slave-holding states were not as she had pictured them, that the novel purported to be not fiction but a record of real life, and that, as such, it was a pack of lies. Quickly, various Southern writers produced answering novels filled with scenes which told the real truth about the slaves and their masters. What is interesting is that the novel was taken to be a factual account of the slave system even by its enemies. We must bear in mind that Southerners were accustomed to political and moralistic attacks on slavery and that they answered these with corresponding arguments. Their reaction to *Uncle Tom's Cabin* implies that the sting of this novel, the reason it was so hated, was that it unfolded such a convincing picture of Southern society.

Mrs. Stowe had certainly meant it that way. As the attacks on her veracity multiplied, so did her determination to prove her own literal accuracy. Even before the serial publication was complete, she wrote a preliminary rejoinder to her accusers which appears as the final chapter in the hard-cover edition. The chapter, entitled "Concluding Remarks," begins candidly,

The writer has often been inquired of, by correspondents from different parts of the country, whether this narrative is a true one; and to these inquiries she will give one general answer.

The separate incidents that compose the narrative are, to a very great extent, authentic, occurring, many of them, either under her own observation, or that of her personal friends.[1]

The following year, 1853, Mrs. Stowe compiled a longer defense which she called *The Key to Uncle Tom's Cabin* and in which she adduced various 'proof-texts'—transcripts of court cases, eye-witness accounts of events on which episodes in the novel were based, handbills which offered rewards for fugitive slaves or mentioned dog hunts. The novel was received in the spirit in which it was intended, as a documentary.

The nature of Mrs. Stowe's self-awareness as a writer, and of her views on the fictional practice of her contemporaries, she herself indicates quite bluntly in her comments on the past life of Augustine St. Clare. St. Clare is introduced as the son of a wealthy Louisiana planter, originally from Canada, and of a Huguenot mother. As a young man he had fallen in love with a beautiful woman whose guardian had wickedly told him that she was about to be married to another. He had thereupon thrown himself into fashionable society and married the cold Marie, only to discover too late that his true love had evaded the schemes of her guardian and still waited for him. He is left a disheartened, ineffectual man. Following the narrative of this trite tale, Mrs. Stowe remarks coolly,

And thus ended the whole romance and ideal of life for Augustine St. Clare. But the *real* remained,—the *real,* like the flat, bare, oozy tide-mud, when the blue sparkling wave, with all its company of gliding boats and white-winged ships, its music of oars and chiming waters, has gone down, and there it lies, flat, slimy, bare,—exceedingly real.

Of course, in a novel, people's hearts break, and they die, and that is the end of it; and in a story this is very convenient. But in real life we do not die when all that makes life bright dies to us. There is a most busy and important round of eating, drinking, dressing, walking, visiting, buying, selling, talking, reading, and all that makes up what is commonly called *living,* yet to be gone through. . . .²

She loves the romantic, the sentimental, the gorgeous, but she knows that after the music of oars and chiming waters comes the flat, bare, oozy tide-mud, and it is this knowledge that she feels most reliable and most familiar. Throughout her writing, and certainly throughout *Uncle Tom's Cabin,* her primary allegiance is to "real life" as she understands the term, that is, real life as distinguished from the false comforts of literature. That this mistrust of fiction reflects the more explicit suspicions of the colonial clergy concerning *belles lettres* is doubtless true. Properly speaking, it reflects the attitude of the late eighteenth century and of Dr. Lyman Beecher and his colleagues that fiction and poetry were desirable as long as they served some elevated purpose. The great example of an admirable author would of course be Milton, but Scott was admired in the Beecher household and so was Byron, in addition to Cotton Mather and the Bible. Yet, despite her familiarity from childhood with some of the best of English literature, Mrs. Stowe did not think of *Uncle Tom's Cabin* at the time she wrote it as a work of literature except in a very secondary sense. She thought of it as a work of salvation. As an author she would have called herself a historian.

The way in which Mrs. Stowe's notion of history affects the message of the novel as well as its style derives from her familiarity with the writing of providential history, a popular form among New England Puritans from the earliest days of the colonies. In this tradition, Mrs. Stowe sees herself as setting down the events of her time in order that her contemporaries and descendants might understand the role of these events in the total scheme of human history from the Fall to the Final Judgment. Thus, she speaks with the prophets of old, reminding the nation of its historical commitments, recording its present struggles, warning of the impending wrath of the Almighty if the nation should betray its covenant and its destiny. The novel is a historical novel in that the events which it records are inevitably events in the unfolding drama of providential history. It is a documentary novel in that these events must be recorded completely accurately. It is a polemic, therefore, because to record the events of the present in their providential perspective is to point the way toward the proper fulfillment of the nation's destiny. Bradford of Plymouth Plantation characteristically sees his band of pilgrims as heroically carrying out an appointed destiny. Later New England writers and orators, ever mindful of their historical obligations, found their contemporaries to have deviated from the ordained course, and exhorted them in the tones of Jeremiah and Amos to return to it or prepare for the rebukes of an outraged God. In essence, then, Mrs. Stowe defines her task as a novelist as that of setting down, in an almost encyclopedic spirit, the institution of American slavery in order to move the nation to recognize, and therefore purge, the corruptions slavery has engendered in the national life. She assumes, correctly, that Southerners as well as Yankees are aware of the nation's covenant with God and she urges all alike to cleanse themselves and renew their historical purpose.

It is no news to anyone that *Uncle Tom's Cabin* is a polemic. Nevertheless, it is useful to clarify the grounds of the argument, and, lest it still be supposed by some that *Uncle Tom's Cabin* is an anti-Southern book, to identify just who is being attacked. This can most readily be done by studying the many references in the novel to the Declaration of Independence and the subjects Mrs. Stowe associates with it. It is also natural to inquire into the remedies, proposed or implied, to which the polemic leads; these are conveyed most clearly through the novel's sentimental heroine, little Eva, and secondarily by the words and example of that "moral miracle," Uncle Tom.

The argument is often introduced by a scene or picture. The

strategy is illustrated by one of the scenes on the boat which is taking Uncle Tom from Kentucky to New Orleans. Among the slaves whom Haley has bought and is taking to market is a young woman named Lucy with a baby, whom Haley sells to a man on the boat. This man explains that his " 'cook lost a youn 'un last week,—got drownded in a wash-tub, while she was a hangin' out clothes,—and I reckon it would be well enough to set her to raisin' this yer.' " [3] Haley steals the baby while Lucy is asleep and sells him. Mrs. Stowe expects the reader's wrath to rise at this tale, and she quickly points the moral.

The trader had arrived at that stage of Christian and political perfection which has been recommended by some preachers and politicians of the north, lately, in which he had completely overcome every humane weakness and prejudice. . . . The wild look of anguish and utter despair that the woman cast on him [when she discovered the sale] might have disturbed one less practised; but he was used to it. He had seen that same look hundreds of times. You can get used to such things, too, my friend; and it is the great object of recent efforts to make our whole northern community used to them, for the glory of the Union. [4]

For the glory of the Union! The ogre, then, is Daniel Webster. Who is to blame? Webster, yes, but also "you" dear reader who allow yourself to rejoice in the glory of the Union.

Mrs. Stowe never makes a point just once. Several pages later, when Haley discovers that the woman has jumped overboard and drowned herself, we are told that Haley's response was

to consider himself an ill-used man, decidedly; but there was no help for it, as the woman had escaped into a state which *never will* give up a fugitive,—not even at the demand of the whole glorious Union. . . .

'He's a shocking creature, isn't he,—this trader? so unfeeling! It's dreadful, really!'

'O, but nobody thinks anything of these traders! They are universally despised,—never received into any decent society.'

But who, sir, makes the trader? Who is most to blame? The enlightened, cultivated, intelligent man, who supports the system of which the trader is the inevitable result, or the poor trader himself? You make the public sentiment that calls for his trade, that debauches and depraves him, till he feels no shame in it; and in what are you better than he? [5]

Thus it is the system itself that is evil, and its most corrupt members are neither the trader nor the slaveholder but rather the pious, educated, respectable citizenry of North and South who self-righteously despise the brutish trader but who are too smug and too selfish to disturb their own complacency on behalf of reform. The polemic attacks the reader.

In the South, according to Mrs. Stowe, the educated, right-minded people are equally as ineffectual as in the North. Augustine St. Clare, who is her type of the "best" Southerner, had inherited, with his brother, Alfred, his father's huge plantation, where he had been so disturbed by the conditions of slavery that he had tried to make various humane improvements. Finally, Alfred and he had had to agree that he was too softhearted to make any money at all as a planter, and Augustine had left the plantation for a large family house in New Orleans. He and his brother are very different temperamentally, but they agree on one thing, that "the first verse of a republican's catechism, 'All men are born free and equal!'" is nonsense. Alfred St. Clare calls it "'one of Tom Jefferson's pieces of French sentiment and humbug. It's perfectly ridiculous to have that going the rounds among us, to this day.'" Augustine agrees that the situation is ridiculous, but for the reason that it is in fact not true; in the society around him all men are simply not free and not equal. Yet, unlike his brother, Augustine believes that they ought to be; he believes in the Jeffersonian principle, but as he confesses to his Vermont cousin "'it's up and down with me,—up to heaven's gate in theory, down to earth's dust in practice.'" [6]

For Mrs. Stowe this point gets, in another way, to the heart of the matter. Augustine St. Clare, like the well educated and idealistic Northern gentleman, believes in certain principles which Mrs. Stowe associates with the Declaration of Independence, principles concerning liberty and inalienable rights, and the consent of the governed. These principles have, she says, lost their force. In the mouths of political orators, particularly those whose hearts swell to the glory of the Union, they have become a mockery of the revolutionary spirit which brought them forth. The Declaration of Independence represents to her mind the true national ideal, of which the rhetoric of the glory of the Union is a horrible perversion.

The educated slaves, she thinks, are fully aware of this corruption of principles. Eliza's husband George, who is the highly literate son of a white planter and a slave mother and is said to have invented a fine machine for cleaning hemp, escapes from a brutal master and meets his former employer in a tavern. The employer, another good-hearted but weak-minded individual, urges George to go back to his master because, as he says, " 'you're running an awful risk' " and " 'going to break the laws of your country!' " To this charitable counsel George replies: " 'My country again! Mr. Wilson, *you* have a country. . . . Haven't I heard your Fourth-of-July speeches? Don't you tell us all, once a year, that governments derive their just power from the consent of the governed? Can't a fellow *think*, that hears such things? Can't he put this and that together, and see what it comes to?' " Mrs. Stowe adds, "Mr. Wilson's mind was one of those that may not unaptly be represented by a bale of cotton,—downy, soft, benevolently fuzzy and confused. He really pitied George with all his heart, . . . but he deemed it his duty to go on talking *good* to him, with infinite pertinacity." [7]

The theme of the corruption of Jeffersonian idealism by the political leaders of the mid-century is first introduced in the novel in an oblique way by Sam, the Shelby's comical slave. He is de-

claiming to the other slaves about his heroism in saving Eliza
from Haley:

'Yer see, fellow-countrymen . . . yer see, now, what dis yer chile
's up ter, for fendin' yer all,—yes, all on yer. For him as tries to
get one o' our people, is as good as tryin' to get all; yer see the
principle's de same. . . .

He develops several elevating arguments, after the manner of
the popular orator, concluding with a rising peroration:

'Yes, my feller-citizens and ladies of de other sex in general, I has
principles,—I'm proud to 'oon 'em,—they's perquisite to dese yer
times, and ter *all* times. I has principles, and I sticks to 'em like
forty,—jest anything that I thinks is principle, I goes in to 't;—I
wouldn't mind if dey burnt me 'live,—I'd walk right up to de stake,
I would, and say, here I comes to shed my last blood fur my principles, fur my country, fur der gen'l interests of s'ciety.' [8]

This scene is immediately followed by the one in which Eliza,
in the middle of the night, comes to the house of Senator Bird
of Ohio, and in which Mrs. Stowe attacks the inhumanity of the
Fugitive Slave Act for which, of course, the good senator has
voted in Washington.

Our good senator in his native state had not been exceeded by any
of his brethren at Washington, in the sort of eloquence which has
won for them immortal renown! How sublimely he had sat with
his hands in his pockets, and scouted all sentimental weakness of
those who would put the welfare of a few miserable fugitives before
great state interests! [9]

In the irony of the slave Sam's proud imitation of the language of his oppressors and the sarcasm of this reference to
Bird's eloquence, Mrs. Stowe continues the argument against
the political rhetoric of her day wherein the language of the past
has so lost its original meaning that it is now used to conceal

the injustice and wickedness of slavery. Not only is the nation guilty of enslaving many of its people; it defends this enslavement in the language of liberty. Moreover, this falsehood is compounded when it is perpetrated by United States senators, the very men who are supposed to be the elected guardians of the republican tradition. Like so many Northerners and Abolitionists, Mrs. Stowe is most outraged by Daniel Webster in whose famous defense of the Compromise of 1850 and in particular of the constitutionality of the Fugitive Slave Act she saw that most hateful of sights, the figure of one of her own kind, a Yankee and a New Hampshire man, turned traitor. The feeling against Webster in the cities of New England was at its most wrathful at exactly the period of the writing of *Uncle Tom's Cabin*. Indeed, the passionate outcry against the Fugitive Slave Act was the seminal force in bringing her to begin the novel. Webster's eloquence alone was enough to infuriate the Abolitionists, and, when coupled with a firmly reasoned legal defense of the provisions of the Compromise, it set them to howling. Only two generations ago, Mrs. Stowe remembers, men had "shed their blood for their principles, their country and the general interests of society." They had spoken with eloquence about liberty and the rights of citizens against tyranny and oppression. Their language and principles had carried them through a victorious war. But now, in 1852, orators such as the infamous Webster have abused and falsified this tradition and have made laws which are the vehicle not of freedom but of oppression. The very concept of the Union itself has become antithetical to that earlier concept of a free and independent nation for which the Revolution was fought. In Sam's slapstick imitation of stump oratory, we hear the hollowness of his models and the insensitivity of those Unionist apologists who parrot phrases which have lost their meaning. The clergy, lawyers, gentlemen, and congressmen whose education and professed idealism should put them most in touch with the original truth of these phrases have lost faith and now deny them. And this betrayal, as Mrs. Stowe sees it, is most odious not in the South but in the North.

It is interesting, in connection with this Revolutionary motif, to consider Edmund Wilson's recent discussion, in *Patriotic Gore,* of the thinking of Alexander Stephens, the Vice-President of the Confederacy. Wilson speaks of Stephens, and to some extent also of Robert E. Lee, as "Romans," referring to their profound and inflexible moral integrity. Yet all Americans were also in the habit of referring to the Founding Fathers as Romans and of making solemn analogies between that ancient republic and their own. Wilson argues that Stephens thought of the Civil War, first and last, as a fight to uphold the integrity of the republican ideal against the imperious encroachments of the tyrannical Washington government. Stephens, like Cato, spoke in the name of the pure, noble statesmen of the early republic.[10]

For both Stephens and Mrs. Stowe, the example of Jefferson and the Founding Fathers dictates opposition to the Unionist policies of the Washington government. Yet, whereas for Stephens the corollary is the rejection of all imposition of one group on another, for Mrs. Stowe the appeal to Jeffersonian principle demands that the government shall abandon its wrong policy in order to impose the right one. Mrs. Stowe's reading of history here, so different from Stephens's, reflects her New England origins. She remembers those Fourth of July celebrations which every year of her childhood began with a reading of the Declaration of Independence. She remembers too that, in their speeches on the glorious Fourth, the village orators roused their audiences to renewed dedication to their heroic Revolutionary past in exactly the same manner as for nearly two centuries the ministers of New England had regularly called for a renewed commitment to the great covenant with God. In Mrs. Stowe's mind at least, it matters not, in 1852, that once upon a time the colonial clergy had denounced Jefferson and his party as atheists.

Much water had flowed under the dam since those days; the devil had allied himself with quite other men in the course of half a century, and for the writer of *Uncle Tom's Cabin* Jeffersonian idealism is part and parcel with the noble example of the past.

Mrs. Stowe's relation to the religious history of New England is in any case complex, as much so as that history had itself become by the time of her birth in Litchfield, Connecticut, in 1811, but it is possible at this point to consider her connection to this history in one respect: the continuation of the formulae of the old Jeremiad into nineteenth-century revival preaching and into *Uncle Tom's Cabin*. In this respect, Mrs. Stowe inherits directly from her father.

Lyman Beecher, D.D. was born in 1775, the son of David Beecher, blacksmith of New Haven. He was a descendant of Hannah Beecher and her son John who had gone to New Haven with the first settlers in 1638. Two days after Lyman was born his mother died of tuberculosis and he was taken to live with his Aunt and Uncle Lot Benton on a farm near Guilford. He entered Yale in 1793 when there was a great enthusiasm among the students for the French rationalists—Voltaire, d'Alembert, Tom Paine, and others—but in 1795 Timothy Dwight replaced the tolerant Ezra Stiles as president of Yale and immediately the most rigorous piety was enjoined. Lyman was converted in one of the student revivals and, after a brief pastorate in Easthampton, Long Island (then part of Connecticut), soon became the Congregational minister in Litchfield. At that time (1810), Connecticut was still under the Standing Order, the legacy of the old Puritan theocracy whereby the Congregational church was tax-supported and all other denominations were not tolerated; and according to which it had ever been the business of the clergy to discourse on public laws and national sins. Thus Lyman entered the ministry in the days when it still held sway not only in matters of the soul but in questions of politics, law, social custom and personal ethics. Under the Standing Order, and when Harriet was born it had been standing for 170 years in Connecticut, the church considered itself authoritative in public as well as in private life.

When, in 1819, the followers of Jefferson defeated the candidates of the Standing Order in Connecticut and all the churches were deprived of state support and religion was declared a matter of private conscience, the energies of the clergy remained bound up with the public welfare. Preaching the gospel became their main activity, and the evangelical message was spread across the land and abroad. Revival sermons called for immediate action; come forward sinners and be saved. The message was personal in that it was addressed to individuals rather than to settled communities, but its content very often included a program for socially uplifting action. One of the most prominent revival preachers in the country in his day, Lyman Beecher belonged to the old public-minded tradition, and led the way in reform causes of all sorts, including Temperance, the Home Mission Society, schools for the blind and many others.

Lyman Beecher's thought and personality were a seminal force in the lives of his children. All of his seven sons eventually entered the ministry, some after considerable resistance. Among his daughters, Catharine became a pioneer crusader in the cause of women's education, and Isabella was a moving, if somewhat turbulent, spirit in the Suffrage movement. Only the second daughter, Mary, stayed out of public life entirely. The nature of his influence on Harriet is suggested in an almost uncanny way by one of his first public tirades. The eager young minister just out of Yale and beginning his first pastorate found himself appalled by the Burr-Hamilton duel and by dueling in general.

Dueling is a great national sin. With the exception of a small section of the Union, the whole land is defiled with blood. From the lakes of the north to the plains of Georgia is heard the voice of lamentation and woe—the cries of widows and the fatherless. This work of desolation is performed often by men in office, by the appointed guardians of life and liberty. On the floor of Congress challenges have been threatened if not given, and thus powder and ball have been introduced as the auxiliaries of deliberation and argument. . . . A duelist may be a gambler, a prodigal, a fornicator, an adulterer, a drunkard and a murderer and not violate the laws of honor.[11]

Fifty years later Harriet Beecher said almost exactly the same things about slavery. It was a national sin; the whole land was defiled with blood (by her time there were apparently no exceptions); daily one heard the cries of widows and the motherless. Moreover, said the daughter, "this work of desolation is performed by men in office," by the defenders of the Fugitive Slave Act and others of those "appointed guardians" who now sacrifice humane feeling to prudent legislation. Just as the duelist may be the worst sort of villain, even a murderer, and not violate the laws of honor, so in 1852, the laws have become so infamous that one positively must be a virtual murderer in order not to violate the Fugitive Slave Act.

To set the argument against slavery in *Uncle Tom's Cabin* in the context of the traditional denunciation of backsliding is to imply that the remedy which Mrs. Stowe proposes is the traditional remedy, the return to the noble example of the past. In political terms this is what she does suggest, although rather vaguely. She would like to see the political leaders of the nation speak and behave as she believes their grandfathers did. But she has no program for the freeing of the slaves. Her remedy is stated in quite other than political terms; it is a religious solution. It relies here too on the example of the colonial past to some extent, yet, in *Uncle Tom's Cabin,* the Christian solution to slavery is expressed primarily in nineteenth-century evangelical terms.

The chapter entitled "Evangeline" introduces the book's evangelical heroine, little Eva. Little Eva is not intended to be realistic in the sense of common or familiar; she is, first and last, extraordinary. She she is sweeter, purer, prettier, frailer, and much holier than anyone else. Mrs. Stowe meets our incredulity head-on: "Has there ever been a child like Eva? Yes, there have been; but their names are always on grave stones. . . ." If this is a perplexing answer, we are given abundant explanation.

It is as if heaven had an especial band of angels, whose office it was to sojourn for a season here, and endear to them the wayward human heart, that they might bear it upward with them in their homeward flight. When you see that deep, spiritual light in the eye, —when the little soul reveals itself in words sweeter and wiser than the ordinary words of children,—hope not to retain that child; for the seal of heaven is on it, and the light of immortality looks out from its eyes.[12]

Eva, the first and most famous of a long line of angelic heroines in the works of Harriet Beecher Stowe, has many interesting attributes. One of them is that she must die. Anticipation of death keeps the halo of the heroine's special goodness bright, and the advent of death completes and justifies the message which she speaks. The "light of immortality" would otherwise fade into common day. Death heightens the idea of a special destiny for which the heroine had to die and gives her an aura of saintliness, even martyrdom.

The most conspicuous attribute of little Eva is her piety. Throughout the book, whenever Eva appears, all humor vanishes from Mrs. Stowe's voice and solemn sentences attest the virtues of the child. An example of Eva's special behavior is her reaction to the story which old Prue has told to Tom about her child's death and which Tom tells Eva who, characteristically, appears with "a crown of tuberoses on her head, and her eyes radiant with delight."

Tom, in simple, earnest phrases, told Eva the woman's history. She did not exclaim, or wonder, or weep, as other children do. Her cheeks grew pale, and a deep, earnest shadow passed over her eyes. She laid both hands on her bosom, and sighed heavily.[13]

Which is to imply that Eva has understood all the sufferings of slavery and the sin and is doing a private penance. Eva is no reformer. To the extent that she represents a "right" response to slavery she stands for a society made up of pure Christians like herself among whom, it goes without saying, there would be no conflict or evil of any kind.

Eva's gospel is simplicity itself. On her deathbed, surrounded by her weeping slaves and parents, Eva delivers her creed with all the public presence of one who had long awaited this moment:

'I sent for you all, my dear friends . . . because I love you. I love you all; and I have something to say to you, which I want you always to remember. . . . I am going to leave you. In a few more weeks, you will see me no more—

. . . I want to speak to you about your souls. . . . Many of you, I am afraid, are very careless. You are thinking only about this world. I want you to remember that there is a beautiful world, where Jesus is. I am going there, and you can go there. It is for you, as much as me. But, if you want to go there, you must not live idle, careless, thoughtless lives. You must be Christians. You must remember that each one of you can become angels, and be angels forever.'

Again she says, " 'I know . . . you all love me.' 'Yes; oh yes! indeed we do! Lord bless her!' " At this point Eva, as it were, breaks bread. She gives them each " 'a curl of my hair; and, when you look at it, think that I loved you and am gone to heaven, and that I want to see you all there.' " For her father there is a special lesson. Eva asks him if he is a Christian, to which he replies, " 'What is being a Christian, Eva?' 'Loving Christ most of all,' said Eva." [14]

The key word is love: She loves them, they love her, she loves Christ, Christ loves everybody; to grasp the meaning of this love is to enter a world of peace and joy both in this life and the next. It is socially as well as spiritually efficacious. Just as each one of them can become an angel, so, when they are all loving Christians, there will be no possibility of conflict among them. This kind of love, essentially parental, is expressed by all the mothers in the book and by Uncle Tom. Tom, on his deathbed, passes on the lesson to young George Shelby who has come too late to bring him back to Kentucky. Speaking first of Chloe and then of his children, Tom says,

'Tell 'em all to follow me—follow me! Give my love to Mas'r, and dear good Missis, and everybody in the place! Ye don't know! 'Pears like I loves 'em all! I loves every creatur', everywhar!—it's nothing *but* love! O, Mas'r George! what a thing 't is to be a Christian!' [16]

Another attribute of the angelical Eva which accompanies this religious love is what Mrs. Stowe calls her naturalness. Eva is a heroine of feeling and her feelings are always spontaneous, unreasoned, intuitive. This is what makes them good. In Edwards's theology, spontaneity is one of the distinguishing features of the holy affections. Mrs. Stowe was certainly well acquainted with Edwards's treatises on the religious affections and on the nature of true virtue, but she was probably more fond of his famous description of his wife as a young girl. Edwards of course believed very much in the doctrine of election, which states that only those few souls are saved who are given special grace. For Edwards that grace chiefly consists in a new heart which God gives to the elected person and which manifests itself in spontaneous piety, spontaneous in the sense that it is caused by God and not by any volitional act of that person or any other person.

Mrs. Stowe's relation to Edwards is decidedly ambiguous. On the one hand, she borrows from him so automatically that she seems unaware of borrowing the idea that true virtue consists in holy affections and is known by the spontaneous expression of these feelings; yet, on the other hand, she discards Edwards's

Calvinistic theology to such an extent that she has Eva tell her assembled friends that they can *all* be angels, a proposition exactly the reverse of Edwards's emphasis on grace and election. Later in her own life Mrs. Stowe was quite explicit about her repudiation of Edwards on this point; she even went so far as to imply that in being so exclusive he had warped and ruined the true faith. It is enough to say here that, when she made her angelical child the most reliable witness and example of true virtue, she was working in the best tradition of Edwards's *Treatise Concerning Religious Affections.*

The extent to which she had modified that tradition is evident in the second group of meanings she associated with the word "natural." Eva is characteristically seen out-of-doors, usually gathering flowers. As the epigraph for the chapter which introduces her, Mrs. Stowe chooses Byron's description of Aurora Raby:

> A young star! which shone
> O'er life—too sweet an image for such glass!
> A lovely being, scarcely formed or moulded,
> A rose with all its sweetest leaves yet folded.

From the moment Eva appears in the novel she is associated with the most unequivocal elements of natural innocence; "an airy and innocent playfulness seemed to flicker like the shadow of summer leaves over her childish face." "She was always in motion, always with a half smile on her rosy mouth, flying hither and thither, with an undulating and cloud-like tread." She is "the fair Evangeline." To the imagination of Mrs. Stowe this affinity between little Eva and the clouds, flowers and sunshine is a mark of Eva's special grace as much as is the natural earnestness of her feelings.

Mrs. Stowe's assumption here that Nature is untainted is, by the standards of both Edwards and traditional New England Puritanism, heretical. Edwards, although a student of Nature as both theologian and scientist, did not forget that it had been included in the Fall. For Edwards Nature offers "images and shadows of divine things," a set of incomplete clues to the mind of the Creator from Whom his creatures—man and the natural world—are estranged. Mrs. Stowe dismisses traditional theology on both counts: physical nature and human nature are both uncorrupt. Mrs. Stowe disbelieves in Original Sin and its consequences. In this she is, however, not especially radical for her time; in fact she is following the revivalist theology of her family and their colleagues who, in exhorting their listeners to come forward, repent and be saved, certainly assumed that a man could, in effect, save himself by an act of his own volition. It is not necessary to an understanding of *Uncle Tom's Cabin* to analyze the theological debates of the mid-century clergy over "moral agency" and the like. Mrs. Stowe was well versed in the controversy, and clearly she agreed with those who believed that, although men did sin, they need not. For Edwards such a belief was vicious heresy; for the Beechers it was common sense.

In discarding the doctrine of Original Sin, in suggesting that *all* little Eva's friends can step forward and be saved by love, Mrs. Stowe has implicitly also discarded the old view of the natural world, that although it was a precious 'hieroglyph' in which God's purposes might be read or apprehended, it was also the 'wilderness,' the abode of the devil, the fallen world corrupted by Adam's sin and manifestly imperfect. For Mrs. Stowe, Nature is not necessarily corrupt, any more than man is. On the contrary, it is simply God's Creation, unspoiled. In this respect Mrs. Stowe shares the Romantic view, that Nature is not only pure but purifying to those who love it.

In a letter to Mrs. Stowe thanking her for sending him her "most noble book," Charles Kingsley remarks that he is happy to see that *Uncle Tom's Cabin* is "a really healthy indigenous growth, autochthonous, and free from all that hapless second and third-hand Germanism, & Italianism, & all the other unreal-

isms."[16] Charles H. Foster, in his study of Mrs. Stowe, quotes
this comment of Kingsley with pleasure and approval as an
estimate of such scenes in the novel as the one in the St. Clare
kitchen or the tough language of the traders, Marks and Haley.
"But, of course," says Foster, "Kingsley went too far. *Uncle
Tom's Cabin* is not free of 'unrealisms.' What we should say is
that it is partly literary-sentimental-pious, partly indigenous."[17]
Foster's antithesis is mistaken. He implies that to be truly indigenous a writer must limit himself to the crude or rustic
aspects of American life because these are truly native and
cannot be called derivative; however, we infer from Foster,
when a writer becomes "literary-sentimental-pious," then he is
turning his back on the American scene and copying foreign
models.[18]

The subtle identification of the American with the rustic and
wild and of the un-American with such a lush combination as
the literary-sentimental-pious is more or less an old habit in this
country. But it is highly misleading. As I shall point out later,
the literary influence of Scott on *Uncle Tom's Cabin* is just as
apparent in the relation of low life scenes to the total composition as it is in the treatment of heroes and heroines. With respect to the un-Americanness of literary-sentimental-pious, that
is nonsense. When Mr. Foster thinks of indigenous religion he
thinks of Puritanism, with which, in the writings of Harriet
Beecher Stowe, he is primarily concerned. But Mrs. Stowe's
Puritanism was a very different thing from that of the colonial
Puritans such as Winthrop and Hooker, or even Cotton Mather.
It had passed through a strange morphology: from the early
days of the Massachusetts Bay Company, through the temperate
climate of the early eighteenth century, into the hot fires and
fierce analyses of Jonathan Edwards where it was virtually
forged anew, and then, through a succession of disciples of Edwards, past the final fall of the Standing Order and into the
voices of revivalists who spread out with the westward migra-

tion to preach personal salvation in the early nineteenth century, not to a chosen band cradled in the hills of New England, but to a huge nation in the throes of a huge dilemma. Lyman Beecher, no less than Finney, Peter Cartwright and the other traveling revival preachers, was interested in immediate conversion of the sinner and in his salvation. To this end they all spoke the most dramatic language they could command, full of fire and brimstone and glory. They were often theatrical and excessively sentimental.

Kingsley goes on to explain in his letter what he himself means by American unrealism and he is quite acute. "Better," says he, "to have written *Uncle Tom's Cabin* than to have been all seven Margaret Fuller Assolis [sic] beautiful unguided souls, wearing themselves out with vain questionings. . . . Your book is a deed." [19] What Kingsley has in mind as unreal is that exotic imported Transcendental philosophy which flourished in gorgeous isolation in Concord, Massachusetts, for a short time and which, in the character of Zenobia in *The Blithedale Romance* said to be drawn from Margaret Fuller, Hawthorne so skillfully contrasts to the pale, sentimental, blonde Priscilla. (Eva is pale and blond to the same rare and wonderful degree as she is sentimental.) The Transcendentalism of Concord was in many cases conspicuously foreign in its borrowings from Fichte, Richter, Cousins and Carlyle. It was, certainly, also native in the uses to which it was put by such as Emerson and Thoreau. The point is that it is quite legitimate to accuse Margaret Fuller of Germanism. It is, on the other hand, entirely wrong to consider the literary-sentimental-pious aspect of *Uncle Tom's Cabin* as foreign. The sentimentality of *Uncle Tom's Cabin* is entirely indigenous, and Mrs. Stowe's readers all over the country in 1852 certainly knew what little Eva was talking about when she spoke the language of evangelical piety.

In *Uncle Tom's Cabin* the creed of pure Christian love is stated directly by little Eva; it is also adumbrated in literary iconology by the imagery of flowers, sunshine, and tears. The novel carries, however, a further development of the message, which is dramatically implied rather than stated. It concerns the mothers in the book. As has been remarked by virtually all readers of *Uncle Tom's Cabin,* Mrs. Stowe dramatizes the evils of slavery largely in terms of its destructive effect on families. There are innumerable instances in the novel of mothers being separated from their children, and all are presented in the most heart-rending manner. More important, mothers are made oracles of moral truth. While little Eva can be said to derive from Edwards's child heroines and yet reject his theology, the central role of the mothers in the novel has no precedent in colonial Calvinism. On the basis of what assumptions, then, does Mrs. Stowe make these mothers the real saviors of society, the most important spokesmen for religious truth? In answering this question, we move deeper than we do with little Eva into the changing aspect of belief in this country from the late colonial period through the mid-nineteenth century.

At the very beginning of the novel, just after the opening scene in which Mr. Shelby has sold Tom and Eliza's son Harry, we are told that Mrs. Shelby is the moral force in the family, the one who makes "benevolent efforts for the comfort, instruction, and improvement of her servants." [20] Ignorant of the sale that has just taken place because her husband dares not admit his weakness to her, she promises Eliza that Harry will never be sold. Eliza runs away and risks death to save her child. When Mrs. Shelby hears of Eliza's escape she is so moved that her husband worries, " 'Come, come, Emily . . . you allow yourself to feel too much.' " To which Mrs. Shelby answers, " 'Feel too much! Am not I a woman,—a mother?' " [21]

As Eliza approaches the house of Senator and Mrs. Bird, we we are shown a scene just before she enters. Mrs. Bird is angrily attacking the Fugitive Slave Act as " 'downright cruel and unchristian. It's a shameful, wicked, abominable law, and I'll break it, for one, the first time I get a chance; and I hope I *shall* have a chance, I do!' " Her husband tells her, " 'we mustn't suffer our feelings to run away with our judgment; you must consider it's not a matter of private feeling,—there are great public interests involved,—there is such a state of public agitation rising, that we must put aside our private feelings.' " In this colloquy we have a clear division of right and wrong. On the woman's side is feeling; on the senator's side is law. On the mother's side is Christian compassion; on her husband's, "judgment." When Mr. Bird says " 'let me reason with you,' " she says she hates reasoning; " 'There's a way you political folks have of coming round and round a plain right thing.' " [22] As it happens, one of the Birds' children has died the year before, and when Eliza suddenly asks Mrs. Bird if she has ever lost a child, all possible protest against the fugitive is silenced. Henceforth, not only is Eliza helped in every possible way, but the reader is given to understand that the victory of feeling over law is a victory for God and humanity.

The next mother story is a short one. At an auction in Washington, Kentucky, Haley stops on his way down to New Orleans. A sixty-year-old slave woman has her "only remaining son" sold away from her. Later, on the steamboat, we have the episode of the young mother who drowns herself when her baby is sold to supply another slave mother whose baby has drowned. As the barge moves along, two white women are overheard in discussion about these incidents, and one is heard to remark, " 'The most dreadful part of slavery, to my mind, is its outrages on the feelings and affections,—the separating of families, for example.' " [23] Old Prue's story later in the book sufficiently illustrates the point.

A more carefully developed aspect of this theme is the relation of Augustine St. Clare to his mother, "a woman of uncommon elevation and purity of character" whose name, Evangeline, he has fondly given to his daughter. St. Clare's essential scepticism was originally explained by his thwarted romance. Mrs. Stowe pictures him as spiritually maimed by this calamity, condemned to be, as he says of himself, "a drifter." It is brought out that, although he deplores slavery as much as does his Vermont cousin, he has no faith that any action on his part might be effective, and no desire to try to remedy a situation the complexity of which seems to overwhelm him. After the death of his daughter, his habitual witty languor changes to a "heavy lethargy of sorrow." His own life becomes completely meaningless to him, and the next life does not seem much better. Mrs. Stowe now offers a more provocative explanation of his state of mind:

> He had one of those natures which could better and more clearly conceive of religious things from its own perceptions and instincts, than many a matter-of-fact and practical Christian. The gift to appreciate and the sense to feel the finer shades and relations of moral things, often seems an attribute of those whose whole life shows a careless disregard of them. Hence Moore, Byron, Goethe, often speak words more wisely descriptive of the true religious sentiment, than another man, whose whole life is governed by it. In such minds, disregard of religion is a more fearful treason,—a more deadly sin.[24]

Thus the very fineness of his sensibility, coupled with his awareness of an ideal he has rejected, has made St. Clare turn against his own better nature. This is his treason and his sin. Mrs. Stowe is reminded of Moore, of Byron, of Goethe.

In St. Clare's case there is a special element, the saintly little Eva, who by dying has become a saint indeed. This death has changed St. Clare to a degree; he has started reading her Bible and has begun steps towards Tom's legal emancipation. Then one evening he comes upon a copy his mother has made of the old Latin hymn, "Dies Irae," which she has arranged from Mozart's *Requiem*. He plays and sings, and then has another interesting and sympathetic discussion with Miss Ophelia about slavery. After a pause he comments, " 'I don't know what makes me think of my mother so much, to-night. . . . I have a strange kind of feeling, as if she were near me. I keep thinking of things she used to say.' " [25] Presently he leaves the house to go down the street to hear the evening news. In a café he tries to stop a fight between two men and one of them stabs him fatally with a bowie knife. The deathbed scene is climactic. After the servants have been asked to leave, St. Clare's eyes finally focus on a picture of his mother. He asks Tom to pray for him, then he murmurs several lines from the "Dies Irae." The end soon follows:

His lips moved at intervals, as parts of the hymn fell brokenly from them.

'His mind is wandering,' said the doctor.

'No! it is coming HOME, at last!' said St. Clare, energetically; 'at last! at last!'

The effort of speaking exhausted him. The sinking paleness of death fell on him; but with it there fell, as if shed from the wings of some pitying spirit, a beautiful expression of peace, like that of a wearied child who sleeps.

So he lay for a few moments. They saw that the mighty hand was on him. Just before the spirit parted, he opened his eyes, with a sudden light, as of joy and recognition, and said *'Mother!'* and then he was gone! [26]

The impression, literally, is that we witness St. Clare passing out of life into the hereafter and greeting his mother as he approaches the other side. His recognition, however, is of more than his mother's identity; he supposedly also recognizes the meaning of her religious faith and the beauty of her love for him. His scepticism is dissolved and his divided spirit healed by this ecstatic glimpse. His mother, at once the messenger and the object of this revelation, typifies the love of Christ. In dying, St. Clare is going "home" where he is loved and belongs. To complete the picture, he is found at death to be wearing "upon his bosom a small, plain miniature case, opening with a spring. It was the miniature of a noble and beautiful female face; and on the reverse, under a crystal, a lock of dark hair . . . poor mournful relics of early dreams, . . ." [27] At his death, therefore, are brought together all the forms of goodness from which in his life he has wandered—his true bride, his mother, and Christian faith. He is released from conflict and delivered unto his mother and his eternal salvation.

After the death of St. Clare, Uncle Tom meets Cassy, a quadroon woman whom Legree has forced for five years to be his mistress. Cassy's story is more varied than Prue's, but just as bitter. After her white father's death by cholera, she was bought by another white man whom she loved and with whom she had two children. Later, however, this "husband" was drawn into gambling and sold her and their children to pay his debts. Her next owner forced her to become his whore by threatening to sell the children, which he finally did anyway. She was then bought by a series of men who wanted her for her good looks. One day she saw her child Henry run to her from out of a crowd. Several men, "'came up to him, swearing dreadfully; and one man, whose face I shall never forget, told him that he wouldn't get away so; that he was going with him into the calaboose, and he'd get a lesson there he'd never forget. I tried to beg and plead,—they only laughed; the poor boy screamed and looked into my face, and held on to me . . . and they carried him in, screaming "Mother! mother! mother!"' " [28] Cassy later attacks her owner with a bowie knife. He beats her up, and sells her. When another nice man buys her and they have a baby, she kills the baby with laudanum to save it from the fate of her other son. The cholera strikes again and kills this owner; she barely survives, only to be bought by Legree.

Cassy is a wild, passionate woman whose maternal agony is made more horrible by the lecheries to which she has been subjected. Her hatred of Legree is as violent as is the man himself, but she has succeeded in making him afraid of her by playing on his superstitions. To understand the nature of his fears and the cunning of her vengeance, we turn to the most significant mother story in the novel, the story of the mother of Simon Legree.

As the tale begins, Legree is already afraid of Cassy who he thinks is possessed by the devil. One day, she had been taunting him with black prophecies when into the room came Sambo, bringing "a witch thing" wrapped in a paper which he had taken from around Tom's neck. When Legree opened the paper, "there dropped out of it a silver dollar, and a long, shining curl of fair hair,—hair which, like a living thing, twined itself round Legree's fingers."

'Damnation!' he screamed, in sudden passion, stamping on the floor, and pulling furiously at the hair, as if it burned him. 'Where did this come from? Take it off!—burn it up!—burn it up!' he screamed, tearing it off, and throwing it into the charcoal. 'What did you bring it to me for?' . . . 'Don't you bring me any more of your devilish things!' [29]

The lock of hair is the one which little Eva, at her death, had given to Tom. But Legree's reaction needs accounting for. Even Sambo and Cassy are amazed at his fury. This episode brings us to the story of Legree's mother.

Hard and reprobate as the godless man seemed now, there had been a time when he had been rocked on the bosom of a mother,—cradled with prayers and pious hymns,—his now seared brow bedewed with the waters of holy baptism. In early childhood, a fair-haired woman had led him, at the sound of Sabbath bell, to worship and to pray. Far in New England that mother had trained her only son, with long, unwearied love, and patient prayers.[30]

The son had proved a rebel and had left home for good to go to sea. He came home only once, and then his mother begged and prayed to him to repent. On that day, "his heart inly relented,—there was a conflict,—but sin got the victory, and he set all the force of his rough nature against the conviction of his conscience." He fled to his ship, and his next news of home was in a letter: "He opened it, and a lock of long, curling hair fell from it, and twined about his fingers. The letter told him his mother was dead, and that, dying, she blest and forgave him." Mrs. Stowe now explains the torment of this New England soul.

There is a dread, unhollowed necromancy of evil, that turns things sweetest and holiest to phantoms of horror and affright. That pale, loving mother,—her dying prayers, her forgiving love,—wrought in that demoniac heart of sin only as a damning sentence, bringing with it a fearful looking for of judgment and fiery indignation. Legree burned the hair, and burned the letter; and when he saw them hissing and crackling in the flame, inly shuddered as he thought of everlasting fires. He tried to drink, and revel, and swear away the memory; but often, in the deep night, whose solemn stillness arraigns the bad soul in forced communion with herself, he had seen that pale mother rising by his bedside, and felt the soft twining of that hair around his fingers, till the cold sweat would roll down his face, and he would spring from his bed in horror. Ye who have wondered to hear, in the same evangel, that God is love, and that God is a consuming fire, see ye not how, to the soul resolved in evil, perfect love is the most fearful torture, the seal and sentence of the direst despair? [31]

Augustine St. Clare's separation from his mother and her faith, and the crippling inner conflict which paralyzes him thereafter, are dim foreshadowings of the sources of Legree's degradation. Legree has become a monster by rebelling against his conscience; he has become brutal by defying the voice of God within him. In St. Clare, the crisis was not severe enough to produce active evil, but it made the man amoral. In Legree, the violent conflict is never resolved. He becomes more and more savage and depraved; yet his better nature will not die and turns, instead, into a source of nightmares and superstitious visions of witches, ghosts and devils. The more Uncle Tom's religious strength appears, the more Legree is driven to beat and destroy him. He apparently cannot stand to witness the martyr's imperviousness to pain. At last Legree recognizes "that it was God who was standing between him and his victim." [32] This is what drives him to kill Tom with a violence commensurate with the violence he has used to destroy his own conscience.

This story comes full circle with the completion of Cassy's vengeance. Some time before, Legree had done some unspecified injury to a slave whom he had then locked in the garret of his house. Ghost stories about the place already flourished. Cassy's plan is to escape by hiding in the garret, which she must first make an invulnerable fortress by terrorizing Legree. She begins hints and complaints that she cannot sleep for all the noises there. Later she jams a bottle into a knothole in the garret wall so that the winds will moan and whistle. She leaves doors open, opens locked ones, and arranges gothic effects. Legree is thoroughly unnerved and will not approach the garret. Then Cassy and Legree's latest young mistress, Emmeline (whose mother had taught her religion and good manners) escape; presently the chase is sounded and the dogs are sent out, but by this time the ladies are safely aloft, where, as Cassy says, they "can make any noise [they] please, and it will only add to the effect." To add to it still further, Cassy takes to walking around the house in a sheet at midnight, to the horror of the servants and the increasing uneasiness of Legree, of whom Mrs. Stowe has this to say:

After all, let a man take what pains he may to hush it down, a human soul is an awful ghostly, unquiet possession, for a bad man to have. Who knows the metes and bounds of it? Who knows all its awful perhapses,—those shudderings and tremblings, which it can no more live down that it can outlive its own eternity! What a fool is he who locks his door to keep out spirits, who has in his own bosom a spirit he dares not meet alone,—whose voice, smothered far down, and piled over with mountains of earthliness, is yet like the forewarning trumpet of doom! [33]

Thus Cassy enacts before Legree's eyes the nightmares of his own soul. The more violently he wars on his conscience, the more these monsters of his guilty imagination surround him in the grotesque impersonations of Cassy. One night when he is asleep she plays her last ghoulish joke: "there came over his sleep a shadow, a horror, an apprehension of something dreadful hanging over him. It was his mother's shroud, he thought; but Cassy had it, holding it up, and showing it to him." He struggled to wake up, and saw that "the door *was* open, and he saw a hand putting out his light."

It was a cloudy, misty moonlight, and there he saw it!—something white, gliding in! He heard the still rustle of its ghostly garments. It stood still by his bed;—a cold hand touched his; a voice said, three times, in a low, fearful whisper, 'Come! come! come!' And, while he lay sweating with terror, he knew not when or how, the thing was gone.[34]

Cassy is impersonating Legree's dead mother! The recognition scene is not quite the same as Augustine St. Clare's, but the mother is still the figure of supernatural power and everlasting love. To Legree's maddened imagination, demons and witches appear where once, in his youth, angels and better spirits had been. The mind of this child of New England, with its habitual belief in supernatural powers and symbols, has been twisted and brutalized to the point where it can conceive only of the powers of evil.

Legree's conscience carries out Cassy's revenge. After this visitation, he starts to drink recklessly and soon becomes sick. "None could bear the horrors of that sick room, when he raved and screamed, and spoke of sights which almost stopped the blood of those who heard him; and, at his dying bed, stood a stern, white, inexorable figure, saying, 'Come! come! come!'" [35] This is the last we hear of Simon Legree.

In Mrs. Stowe's analysis, then, Legree's crimes are the issue of a soul at war with its own former faith, frenzied by guilt, and driven to ever greater enormities in its desperate flight from a God who, though rejected, is still believed in. Once the image of that God has been sown in the mind of the child, the man can never be freed from its power. Rebellion can only produce a savage inner conflict. The imagination can only conceive fiercer devils and more terrible cruelties. Preying alike upon himself and others, the man becomes a moral monster. Legree's mother was his good angel. Through her offices this angry God can be approached as a God of love. Like the mother of St. Clare, she both teaches and exemplifies the gospel of love. According to Mrs. Stowe, "Not in the riches of omnipotence is the chief glory of God; but in self-denying, suffering love!" [36] This same quality of self-denying love is repeatedly attributed to mothers in *Uncle Tom's Cabin* and virtually everywhere else in her writings. It is the keynote of Uncle Tom's martyrdom. It is to Mrs. Stowe the essential Christian virtue.

The dramatization of the evils of slavery through its destructive effect on families in the novel implies that the rehabilitation of the nation should come about through a recognition of the sacred ties of family love. When the nation learns to see itself as a family and when its hostile members recognize each other as brothers, then will the wrathful God of Jeremiah, who now threatens such awful doom, show himself to be a kindly father. The lost sheep will be gathered into the fold, all members of the nation will be the loving children of their parents on earth and their father in heaven, and wars shall cease. The millennium shall have come. *Uncle Tom's Cabin* summons the nation to encompass the Kingdom of God.[37] To this end the novel itself encompasses, with Dickensian vitality and Whitmanesque sweep, the whole of that mid-century society which was on the verge of losing its soul to save its legal boundaries. As Mrs. Stowe sees the Union of 1852, and as she presents it in *Uncle Tom's Cabin*— in clear detail, huge, diverse, yet coherent in that the anguish of slavery touches everyone—it can redeem its destiny only by giving up Webster's brutal compromise in favor of another kind of Union, a more perfect union, bound together by Christian love.

# CHAPTER 2

# Dred: *and Harry Gordon's Dilemma*

*J*udging from the opening chapters of *Dred,* published in 1856, one might conclude that in the four intervening years since *Uncle Tom's Cabin* Mrs. Stowe had relaxed the pressure for immediate entrance into the millennium and had found herself in a conciliatory, even nostalgic mood. *Dred* is set entirely in North Carolina, and the author's descriptions of the beauty of the Gordon and Clayton plantations could satisfy the fondest defender of the region. Herself a passionate gardener, Mrs. Stowe allows her imagination to linger over flowers and blossoming trees which would grow in that warm air and fertile soil but would not thrive in New England even in her indoor greenhouses. Over and over in the novel she indulges in amorous descriptions of the Southern scene. Even toward the end she cannot resist giving another account of the Clayton plantation, the name of which is Magnolia Grove.

The place derived its name from a group of these beautiful trees, in the centre of which the house was situated. It was a long, low cottage, surrounded by deep verandas, festooned with an exuberance of those climbing plants which are so splendid in the southern latitude. The range of apartments which opened on the veranda where Anne and Nina were sitting was darkened to exclude the flies; but the doors, standing open, gave picture-like gleams of the interior. The white, matted floors, light bamboo furniture, couches covered with glazed white linen, and the large vases of roses disposed here and there, where the light would fall upon them, presented a background of inviting coolness.[1]

It would seem that Mrs. Stowe is going out of her way to flatter the legend of the Old South. Actually, she takes the opportunity in the author's preface to give two reasons for her choice of setting. She mentions first the "merely artistic" consideration, which she holds to be of inferior importance. I shall discuss it in the following chapter. To her, "the highest" value of the Southern setting is that it draws attention to the "moral bearings" of a subject which is in reality a national one, namely the crisis over slavery. "If ever a nation was raised up by Divine Providence, and led forth upon a conspicuous stage, as if for the express purpose of solving a great moral problem in the sight of all mankind, it is this nation. God in his providence is now asking the American people, Is the system of slavery, as set forth in the American slave code, *right?*" Once again in *Dred,* as in *Uncle Tom's Cabin,* the author conceives of herself as the providential historian.

As I have said, *Uncle Tom's Cabin* is a work of providential history which seeks to document the contemporary scene in order to move its readers to return the nation to its true historical course by purging it of the sin of slavery. The definition of the nation's destiny as stated and implied in the book's argument is significantly different from what it was in the Puritan historians: *Uncle Tom's Cabin* argues for the evangelical ideal of a society bound together by brotherly love, not for Bradford's or Cotton Mather's Christian Commonwealth. Moreover, the message is spoken and exemplified by secular characters—the angelic heroine and the self-denying, pious mothers—rather than by the clergy or the official leaders of society; indeed these secular apostles preach love against law, an antithesis which would have been highly sinister in the judgment of any good Puritan. Mrs.

Stowe has used the framework of providential history to point towards a destiny which the colonial historians never framed or desired. Nonetheless, she does rely on the old documentary method and the old rhetoric of the Jeremiad to move her readers, and she is quite right in assuming that the Southern reader belongs to this tradition as much as does the Yankee. She is also right in thinking that the evangelical gospel was the common religious experience of both North and South.

As providential history appealing to its readers to cleanse the sins of the nation, *Dred* provides a measure of the extent to which Mrs. Stowe's outlook on slavery changed in the troubled years between 1852 and 1856. The second slavery novel is not nearly so single-minded. The providential historian, although she makes a fascinating exploration of the "great moral problem" which the nation is called upon to solve, does not point to a lesson or urge a solution. Rather, Mrs. Stowe seems to dramatize her own fearful uncertainty through a sort of debate between several conflicting lines of argument.

*Dred* does restate the gospel of evangelical love; the case is put by Milly, an old slave woman who, although she has lost no less than fourteen children to sale or death, urges the cause of Christian love as it is argued in *Uncle Tom's Cabin*. Yet Mrs. Stowe, while she clearly endorses Milly's message, has apparently lost confidence in its strength to prevail. Hence, she introduces into American fiction two very modern characters: Dred, the militant black rebel, and Harry Gordon, the man in the middle, the son of the white planter and his mulatto mistress and, thus, the half brother of the white heir and of his sister, the novel's heroine. The focus of Mrs. Stowe's analysis of the problem of slavery in this novel is her portrayal of Harry Gordon's dilemma, the desperate difficulty for him of choosing between Dred's call for vengeance and Milly's plea for patience. Before she comes to Harry's story, however, Mrs. Stowe disposes of another alternative which had been put forward as a possible solution to the "great moral problem" of her time.

Edward Clayton and his sister, Anne, have put into effect a program of reform at Magnolia Grove which assumes an extremely patronizing attitude toward the slaves, essentially that they are "childish" docile darkies, and consists in subjecting them to a benevolent education in the ways of white society. Anne Clayton explains their method to Nina, who is surprised that none of the cabinets or closets in the house is locked: " 'I called them [the slaves] all together, and I said to them, "Now, people have always said that you are the greatest thieves in the world; that there is no managing you except by locking up everything from you. But I think differently. I have an idea that you can be trusted." ' " [2] According to Anne the slaves were so inspired by her high opinion of them that they forthwith stopped stealing forever. Edward Clayton, trying "all he could to awaken self-respect" built "that pretty row of cottages you saw down at the quarters. He put up a large bathing-establishment" as well, and Anne explains that, by encouraging the first few to use it, they succeeded in spreading "neatness and order" among the slaves. Further, Edward "has instituted a sort of jury trial among them." Anne speaks bravely of her discouraging moments in the administration of these reforms, but concludes that " 'if there is a missionary work in this world, it is this.' " Evidently the Claytons intend to transform the dark and, as they often called them pityingly, "barbarous" heathen into scrubbed and happy citizens. The extent of their dreams is not, however, fully manifest until Anne takes Nina to visit the school house where she instructs the slave children. "They passed onward into a grove of magnolias which skirted the back of the house, till they came to a little building, with the external appearance of a small Grecian temple, the pillars of which were festooned with jessamine." Now we are in Mrs. Stowe's Utopia.

Anne stepped to the door and rang a bell, and in about ten minutes the patter of innumerable little feet was heard ascending the steps, and presently they came streaming in. . . . All were dressed alike, in a neat uniform of some kind of blue stuff, with white capes and aprons.

They filed in to the tune of one of those marked rhythmical melodies which characterize the negro music, and moving in exact time to the singing, assumed their seats, which were arranged with regard to their age and size. As soon as they were seated, Anne, after a moment's pause, clapped her hands, and the whole school commenced a morning hymn, in four parts. . . .[8]

The Claytons' sceptical neighbor, Mr. Bradshaw, who is also on the tour, is moved to tears by this performance. Thus do the Claytons propose to convert the doubters among their countrymen to follow their pious example. Thus shall the nation be saved and the slaves be made over in the image of their faithful masters; one and all shall lift up their voices in a Christian hymn (in four parts) in a "Grecian temple festooned with jessamine," and live happily ever after.

To this sentimental reformer's rhapsody, however, the other characters in the novel give no allegiance. In fact, it is Edward's and Anne's father, Judge Clayton, who most articulately opposes their program on the grounds that the law is slavery, right or wrong. In an appellate decision by Judge Clayton reversing a lower court's endorsement of Edward Clayton's high-minded defense of a slave woman who had been cruelly treated by a white, the father repudiates the son in words taken from an actual case which had been decided by Judge Ruffin of North Carolina. The effect of the scene in the courtroom, and of an interview following it in which Judge Clayton explains his actions and obligations, is to shift the emphasis of the novel from idealistic daydreams and to put the burden of slavery on the Southern society as a whole. Clearly Mrs. Stowe is addressing a Southern audience in *Dred,* as she was not in *Uncle Tom's*

*Cabin,* and her desire is to stir the South to initiate reform, particularly in the slave code.

*Dred* is a peculiar novel. It opens in an easygoing manner which gives promise of a pleasant little tale set in a lush plantation background and allowing for the free play of romantic incident. When she is not embellishing the "Byronic" attractions of her leading characters, the author demonstrates a satirical skill as adroit as it is incompatible with the heavy-handed ironies and solemn lessons of *Uncle Tom's Cabin.* The high-minded reforms of the Claytons' model plantation are not severely urged upon the reader; it is all too good to be true, and the reader feels little insistence that he go and do likewise. The emotional imperatives of *Uncle Tom's Cabin* are gone; its melodramatic intensity is replaced by a mood of romantic adventure and satirical gaiety. Yet when the novel ends five hundred pages later, we have witnessed brutalities more savage than anything in *Uncle Tom's Cabin* and have heard prophecies of doom and vengeance which make the horrors of Legree's plantation seem mild. The change in both the style and direction of the novel occurs quite abruptly halfway through with the sudden introduction of the wild pariah of the Great Dismal Swamp, Dred.

The cause of the change, like the avowed inspiration of *Uncle Tom's Cabin,* by the passage of the Fugitive Slave Act, was a national, political event, in this case the beating in the Senate of Charles Sumner by Preston Brooks of South Carolina in defense of the honor of Senator Butler who had been attacked by Sumner in his speech, "Crime against Kansas." The impact of the event was of course cumulative and was further sharpened three days later by the Pottawatomie massacre carried out by John Brown and his sons against five pro-slavery men in Pottawatomie, Kansas. A third factor was the sensational "slave auction" conducted by Henry Ward Beecher in Plymouth Church following the protest meeting in Brooklyn against the attack on Sumner. The inflammatory effect of these events, which occurred in a period of two weeks, was, as her biographer puts it, to make Mrs. Stowe, then nearing what proved to be the middle of her second novel, suddenly feel "herself borne by the inspiration which had carried her so triumphantly through *Uncle Tom's Cabin.*" The result of this new impulse was not only to ruin *Dred* as a work of art, as we shall presently see; it also profoundly affected the moral and political arguments the novel was to put forward. Mrs. Stowe abandoned the attempt to stir up reform sentiment by means of polite fictional persuasion. Out of her distress, she conceived of Harry Gordon's tragic dilemma. Moreover, she also felt the need to speak in the voice of Dred, the prophet of doom and destruction.

As a character, Dred is a most improbable mixture of savagery and bombast. He spoils the book because, from the time of his appearance at the camp meeting, he is the central figure in the novel and yet none of the other characters has any relation to him, with the exception of the slaves who escape to his lair in the swamp and simply tell him their stories, and of Harry Gordon who knows Dred in an impersonal way and listens to him talk. Dred's talk is the worst thing about him from "the merely artistic point of view," although it is clearly his greatest fascination for Mrs. Stowe, who writes him long speeches in the idiom of the Old Testament prophets to whom she proudly compares him.

Yet, despite the suffocating effect of his monologues, Dred is an interesting character, far more interesting in conception than his venerable predecessor, Uncle Tom. Physically, he is stupendous.

He was a tall black man, of magnificent stature and proportions. His skin was intensely black, and polished like marble. . . . [The] neck and chest [were] of herculean strength[, and] the shoulders showed the muscles of a gladiator. . . . The large eyes had [a] peculiar and solemn effect of unfathomable blackness and darkness. . . . But there burned in them, like tongues of flame in a black pool

of naptha, a subtle and restless fire that betokened habitual excitement to the verge of insanity . . . and the whole combination was
such as might have formed one of the wild old warrior prophets of
the heroic ages.[4]

His clothing is coarse and crude, but he wears a "loose shirt of
red flannel," and "a fantastic sort of turban, apparently of an
old scarlet shawl." He carries a rifle, a bowie knife and a hatchet.
He is the very type of savage spendor, noble not in natural
Rousseauistic goodness but rather in his outlandish defiance. He
reminds one of the characters in *Moby Dick,* but less of the
dark-skinned harpooners to whom he is more physically similar
than of their dreadful captain in whose ruthless bitterness of
soul he shares.

Mrs. Stowe even begins to sound like Melville as she describes
her ferocious hero. Speaking of the Old Testament stories from
which Dred draws his rebellious inspiration, she cites as his
favorites, "the wrathful denunciations of ancient prophets against
oppression and injustice. He had read of kingdoms convulsed
by plagues; of tempest, and pestilence, and locusts; of the sea
cleft in twain. . . ." Most Melvillean of all, Dred "thrilled with
fierce joy as he read how Samson, with his two strong arms,
pulled down the pillars of the festive temple, and whelmed his
triumphant persecutors in one grave with himself."[5] Like Ahab,
Dred is a man driven by hatred, a man maimed in his soul by
the violence of his persecutors and by the violence of his own
desire to destroy them. As he listens to the grotesque and brutal
stories which are told to him by the slaves who have escaped
their pursuers and reached his hidden home in the swamp,
each of their encounters with the forces of white oppression becomes his own and he raises the cry to Jehovah to punish "this
evil nation." He is a man possessed and maddened by his own
heart's hatred, and often the intensity of that demonic passion
will hold him ferociously still, "his eye fixed before him on
vacancy, the pupil swelling out in glassy fullness, with a fixed,

somnambulic stare." In short he is a monomaniac, engulfed by an errand of vengeance against an evil whose enormity has become coexistent with creation itself.

This is not a matter of literary influence. There is no evidence that Mrs. Stowe had read *Moby Dick* by the time she was writing *Dred*. We are speaking here of a confluence of imaginative sources and perspectives, and the important thing is to observe in Mrs. Stowe's work of the 1850s many of the same themes and preoccupations with which we are familiar from other works of that notable literary decade. We can, then, simply recognize the similarity between Dred's obsessive defiance of a society become deadly in its apotheosis of whiteness and Ahab's maniacal pursuit of the deadly white whale. That the American imagination in the 1850s was powerfully attracted by the figures and forces of wild violence, that it was both horrified and heroically proud to sound its "barbaric yawp over the rooftops of the world," is, more or less, common knowledge. We also know that for mid-nineteenth-century Americans the overwhelming sense of the vastness and wildness of their newly possessed continent was further complicated by the old seventeenth-century Puritan attitude toward the wilderness, an attitude in itself a mixture of fear of the evils and temptations which the wilderness held and of reverence for the wonderful symbolism of God's handiwork in nature. Intervening was the eighteenth-century confidence in unspoiled nature as a source of strength and wisdom and goodness to man and society, a confidence very much shared in this country by Jefferson, his contemporaries, and his later followers. Hence, by the 1850s, with the flamboyant enthusiasm for "Manifest Destiny" and "Nature's Nation" ringing in their ears, Melville and Mrs. Stowe both had need to question "those awful affinities which bind us to that unknown realm," [6] the realm behind the physical objects of our corporeal life, the realm of darkness and death, and possibly too of radiant salvation. Nothing could be more characteristic of the mid-century literary concern over the true significance of nature for American society than Mrs. Stowe's choice of metaphor to describe Edward Clayton's precarious position as an active opponent of slavery. "He who glides dreamily down the glassy surface of a mighty river floats securely, making his calculations to row upward. He knows nothing what the force of that seemingly glassy current will be when his one feeble oar is set against the whole volume of its waters." [7] The implication is that to set oneself against the forces of slavery and the status quo established by the Compromise of 1850 is to invite torrential destruction. Melville implies the same.

When I said earlier that none of the other characters in *Dred* has faith in the reform projects of Edward Clayton and his sister, I did not mean that Mrs. Stowe herself scorns their good intentions. On the contrary, she endorses everything Clayton does, from his model plantation at Magnolia Grove to his courthouse battle against his father and the law. When she makes him a martyr to the system, she is pleading as forcefully as she can for the leaders of Southern society to follow Clayton's initiative of change. Yet after the beating of Sumner and the events of the following two weeks, her fears that this will not happen have become so strong that she can make Clayton only an admirable but inneffectual victim of the system and of his own good intentions. Following the metaphor of the glassy, treacherous river, she goes on to clarify Clayton's difficulty.

It was the fault of Clayton, and is the fault of all such men, that he judged mankind by himself. He could not believe that anything, except ignorance and inattention, could make men upholders of deliberate injustice. He thought all that was necessary was the enlightening of the public mind, the direction of general attention to the subject.[8]

Clayton assumes that men desire social justice. He assumes that, because men are basically decent and rational, they can be persuaded to adopt practical means to the end of obtaining the goods they wish for their society. By the summer of 1856, Mrs. Stowe doubts whether in fact most men do desire justice. Hence, the entrance of Dred, who assumes no such thing.

Dred's violent bitterness is the product of despair. Like his assumptions, his program of action is the opposite of Clayton's. Dred is a revolutionary. To his tormented mind, the nation has already committed itself to a course of injustice from which it has lost the will and the power to redeem itself. He therefore feels himself to be the agent and spokesman for God's utmost wrath, and he proposes to his hunted followers in the swamp a course of bloody destruction against the whole of society. Ever mindful of her role as providential historian, Mrs. Stowe supports Dred's schemes with footnotes on Nat Turner's rebellion in 1831. Moreover, each one of the gruesome stories which the runaways tell to Dred is footnoted from case histories. According to the record at least, Dred's program of inspired terrorism is both possible and justified.

Certainly Mrs. Stowe finds Dred noble and awesome. The fact that she constantly compares him to the "wild old warrior prophets" whose mighty example had been revered by New Englanders for over two hundred years is evidence enough that she sees him as heroic. The fact that she compares the Negroes as a race to the ancient Israelites suggests the further analogy of Dred as the Mosaic leader guiding his oppressed chosen people out of captivity. And when Mrs. Stowe adds to these associations the heroic revolutionary past of the United States, we can no longer doubt that she feels Dred's own desperation within herself.

Though the slaves of the South are unable to read the Bible for themselves, yet most completely have its language and sentiment penetrated among them, giving a Hebraistic coloring to their habitual mode of expression . . . for none of us may deny that, wild and hopeless as this scheme was, it was still the same in kind with the more successful one which purchased our fathers a national existence.[9]

She sees the Negroes, like the Jews, as a nation in bondage and she shares the defiant anger of Dred against their "triumphant persecutors." Nevertheless, Mrs. Stowe is as much afraid of the consequences of this violent anger as she is in sympathy with its motives. She fears that the disease has become so poisonous that the purgative bloodletting will kill the patient, and of course she does not share Dred's willingness to annihilate the entire society.

Hence, in addition to Clayton's and Dred's answers to the unbearable system of slavery and the tyranny of its enlightened supporters, another voice is heard in the novel and a third response is given: that of the old slave woman, Milly. Hers is a classic among Mrs. Stowe's mother's stories. As told in first-person narrative to Nina Gordon, Milly was the mother of thirteen children, all sold away from her by the time she had her last child, a boy named Alfred, whom Nina's aunt, "Miss Harriet," promised not to sell, but whom she did sell when the Joneses near-by offered her "a great deal of money for him." Milly's "heart was like a red-hot coal." On the following Sunday morning she took the new coat and shoes she had bought for Alfred, "'cause he was a handsome boy, and I wanted him always to look nice,'" and started over to the Joneses to see what had become of him. On the way over she meets a younger woman, Huldah, who lives on the Jones's place, and learns that Alfred is dead.

'And she told me it was dis yer way. Dat Stiles—he dat was Jones's overseer—had heard dat Alfred was dreadful spirity; and when boys is so, sometimes dey aggravates 'em to get 'em riled, and den dey whips 'em to break 'em in. So Stiles, . . . was real aggravating to him; and dat boy—well, he answered back, just as he allers would be doing, 'cause he was smart, and it 'peared like he could n't keep it in. And den . . . Stiles was mad, . . . and den Alfred, he cut and run. . . . And just den young Master Bill come along, and wanted to know what was de matter. So Stiles told him, and he took out his pistol, and said, "Here, young dog, if you don't come back before I count five, I'll fire!"

"Fire ahead!" says Alfred; 'cause you see, dat boy never knowed what fear was. And so he fired. And Huldah said he just jumped up and give one scream, and fell flat. . . . I did n't say a word. . . . I walked . . . straight home. I walked up into missis' room, and she was dressed for church, sure enough, and sat dere reading her Bible. I laid it right down under her face, dat jacket. "You see dat hole!" said I; "you see dat blood! Alfred's killed! *You* killed him; his blood be on you and your chil'en! O Lord God in heaven, hear me, and render unto her double!"' [10]

Thus Milly has experienced in her own life the bitterest agonies for which Dred seeks vengeance. She has as much cause for hatred and rebellion as he does, and, at first, just after Alfred is killed, she is frantic with grief and seeks out God to avenge her.

'I tell you, I sought de Lord early and late. Many nights I have been out in de woods and laid on de ground till morning, calling and crying, and 'peared like nobody heerd me. Oh, how strange it used to look, when I looked up to de stars! winking at me, so kind of still and solemn, but never saying a word! Sometimes I got dat wild, it seemed as if I could tear a hole through de sky, 'cause I must find God; I had an errand to him, and I must find him.'

Yet in the end Milly is Dred's only effective opponent, because, succeeding her rage, comes a new emotion, almost expiatory, of Christian forgiveness. As she herself tells it, one night at a camp meeting she heard in a sermon how God had given up His own son.

'O Lord, what a story dat ar was! And den, how dey took him, and put de crown of thorns on his head, and hung hum up bleeding, bleeding, and bleeding! . . . I saw him, suffering, bearing with us, year in and year out—bearing—bearing—bearing so patient! 'Peared like, it wa'n't just on de cross; but, bearing always, everywhar! Oh, chile, I saw how he loved us!—us *all*—all—every one on us!—we dat hated each other so. . . . Oh, chile, I saw what it was for me to be hatin', like I'd hated. "O Lord," says I, "I give up! O Lord, never see you afore; I did n't know. Lord, I's a poor sinner! I won't hate no more!" And oh, chile, den dere come such a rush of love in my soul! Says I, "Lord, I ken love even de white folks. . . . Ah, chile, we must n't hate nobody; we's all poor creatures, and de dear Lord he loves us all." '

This is, of course, the same message and the same solution to the national dilemma as is presented by little Eva and Uncle Tom. It differs, apart from the superior narrative style, in that Milly has felt and acknowledged the hatred and bitterness against white society which moves Dred. Neither Uncle Tom nor little Eva ever acknowledges any other attitude than universal love; neither is aware of evil to the extent of hating it. Thus, Milly's experience is dramatically much more convincing, as well as much more artfully told. Milly's own manner in telling the story is neither grotesque, as is Old Prue's, nor sentimental as Uncle Tom and little Eva so often are. Milly is more detached as she describes her own sufferings than anyone in *Uncle Tom's Cabin,* and for this reason she is both more admirable and more persuasive. She is old; she is ironic; she is a big woman who has watched and suffered in this vale of tears so long that she has lost some of the painful sense of her own troubles and gradually assumed the burdens of those around her. With noble patience she urges the others, Negro and White, to forbear and endure.

Milly's role becomes most important in connection with her rivalry with Dred for the confidence of Harry Gordon. Harry Gordon is the most interesting character in the novel, for he is the descendant of that ancestral Thomas Gordon, Knight, and the son of Nina's father, Colonel Gordon, and of "a beautiful Eboe mulatress." [11] Harry is so intelligent, well educated and able that no one on the plantation even pretends to command him; "he proceeded, to all intents and purposes, with the perfect ease of a free man." Ironically, he is so much the son of the Gordons that, "had he not been possessed of a good share of the thoughtful, forecasting temperament derived from his Scottish parentage, he might have been completely happy, and forgotten even the existence of the chains whose weight he never felt." The difficulty originates with Harry's white brother, Tom. "It was only in the presence of Tom Gordon—Colonel Gordon's lawful son—that he ever realized that he was a slave. From childhood there had been a rooted enmity between the brothers, which deepened as years passed on. . . ." [12] Tom Gordon is a brutal man, a drinker and profligate, though endowed with the same intelligence and sensibility as Harry. Tom shows that he has been corrupted by the slave society, which indulged him as a child in his every hostile gesture toward the slaves and particularly toward his mulatto half brother. Thus far in Mrs. Stowe's definition of the relationship of the half brothers, we are able to recognize a situation parallel to the one in *Pudd'nhead Wilson,* and similar, in the central pattern, to Cable's story of the half brothers Grandissime.

The situation in *Dred* also closely resembles that of Faulkner's pair of brothers in *Absalom, Absalom!* in that Harry and Tom come to blows over their sister. In fact, there is a sort of double triangle: first with Nina, the sister of both men; second with Harry's French quadroon wife after whom Tom lusts. These relationships are not identical to those in any of the three novels to which I have compared them, but it is nevertheless remarkable that Mrs. Stowe should have conceived in the mid-fifties what became an almost archtypical configuration in novels about the South thirty, forty and seventy years later.

Harry's dilemma, about which Dred and Milly give conflicting advice, is whether to yield to his passionate rage over

Tom Gordon's treatment of himself and his wife and join forces with Dred, and in so doing make himself the enemy of Nina Gordon to whom he is devoted; or, to stay by Nina's side and be forced to call himself a coward and a betrayer of his race. Dred is unconditional in his demand that Harry see the racial struggle in its true desperate light and that he commit himself to violent rebellion. Dred accuses Harry of leading the soft life at the Gordon plantation and of hiding his eyes from the sufferings of other slaves. On the occasion of one encounter between the two men, Milly happens along the path through the wilderness which leads to Dred's hut. She urges patience and restraint. "'Cause you hate Tom Gordon, does you want to act just like him?'" More telling still is Milly's argument about Nina, because it is Nina who has bought Harry's wife, Lizette, after a considerable struggle with some lawyers whom Tom has hired to buy her for himself. Thus Milly makes a telling point when she says to Harry, "'Why, chile, would you turn against Miss Nina? Chile, if they get a-going, they won't spare nobody. Don't you start up dat ar tiger; 'cause, I tell ye, ye can't chain him, if ye do!'"

The argument is profoundly serious.[13] Dred accuses Harry of being a willing slave, both to the false consolations of religion and to his own soft-hearted fears of violence:

'Look here, Harry, . . . did your master strike you? It's sweet to kiss the rod, is n't it? Bend your neck and ask to be struck again! —won't you? Be meek and lowly! that's the religion for you. You are a slave, and you wear broadcloth, and sleep soft. By and by he will give you a fip to buy salve for those cuts! Don't fret about your wife! Women always like the master better than the slave! Why should n't they? When a man licks his master's foot, his wife scorns him,—serves him right. Take it meekly, my boy! "Servants, obey your masters." Take your master's old coats—take your wife when he's done with her—and bless God that brought you under the light of the gospel!'

Frantically Harry cries out that he will do as Dred tells him, but Dred has vanished into the thicket, leaving Harry alone with his anger and shame.

There was an uprising within him, vague, tumultuous, overpowering; dim instincts, heroic aspirations; the will to do, the soul to dare; and then, in a moment, there followed the picture of all society leagued against him, the hopeless impossibility of any outlet to what was burning within him. The waters of a nature naturally noble, pent up, and without outlet, rolled back upon his heart with a suffocating force. . . .

At this moment Milly appears in the path. Unlike Dred who says, " '*I* am a free man! Free by this,' holding out his rifle," she tells him " 'dere's a blood of sprinkling dat speaketh better things dan dat of Abel. Jerusalem above is free—is free, honey. . . .' " Harry replies that her faith " 'may do well enough for old women like you,' " but that for him it is too difficult. Besides, how is she so sure that they will all be restored in heaven? Milly simply answers that she is sure, and adds, " 'Chile . . . I ain't a fool. Does ye s'pose dat I thinks folks has any business to be sitting on der cheers all der life long, and working me, and living on my money?' " She reminds him that she knows his bitterness well, but urges him to avoid Dred's course of defiance. " 'Don't you do nothing rash and don't you hear *him*. Dat ar way out is through seas of blood." Finally she reminds him that in turning against Tom, the brother he hates, he will also be turning against Nina, the sister he loves and has promised their father to protect. Thus, Harry confronts a tragic problem.

Toward the end of the novel, there is a good deal of conversation among the Claytons and their friends about freedom, a free country, free speech, the Declaration of Independence, and so on. In the course of these discussions, most of which add nothing new to their counterparts in *Uncle Tom's Cabin,* an interesting note is struck by one of Judge Clayton's friends, a lawyer named Frank Russell. " 'Nobody,' says Russell, 'is absolutely free, except Robinson Crusoe, in the desolate island; and he tears all his shirts to pieces and hangs them up as signals of distress, that he may get back into slavery again.' " [14] Dred has been specifically associated with Crusoe's kind of freedom, the kind that makes one an isolated outcast. Certainly Dred does not signal his distress. He boasts of his savage life. He is proud that he sleeps "on the ground, in the swamps" whereas Harry sleeps "in a curtained bed"; he jeers at Harry for "eat[ing] the fat of the land," when he has "what the ravens bring me." [15] Hence, Harry's problem is more than just a Negro's problem; in seeking the path out of society's confinements and tyrannies toward true freedom, he encounters the same risk as a white man would run, the risk of which Thoreau and Melville and Hawthorne were all so powerfully aware. He risks cutting himself off from, in a sense, annihilating society altogether, and thus denying for all others the human dignity and the heroic possibility he has sought for himself. Alone in his solitary victory, he would then become a creature of the wilderness in fact, desolate, perhaps barbaric.

The possibility that a man could be brutalized by life in the wilds was well realized on the frontier. Travellers were often appalled at the savagery of the conditions of life there and at the habits and especially the amusements of the frontiersmen. The predicament of Robinson Crusoe had special seriousness for mid-century America. One thinks of Thoreau's sly boast that he was tempted to eat a raw woodchuck, and certainly of Melville's various savages, noble and not so noble. It is significant that Mrs. Stowe's involvement with Harry and Dred led her to imagine their response to this problem. Though Mrs. Stowe's analysis of the psychological risks of freedom does not explore the subject farther than it was taken by other mid-century writers, her discussion is distinguished by the fact that it is conducted from the point of view of Harry Gordon and Dred, rather than from that of, say, Thoreau.

Harry has another problem he might have shared with his white contemporaries. He is asked to choose between the revolutionary program of Dred and Milly's faith that true freedom lies not in social reform or rebellion but in Christian compassion and forebearance. Any American of the 1850s might be torn between a desire for radical social change (especially in the system of slavery) and a conscientious rejection of violent class or civil warfare. Moreover, as is clear from her letters, as well as implied in the novel, Mrs. Stowe saw the American struggle over slavery as an extension of the European revolutions of the 1840s. Harry's choice between revolution and patience is to that extent similar to the choice any man of conscience would have faced at the time.

Finally, Harry's problem is personal and peculiar to his racial heritage. Like Joe Christmas, he is divided against himself. Harry cannot honestly suppress either loyalty to the white society and his white father and sister, or sympathy with the bitterness and defiance of Dred. And in this ordeal, neither Dred's nor Milly's advice meets his need.

Thus the failure of *Dred* as a novel owes much to the success with which Mrs. Stowe had articulated and understood the complexities of her subject. In *Dred,* she did no more than to project in fiction the scope of the dilemma, and to dramatize it in characters and situations—the debate between Dred and Milly, the relations of the three Gordon children—which have proved very durable indeed. It is remarkable that so much that has been central to the literature of the South from Twain and Cable through Faulkner should have been focal to a novel published in 1856.

What, then, is the upshot of all this? For what attitude or program of action does Mrs. Stowe argue in this novel? What is the providential historian and scribe of the Lord telling us to do about the great moral problem of slavery?

The message of *Uncle Tom's Cabin,* that the crisis over slavery can be resolved only by Christian love, is restated in the second novel by Milly, and Mrs. Stowe clearly supports her. The difference between the two novels comes chiefly from the fact that Mrs. Stowe has changed not the answer but the question; she has redefined the problem, and hence, the old solution of Christian love, although more forcefully argued by Milly than by Little Eva or Uncle Tom, is not so convincing. What happened was that, first, Dred had become a plausible, even fascinating, and certainly frightening figure to Mrs. Stowe. Second, Harry Gordon's situation had occurred to her.

The problem, as Mrs. Stowe articulates it in Harry Gordon's dilemma—shall he choose rebellion or patience? shall he tolerate his vicious brother for the sake of his honorable sister?—is to discover what are the means to, and limits of, freedom for any man. What, indeed, is freedom, and how can it be won for the individual and in society? Does honor demand rebellion against one's oppressors or does love have a greater claim, enjoining forebearance, urging the dignity of all men? Harry Gordon does not answer these questions.

The polemic in *Dred* does not advocate any particular solution to the great moral problem, but consists instead of a dramatic debate in which the author cannot assign clear victory to anybody. It would be nice if the Claytons' dreams came true, but they probably will not. It is true that Christian love might bind all men together as brothers, but most men may not wish to be bound. Dred's program of revolutionary destruction appears to be both possible and justifiable. Harry Gordon, who not only seeks his own freedom, but is also sensitive to the claims of both Nina and Milly, and of his suffering fellow slaves, does not know what to do.

Mrs. Stowe does not know what Harry should do either, and as a result, the novel is inconclusive not only with respect to its message, but also from 'the merely artistic point of view.' As a novel, it has no proper ending. The plot achieves no satisfactory resolution but tends to trail off into a welter of legal documents and various testimonials taken from the newspapers and political tracts of the time. Mrs. Stowe cannot build up to an ending comparable to Uncle Tom's final statement of love for his oppressors or to the reunion in freedom of George and Eliza. Although her ability to construct a plot was rather low on the list of her talents as a writer, Mrs. Stowe did have a powerful imagination, powerful enough to recognize that no happy ending was conceivable for her second novel, powerful enough, perhaps, to see that events themselves were quickly superceding the possibilities of fiction to contain her subject. The disintegration of this novel at the end, and its failure to impose even a spurious fictional pattern on the arguments over slavery, suggest the disintegration of the nation during the next five years and anticipate the chaotic failure of all argument and all bonds that finally led to Civil War. Today, Harry Gordon is still receiving conflicting advice. History has given us some insight into his, and Mrs. Stowe's dilemma.

# CHAPTER 3

# The Merely Artistic Point of View

Thus far I have been discussing the two slavery novels in terms of their presentation of the nature and problems of the slave system and the arguments they adduce for possible responses to the national crisis. The novels are historical in that they record contemporary events in the manner of the providential historian and in that they consequently propound arguments for the proper solution to contemporary problems in the context of the historical commitment of the nation to its covenant with God. Following Mrs. Stowe's own set of priorities, I have dealt first with the "great moral problem" which, as the scribe of the Lord, it was her duty to record and to which she offered various possible solutions. Having examined these arguments in some detail, I should like now to consider the two novels from what Mrs. Stowe called in the preface to *Dred* "the merely artistic point of view."

Artistically too the novels are historical; that is, they belong to the tradition of the historical romance in the manner of Scott and his American followers, Cooper, Simms, Kennedy, Cooke, and others. Mrs. Stowe's use of some of the conventions of the historical romance is often as different from her models as is her imitation of the providential history or the clerical Jeremiad, but only if we appreciate her artistry in the practice of the genre can we evaluate her achievement even as a polemicist, much less as a novelist.

One of Scott's concerns in the composition of his own novels was to secure what he called 'verisimilitude.' Since the events of the novel and the actions of the major characters were often highly romantic or based on events of the distant past, the reader needed to be brought in touch with the story by a continuous background of setting, incident and minor character to allow him to believe in the tale. This descriptive background was used by Scott not only to gain the reader's credence, but also to create an atmosphere which would make the tale come alive with excitement, suspense, or whatever emotion Scott wished to evoke. This double use of descriptive background to verify events and to stir the reader's poetic imagination is one of the skills which Mrs. Stowe, who could recite Scott's novels by the chapter, learned from the great romancer.

A good example of her use of this technique comes early in *Uncle Tom's Cabin,* in the famous episode of Eliza crossing the ice on the Ohio River in her flight from Marks and Loker. The ice was beginning to thaw and had broken up into big chunks; the melting snow had made the water run high and fast. Eliza had been chased down the bank to the water's edge when, "with one wild cry and flying leap, she vaulted sheer over the turbid current by the shore, on to the raft of ice beyond."

The huge green fragment of ice on which she alighted pitched and creaked as her weight came on it, but she staid there not a moment. With wild cries and desperate energy she leaped to another and still another cake;—stumbling—leaping—slipping—springing upwards again! Her shoes are gone—her stockings cut from her feet—while blood marked every step. . . .[1]

The story, for all its extravagance, is based on excellent observation. Mrs. Stowe well knows that the agitated water beneath will make the ice chunks look green; that the current is often particularly fast right next to the shore; that the ice would not be smooth but rather rough and cutting. Eliza herself is said to be frenzied and her crossing is made a feat of utter desperation. The story is one of the things in the novel which was challenged as untruthful, but the author insisted that she had heard of such an escape when she was living in Cincinnati, and she includes the episode in *The Key to Uncle Tom's Cabin*. True or false, it is made plausible as well as sensational by a supporting description which the reader automatically verifies from his own experience.

It might be more accurate to say that the reader is brought into the episode in such a way that it becomes his own experience. The camera, as it were, follows Eliza; we see the ice up close, we see her bleeding feet. We are close enough to hear the ice creak as she jumps onto it. We see and hear and feel what she does and, in this specific sense, we not only believe in her flight, we are also able to identify with her during it. This is precisely the function of verisimilitude in the historical romance: not only to convince us of the tale but to include us, imaginatively, in its sights and sounds and drama. Another example of the same technique comes just before the crossing of the Ohio when Eliza is being taken from the house of Senator Bird, who pities her but will take no risk on her behalf, to the house of a neighbor for help and protection. The night journey along a muddy log road is so vividly and graphically done that the reader, who again feels that he is there, not only believes the account, but actually learns from it what overland travel was like in the countryside in those days. It is undoubtedly this sort of scene painting, which Mrs. Stowe learned from Scott, which creates the impression that the novel is not fiction but a documentary. The vitality of the novel's settings and incidental descriptions is the source of much of its power. Like Scott, she achieves not only credibility but, further, an imaginative reality more potent than mere factual realism.

Our sense of place is deepened by descriptions which include not only physical features of the land but also the mood and style of the life there. As might be expected from her New England background, Mrs. Stowe does a particularly sensitive rendering of a Vermont village.

Whoever has travelled in the New England States will remember, in some cool village, the large farmhouse, with its clean-swept grassy yard, shaded by the dense and massive foliage of the sugar maple; and remember the air of order and stillness, of perpetuity and unchanging repose, that seemed to breathe over the whole place. . . . Within, he will remember wide, clean rooms, where nothing ever seems to be doing or going to be done, where everything is once and forever rigidly in place, and where all household arrangements move with the punctual exactness of the old clock in the corner. In the family 'keeping room,' as it is termed, he will remember the staid, respectable old book-case, with its glass doors, where Rollin's History, Milton's Paradise Lost, Bunyan's Pilgrim's Progress, and Scott's Family Bible, stand side by side in decorous order, with multitudes of other books, equally solemn and respectable. There are no servants in the house, but the lady in the snowy cap, with the spectacles, who sits sewing every afternoon among her daughters, as if nothing ever had been done, or were to be done,—she and her girls, in some long-forgotten fore part of the day, *'did up the work,'* and for the rest of the time, probably, at all hours when you would see them, it is *'done up.'* The old kitchen floor never seems stained or spotted; the tables, the chairs, and various cooking utensils, never seem deranged or disordered; though three and sometimes four meals a day are got there, though the family washing and ironing is there performed, and though pounds of butter and cheese are in some silent and mysterious manner there brought into existence.[2]

This short account is neither superficial nor caricature. It is not a description of white steeples and quaint eccentrics, but is rather a beautifully lucid glimpse into the heart of that stillness in a New England village which the casual visitor might mistake for inactivity. It alludes to a regional past and way of life deftly and truthfully. Once again the reader recognizes authenticity, and, if he does not recognize it, he feels that he is learning the truth.

Moreover, the settings in *Uncle Tom's Cabin* are usually not fictitious, but use actual place names—New Orleans, Cincinnati—and refer to real people—Webster—in the manner of the historical novel. Descriptions of interiors such as inns and taverns, kitchens or parlors are drawn as literally as possible after those within Mrs. Stowe's own experience. Even, as happens more often than the reader is aware, when the scene is not one she had observed herself, she relies on the information she has from her friends or family to create an authentic picture.

The immense geographic backdrop of *Uncle Tom's Cabin,* so exactly described and so important to the novel's verisimilitude, is not the conception of a secluded New Englander's fancy. Mrs. Stowe had lived in Cincinnati for the eighteen years immediately preceding the writing of the novel, and it is only necessary to remember what Cincinnati was like during the two decades from 1832 to 1850 to understand how naturally she would conceive of such large variety. In the 1830s and 40s there was probably no other place in the country where one could simultaneously observe so much diverse activity. Cincinnati was one of the main inland ports from which the ever increasing numbers of westward pioneers continued their journey toward the Mississippi. As a port it also saw a traffic of slave barges on their way 'down the river' to New Orleans and ferry boats going back and forth to the planter area of northern Kentucky. The city itself developed quickly into a pork packing center and a market for the surrounding territory, while at the same time trying to provide itself with a duly sober cultural life of concerts, literary clubs, and the like. Cincinnati was the scene of Abolitionist riots and ghastly epidemics; it was a main junction on the Underground Railroad; its population reflected almost every color, kind, and class of people then to be found in the United States.

Mrs. Stowe went to Cincinnati at the age of twenty-one with most of her brothers and sisters and her father when he decided to journey thither to become the first president of Lane Theological Seminary in order to help to save the west from barbarism and the Pope. She taught with her older sister Catharine in a school they started in a suburb of the city; she married one of her father's first two colleagues and bore him seven children there, one of whom died in the cholera epidemic the year before they left to return to New England. She took in boarders and frequently had Negro servants in the house in addition to her pupils and children, and it was in Cincinnati that she first wrote short stories and sketches to supplement her husband's often unpaid salary. These stories are, however, not about Cincinnati life nor about slavery, but go back to scenes and especially people Mrs. Stowe had known and heard about as a child in Litchfield, Connecticut. She said very little, even in her letters at the time, of her impressions of people or politics in this fascinating, chaotic city. Her life there seems in fact to have been difficult, poor and unhappy, a round of chores and worries which took all her best energies. Nevertheless, it is apparent to any reader of *Uncle Tom's Cabin* that its author had been an interested and careful observer of the various conflicts and dramas of the national life as they played through the life of the city during those eighteen years.

Mrs. Stowe's early and devoted familiarity with the Waverly novels, in addition to stimulating what proved to be a great talent for setting and description, led to her ease in handling a large cast of characters, especially minor characters, to further verify and enliven the action of a plot. In *Uncle Tom's Cabin; or, Life Among the Lowly,* the role of minor characters and incidents is of major significance.

Character and setting are often complementary. Sometimes, as with Miss Ophelia, the cousin of Augustine St. Clare but a native of that still Vermont village already described, the characters are very much a product of their region, though products in a rather interesting psychological way. Miss Ophelia, or as her cousin calls her simply, "Vermont," is a New Englander not in the sense of being preachy or moralistic but in the sense, implied in the description of the place itself, of being orderly to the bottom of her soul. As soon as she arrives at her cousin's Louisiana house she addresses herself as chief housekeeper to straightening up the kitchen, the traditional pride of all New England women, but in this case the domain of the black cook Dinah who proves impervious to Miss Ophelia's attentions. Contrasted to this industrious maiden lady from Vermont is Marie St. Clare, mistress of the house, who at the time of her marriage had been "the reigning belle of the season," and had, says Mrs. Stowe, "consisted of a fine figure, a pair of splendid eyes, and a hundred thousand dollars." Marie St. Clare is defined by "a selfishness the more hopeless, from its quiet obtuseness, its utter ignorance of any claims but her own. From her infancy, she had been surrounded with servants, who lived only to study her caprices." After the birth of her daughter, she became jealous and "regarded her husband's absorbing devotion to the child with suspicion and dislike; . . ."

From the time of the birth of this child, her health gradually sunk. A life of constant inaction, bodily and mental,—the friction of ceaseless ennui and discontent, united to the ordinary weakness which attended the period of maternity,—in course of a few years changed the blooming young belle into a yellow, faded, sickly woman, whose time was divided among a variety of fanciful diseases, and who considered herself, in every sense, the most ill-used and suffering person in existence.[3]

Although these lines may seem to us somewhat heavy-handed, they are the beginning of a portrait of Marie St. Clare as a sick, helpless, spectral queen of Southern chivalry, a portrait to the substantial truth of which we have testimony from Faulkner, W. J. Cash, and many others.

The variety of the Negro characters in the novel and the deftness with which they are drawn is more remarkable still in that, with the occasional exception, Negro characters are absent from American fiction before the Civil War. *Uncle Tom's Cabin* includes a great many Negroes, clearly characterized and quite different from each other, whose cumulative presence complements and extends the large cast of white characters and vastly enhances the effect of a comprehensive national dramatis personae. A brief but appealing episode early in the novel shows how these characters—we except George and Eliza Harris and Uncle Tom himself—are typically presented. Sam and Andy, slaves of the Shelbys in Kentucky, set about to delay the trader Haley from pursuing Eliza and her son, who have run away the previous night. Their clownish tricks scare off the horses and waste the morning and Haley gets started only after lunch, accompanied by Sam and Andy who are sent along to show him the roads. Sam helpfully begins:

'Now, der's two roads to de river,—the dirt road and der pike,—which Mas'r mean to take? . . .
'Cause,' said Sam, 'I'd rather be 'clined to 'magine that Lizy 'd take de dirt road. bein' it's the least travelled.' . . .
'If yer warn't both on yer such cussed liars, now!' [Haley] said, contemplatively, as he pondered a moment. . . .
'Course,' said Sam, 'Mas'r can do as he'd ruther; go de straight road, if Mas'r thinks best,—it's all one to us. Now, when I study 'pon it, I think de straight road de best, *deridedly.*'

Haley of course chooses the dirt road, although Sam remarks, " 'Now I think on 't, I think I hearn 'em tell that dat ar road was all fenced up and down by der creek, and thar, an't it, Andy?' " Andy is uncertain, being too young to remember the event and having only " 'Hearn tell.' " After about an hour's ride the road runs into the barnyard of a large farm and Sam enjoys his joke on the trader. " 'Wan't dat ar what I telled Mas'r? . . . How does a strange gentlemen spect to know more about a country dan de natives born and raised?' " [4]

Sam is an interesting character, who later gives that notable imitation of grandiose political oratory. He and Andy are lackadaisical and obviously well treated slaves who belong to the mild, healthy society of the northern Kentucky plantations. Their tricks and chatter provide a nice comic interlude which relieves the potential melodrama of the chase and keeps the action on the plane of relaxed social comedy. The very casualness of their role, the near triteness of the joke, and the relative insignificance of the episode typify the way in which Mrs. Stowe often takes for granted the exits and entrances of a multitude of Negro characters in the novel. The easy familiarity with which Mrs. Stowe treats her many Negro characters in *Uncle Tom's Cabin* does of course implicitly affirm what the Supreme Court was soon to deny, namely that they are "persons." They are, moreover, often found in the sort of scene just described where the reader is allowed to relax for a moment from the main action and enjoy a comic diversion. Mrs. Stowe's use of such short comic interludes to modify the pace of the main action is again a device of the historical romance. What strikes one often, as in the scene above, is that these minor and comic characters turn out to be the slaves. Nobody had done that before. Cooper stuck to Indians.

The extent to which Mrs. Stowe differentiates among the Negro characters in matters of dress, personality, speech, and even color, can be briefly suggested by a scene in the slave warehouse in New Orleans where Augustine St. Clare has sent all his servants after the crushing death of his daughter, Eva. Legree has come up to town to buy slaves and has brought with him Sambo and Quimbo, his two black lieutenants. Sambo is "full black, of great size, very lively, voluble, and full of trick and grimace." Uncle Tom and Adolph, St. Clare's dapper valet, are sitting together when Sambo approaches Tom first, who tells him he is to be sold at the auction.

'Sold at auction,—haw! haw! boys, an't this yer fun? I wish't I was gwine that ar way!—tell ye, wouldn't I make em laugh? But how is it,—dis yer whole lot gwine to-morrow?' said Sambo, laying his hand freely on Adolph's shoulder.

'Please to let me alone!' said Adolph, fiercely, straightening himself up, with extreme disgust.

'Law, now, boys! dis yer 's one o' yer white niggers,—kind o' cream color, ye know, scented!' said he, coming up to Adolph and snuffing. 'O Lor! he'd do for a tobaccer-shop; they could keep him to scent snuff! Lor, he'd keep a whole shope agwine,—he would!'

'I say, keep off, can't you?' said Adolph enraged.

'Lor, now, how touchy we is,—we white niggers! Look at us, now!' and Sambo gave a ludicrous imitation of Adolph's manner; 'here's de airs and graces. We's been in a good family, I specs.'

'Yes,' said Adolph; 'I had a master that could have bought you all for old truck!'

'Laws, now, only think,' said Sambo, 'the gentlemens that we is!' [5]

Some people object that the slaves in *Uncle Tom's Cabin* are minstrel show darkies. This is a misleading criticism. First, as is evident in the preceding passage, they are not all alike, and they quarrel in a way far too serious for the mirth of old Jim Crow. Second, to the extent that the Negro characters in the novel are stereotypes, they are certainly no more so than the whites. If Sam and Andy's prank on Haley is minstrel stuff, then Haley is surely a stage villain and Shelby and St. Clare are stereotypes of the Southern planter. Indeed, we can find a good many of the literary offenses of James Fenimore Cooper in *Uncle Tom's Cabin,* as we can in most of the historical romances of the first half of the nineteenth century.

*Uncle Tom's Cabin* was serialized in a sheet called the *National Era* which was founded in 1847 in Washington by Dr. Gamaliel Bailey whom Mrs. Stowe had known in Cincinnati, and who had already published several of her previous "sketches." On March 9, 1851, she wrote to Bailey suggesting her current story which was to be about "the 'patriarchal institution,' written either from observation, incidents which have occurred in the sphere of my personal knowledge, or in the knowledge of my friends. I shall show the *best side* of the thing, and something *faintly approaching the worst.*" The letter goes on to tell him a little about her method.

My vocation is simply that of *painter,* and my object will be to hold up in the most lifelike and graphic manner possible Slavery, its reverses, changes, and the negro character, which I have had ample opportunities for studying. There is no arguing with *pictures,* and everybody is impressed by them, whether they mean to be or not.[6]

The last chapter of *Uncle Tom's Cabin* reiterates all of the points Mrs. Stowe had made in the letter to Bailey, but at much greater length. She insists on the novel's authenticity to the point of citing Eliza, Uncle Tom, old Prue, and Simon Legree as transcriptions of real people. She repeats here also her motive for writing, namely the passage of the Fugitive Slave Act (1850) and the succeeding discussions among pious Northerners about what their Christian duty required with respect to the remanding of slaves. Mrs. Stowe there and then concluded that "These men and Christians cannot know what slavery is; if they did, such a question could never be opened for discussion. And from this," she says in retrospect, "arose a desire to exhibit it in a *living dramatic reality.*"[7]

The use of pictorial verisimilitude in setting and character is not limited by Mrs. Stowe to the purposes of credibility and poetic atmosphere. Her pictures point a moral. To show slavery in "living dramatic reality" is to conduct an argument with the reader (and with Daniel Webster). In the course of this argument, the skills of the historical romancer in describing a scene, come to the aid of, and are often blended with, the documentary style of the providential chronicler whose duty it is to record the events of her time. Mrs. Stowe's readers were not only familiar with the novels of Scott and his American followers, and hence susceptible to Mrs. Stowe's skillful adaptation of those conventions; they were also quite used to the tones of clerical exhortation in which backsliding was lamented and the audience was urged to return to its covenant and its national destiny. Hence, Mrs. Stowe hit her readers coming and going.

To illustrate the way in which Mrs. Stowe blends her documentary method and its moral argument with the practice of the novelistic genre painter, I should like to quote the familiar passage describing a scene in the kitchen of the St. Clare house in New Orleans. This scene will also give us further insight into her use of the conventions of the historical romance. The episode turns on the relations between the slaves and their masters and, more immediately, among themselves, although in the house of Augustine St. Clare this does not mean, as it does with Simon Legree, that the masters are wicked and brutal and the slaves are huddled together, wrathful and oppressed. Not at all. Here the master is sophisticated and indulgent, and the conditions of slavery reflect the tone of the white society around it.

The scene in the kitchen takes place the evening before a ball. Present are Dinah, the black cook; the proud and pampered Adolph; Jane, Marie St. Clare's spoiled personal maid; Rosa, a chambermaid; and various Negro children. Miss Ophelia happens to be in the kitchen too at the moment when the children spy old Prue, " 'a coming, grunting along like she allers does.' "

Prue had a peculiar scowling expression of countenance, and a sullen, grumbling voice. She set down her basket, squatted herself down, and resting her elbows on her knees said,

'O Lord! I wish't I's dead!'

'Why do you wish you were dead?' said Miss Ophelia.

'I'd be out o' my misery,' said the woman, gruffly, without taking her eyes from the floor.

'What need you getting drunk, then, and cutting up, Prue?' said a spruce quadroon chambermaid, dangling, as she spoke, a pair of coral ear-drops. . . .

'Ye think ye're mighty fine with them ar, a frolickin' and a tossin' your head, and a lookin' down on everybody. Well, never mind,—you may live to be a poor, old, cut-up crittur, like me. Hope to the Lord ye will, I do; then see if ye won't drink,—drink,—drink,—yerself into torment; and sarve ye right, too—ugh!' and, with a malignant howl, the woman left the room.

'Disgusting old beast!' said Adolph, who was getting his master's shaving-water. 'If I was her master, I'd cut her up worse than she is.'

'Ye couldn't do that ar, no ways,' said Dinah. 'Her back's a far sight now,—she can't never get a dress together over it.'

'I think such low creatures ought not to be allowed to go round to genteel families,' said Miss Jane. 'What do you think, Mr. St. Clare?' she said, coquettishly tossing her head at Adolph.

It must be observed that, among other appropriations from his master's stock, Adolph was in the habit of adopting his name and address; and that the style under which he moved, among the colored circles of New Orleans, was that of *Mr. St. Clare*.

'I'm certainly of your opinion, Miss Benoir,' said Adolph.

Benoir was the name of Marie St. Clare's family, and Jane was one of her servants.

'Pray, Miss Benoir, may I be allowed to ask if those drops are for the ball, to-morrow night? They are certainly bewitching!'

'I wonder, now, Mr. St. Clare, what the impudence of you men will come to! . . . I shan't dance with you for a whole evening, if you go to asking me any more questions.'

'O, you couldn't be so cruel, now! I was just dying to know whether you would appear in your pink tarletane,' said Adolph. . . .

'Come,—clar out, you! I can't have you cluttering up the kitchen,' said Dinah; 'in my way, foolin' round here.'

'Aunt Dinah's glum, because she can't go to the ball,' said Rosa.

'Don't want none o' your light-colored balls,' said Dinah; 'cuttin' round, makin' b'lieve you's white folks. Arter all, you's niggers, much as I am.'

'Aunt Dinah greases her wool stiff, every day, to make it lie straight,' said Jane. . . .

'Well, in the Lord's sight, an't wool as good as har, any time?' said Dinah. 'I'd like to have Missis say which is worth the most,—a couple such as you, or one like me. Get out wid ye, ye trumpery,— I won't have ye round!' [8]

This scene is neither didactic nor sentimental. It is comic, even in the case of old Prue whose life history is easily as gruesome as Uncle Tom's; it is also undeniably authentic in its brilliant rendering of the private mimicry and quarreling which rings doubly true for being invisible to the eye of the ordinary visitor. One cannot match the irony of Dinah's appeal to "the Missis" until thirty years later when Roxy, in *Pudd'nhead Wilson,* justifies her baby switching on the ground that "white folks done it." It is the effect of utter candor in this dialogue which makes it seem realistically to hold the mirror up to nature, the candor of Jane's and Adolph's condescension to Dinah and of their self-conscious imitation of their masters' idiom and custom.

It was one of the conventions of the American historical novel that the story should be presented on a split-level stage. The upper part is allotted to respectable more or less upper class characters who speak perfect and often pompous English, who dress in the fashionable equivalent of buckles and brocades, and whose education has made them familiar with European tastes and ideas. On the lower stage are enacted the scenes which concern those characters called lowly: servants, or, more often, rustics of some sort—farmers, woodsmen, sailors. They would be uneducated, but nevertheless wise in the ways of woodcraft, Indian fighting, tricky navigation, or, if women, in cake-baking, and household lore. These people typically wear homespun and they speak a language, often a dialect, which is according to this tradition at once realistic and patriotic. An excellent example, and in a sense a prototype, of this character is Jonathan in

Royall Tyler's play *The Contrast* (1778). In the novels of Cooper one thinks of Peter Coffin and, of course, of Natty Bumppo.

It is often observed by students of American literature that the upper class characters suffer from stiffness and imaginative dryness due to their derivative literary origin, or, perhaps to the desire of the author to make his American heroes and heroines measure up to English gentility. The low life scenes, on the other hand, are often fast-moving, entertaining interludes in which the authentic native idiom and the imaginative energy of new American characters is exactly expressed. While our writers were still imitating foreign models in their allegedly principal characters, they were busy creating an original cast of characters and were experimenting with new uses of landscape and with various kinds of native vernacular speech in the low life scenes.

With this tradition in mind, we can put ourselves in the place of the reader of *Uncle Tom's Cabin* in 1852. We would expect in the low life scenes veracious social comedy, spicy native characters and talk, a rollicking glimpse of real life doubly real because the respectable observers are gone. And we get in the scene in the St. Clare kitchen just what we expected: dialect, animated argument, grim, even sordid, detail about old Prue, and an unmistakable sense of psychological truthfulness in the relations of the different characters to one another and to their place in the pecking order. Hence the effect of authentic reportage. The only unexpected element is that the characters are all Negroes. Hence, too, the force of the moral argument when Mrs. Stowe continues the scene.

After the group in the kitchen disperses, it turns out that Uncle Tom has followed Prue out the back door. He offers to carry her basket, but his real desire is to save her soul from what he considers her blaspheming. Prue tells him she will not stop drinking because " 'I knows I'm gwine to torment. . . . Ye don't need to tell me that ar. I's ugly,—I's wicked,—I's gwine straight to torment. O, Lord! I wish I's thar!'" Tom is so patient and persistent that she is forced to tell him her whole story.

'Where was you raised?' said Tom.

'Up in Kentuck. A man kept me to breed chil'en for market, and sold 'em as fast as they got big enough; last of all, he sold me to a speculator, and my Mas'r got me o' him.'

'What set you into this bad way of drinkin'?'

'To get shet o' my misery. I had one child after I come here; and I thought then I'd have one to raise, cause Mas'r wasn't a speculator. It was de peartest little thing! and Missis she seemed to think a heap on 't, at first; it never cried,—it was likely and fat. But Missis tuck sick, and I tended her; and I tuck the fever, and my milk all left me, and the child it pined to skin and bone, and Missis wouldn't buy milk for it. . . . She said she knowed I could feed it on what other folks eat; and the child kinder pined, and cried, and cried, and cried, day and night, and got all gone to skin and bones, and Missis got sot agin it, and she said 't wan't nothin' but crossness. She wished it was dead, she said; and she wouldn't let me have it o' nights, cause, she said, it kept me awake, and made me good for nothing. She made me sleep in her room; and I had to put it away off in a little kind o' garret, and thar it cried itself to death, one night. It did; and I tuck to drinkin', to keep its crying out of my ears! I did,—and I will drink! I will, if I do go to torment for it! Mas'r says I shall go to torment, and I tell him I've got thar now!' [9]

The ordinary reader, after having been put in a relaxed and credulous frame of mind by the scene in the kitchen and the hoarse dialect of old Prue, reads this tale as a continuation of the earlier part of the scene and consequently believes every word of it. Thus, we are swayed by Prue's story before we have a chance to remind ourselves that she might well be drunkenly exaggerating or that her case may not be typical of the treatment of slaves in the South. The argument is, of course, harder to resist in this form than it would be if delivered in the rhetoric of Abolitionists or through the formal debates of politicians.

Because of the particular way in which the low life scenes and characters of historical romance had come to be treated in America, the portrayal of "life among the lowly" in *Uncle Tom's Cabin* was especially disturbing. Although Mrs. Stowe retains the stock low life figures and situations to some extent, she introduces a new and startling variation on the conventions by often making these characters and scenes deal entirely, or mainly, with the slaves. In just the places where the American reader had come to expect the especially native product, he found a native he had, in literature at least, overlooked. We must put ourselves in the position of Mrs. Stowe's readers then, and remember the popularity of the genre and the power of its conventions, if we are to understand the extraordinary drama she created for her audience.

Finally, it is worth mentioning that Mrs. Stowe changes the traditional functions of dialect. Again, she partly stays within the convention, using dialect for local flavor and to enhance the effect of authenticity. On this score too, she commits some of Cooper's famous offenses. Sam will say "the" in one sentence and "de" in another; or he will mix "never" and "neber." Old Prue is more consistent, but there are, all through the novel, these obvious lapses where dialect appears, as well as the more serious confusion of Yankee with Negro idioms. Such errors do not, however, impair the main effect of the dialect any more than do the presence of the various other offenses of the historical romancer which Mrs. Stowe commits with Cooper and against all of which in general and those of the master, Scott, in particular, Twain was in indignant revolt.

There are several kinds of dialect in the novel. The most unusual for the time was that of the slaves, but Haley, Marks and Loker speak a tough river slang, the Canadian Quakers are given a very pure 'thee' and 'thou' language, and the preachers in the novel sound their clerical jargon with a vividness that only a woman who was daughter, wife, sister and mother of ministers could command. Indeed all the characters in the book are given, to a greater or lesser extent, a typical way of speaking. Thus the convention of the double stage found in earlier American historical romances is further modified. Although the cast of characters ranges geographically, racially, and socially through a very wide spectrum, the stage is continuous and the use of dialect and special idiom in characterization is not reserved for the low life characters alone. In this respect, the double stage is abandoned entirely and with it the self-conscious decorum of the polite characters. The Shelbys and St. Clares are every bit as native in word and deed as are the traders, servants and field hands.

The more important modification of convention is, however, the one illustrated by the scene in the St. Clare kitchen. Because of the fact that the historical romance in this country had developed the habit of retaining a rather transatlantic gentility for the heroes and heroines and of giving to the low life characters the authentic vernacular flavors of the new world, American readers had come to look to the latter for what was peculiarly and intimately their own. When Mrs. Stowe conceived innovation in that convention—when she used comic, low life scenes to portray not backwoods rustics or homespun patriots, but slave cabins and slave quarters, the planter's kitchen or the auction warehouse—she showed herself worthy of Lincoln's greeting: "So you're the little lady who started this big war."

It is easy for us to forget, dazzled as we are by the masterpieces of the 1850s, that the American reader of the mid-century had read far more historical romance, American and English, than he had read of whalers, Walden Pond or the Salem Custom House. Mrs. Stowe's audience, although most of them could probably not recite Scott's novels as she could, were far more familiar with them and their American variants than with any other form of fiction. When we think of Mrs. Stowe's predecessors in the genre in America, we can recognize in her first novel the sources of its power to move and persuade its audience. We can also appreciate that, from the merely artistic point of view, *Uncle Tom's Cabin* is an achievement of great subtlety and originality.

*Dred* is also a historical romance. In the author's preface, having explained her main interest in the Southern setting as the stage whereon the great events of providential history are being enacted, Mrs. Stowe also cites its "merely" literary value. On this theme she clearly speaks as the experienced romancer:

. . . there is no ground, ancient or modern, whose vivid lights, gloomy shadows, and grotesque groupings, afford to the novelist so wide a scope for the exercise of his powers. In the near vicinity of modern civilization of the most matter-of-fact kind exist institutions which carry us back to the twilight of the feudal ages, with all their exciting possibilities of incident.[10]

When Mrs. Stowe thinks of romance and glamor, she tends to think of Byron. The heroine of *Dred,* Nina Gordon, is descended from one of "the first emigrants to Virginia, in its colonial days, . . . one Thomas Gordon, Knight, a distant off-shoot of the noble Gordon family renowned in Scottish history."[11] Her fiancé, Edward Clayton, scion of a neighboring plantation, is "one of your high-and-mighty people—with such deep-set eyes—eyes that look as if they were in a cave—and such black hair! And his eyes have a desperate sort of sad look, some-times—quite Byronic."[12] Thus it seems clear at the beginning of the novel that Mrs. Stowe is not going to stint on any of the gratifications of the luxurious setting, dashing Byronic lovers, or rich, thrilling, even improbable incident which the Carolina background can provide in the service of romance.

Frequently in the first half of *Dred* the work of supplying the descriptive background of historical romance leads Mrs. Stowe into a satirical treatment of her minor characters. This satirical tone gives us added confidence in her tale as a picture of "real life" which once again enhances both fictional verisimilitude and political argument. An instance of this lighter tone, so different from the mood of *Uncle Tom's Cabin,* is a colloquy between Nina Gordon and her Aunt Nesbit, a former belle turned pious fraud.

When Nina visits her aunt's bedroom one morning and finds her going over numerous laces and silks, the aunt instructs her niece, " 'I have been through all this, Nina . . . and I know the vanity of it.' " Aunt Nesbit rehearses a solemn lesson about the folly of the beauties of the earth. When Nina protests, the good woman concludes, in perfect imitation of the clerical formula, " 'That's the opposition of the natural heart, my dear.' " What is satirized in Aunt Nesbit is false religion, or, to be more explicit, what Mrs. Stowe takes to be the decadence of the major Protestant denominations, especially in the South. When "the Rev. Mr. Orthodoxy" preaches that "selfishness is the essence of all moral evil," Mrs. Stowe comments that Aunt Nesbit did not apply the point to her own state of mind; neither, we are left to infer, did the minister.[13]

One of the major themes of *Dred* is the failure of the large Protestant churches adequately to respond to the "great moral problem" of slavery. As in *Uncle Tom's Cabin,* the leading spokesman for religious truth is a secular figure, Milly, but where in *Uncle Tom's Cabin* the failure of the clergy is only implicit and is suggested chiefly by their conspicuous absence, *Dred* mounts a sweeping attack on a variety of men who, in Mrs. Stowe's view, were daily betraying their calling. She begins early in the novel by showing the malevolent influence of wrong headed theology on a dull-witted layman, Mr. Jekyl. The point of the attack is ultimately to demonstrate the harm done to simple minds by President Edwards (making it a continuation of her quarrel with him) and incidentally to show the treachery of the local clergy in allowing a man like Jekyl to think and act as he does. The strategy of the attack is much the same as Mrs. Stowe had used in Sam's parody of the rhetoric of the Unionist orators. Again with Jekyl, we hear a perverted use of language which once meant, and ought still to mean, something else. And although Mrs. Stowe ultimately blames Edwards for using language and pressing arguments which ordinary minds are bound to misunderstand, she still cannot suppress her contempt for the degradation of this once lofty language in the mouth of Mr. Jekyl.

[Jekyl's] favorite subject of all was the nature of true virtue; and this, he had fixed in his mind, consisted in a love of the greatest good. According to his theology, right consisted in creating the greatest amount of happiness; and every creature had rights to be happy in proportion to his capacity of enjoyment or being.

We notice that the word "right" meaning moral good is twisted into the word "rights" meaning legal prerogative. Continuing,

He whose capacity was ten pounds had a right to place his own happiness before that of him who had five, because, in that way, five pounds more of happiness would exist in the general whole.

Thus legal rights are reduced to a commercial measure; the value of the soul corresponds, like that of a sack of flour, to its weight.

Mr. Jekyl's belief in slavery was founded on his theology. He assumed that the white race had the largest amount of being; therefore, it had a right to take precedence of the black.

Not only did he consider the white race justified, even obligated, to please itself at the expense of the black; he also found the lot of the slave, thus condemned to misery, entirely tolerable. In this, his perversion of Edwards is especially striking:

Thus, Mr. Jekyl considered that the Creator brought into the world yearly myriads of human beings with no other intention than to make them everlastingly miserable; and that this was right, because his capacity of enjoyment being greater than all theirs put together, He had a right to gratify himself in this way.[14]

I shall deal with Mrs. Stowe's quarrel with Edwards more thoroughly in the next chapter in discussing the New England novels in which it plays so large a part, but it is useful to mention the attack on Mr. Jekyl in *Dred* not only to illustrate Mrs. Stowe's further use of rhetorical satire but also to emphasize the continuity of the issue in her writing. It will be central again in the discussion of Byron.

Although the many-sided attack in *Dred* on the decadence of the Protestant clergy could quite properly be said to belong to Mrs. Stowe's analysis of the "great moral problem" of slavery rather than to "the merely artistic point of view," her method of conducting the attack is far more significant than the substance of her charges. As regards the latter, she accuses the brethren of incompetence, hypocrisy, cowardice and either a villainous acquiescence in the system of slavery or, worse, direct participation. The one exception is Fr. Dickinson who takes his vows seriously but is utterly ineffectual in trying to act on them. Like the high-minded reformer, Edward Clayton, he is helpless.

The overriding concern of Mrs. Stowe's life was the Christian religion in all the aspects by which she knew it. At home, as a child, she learned the whole story of the colonial churches and of the theological and political controversy in which her father and his colleagues engaged in the early nineteenth century. She later became interested in the Catholic church, mainly in Italy, and in 1864 joined the Episcopal church in Hartford. Her reading and writing were often on religious subjects and her whole outlook was from the vantage point of one chiefly concerned for religious issues. Thus, when we think about Mrs. Stowe's involvement with slavery and the national crisis of the

1850s, we ought to remember that she was interested in slavery because it presented a great moral problem to the churches, the private conscience, and society at large; she did not acquire an interest in Christian doctrine and ethics because of the crisis over slavery. In other words, her concern with the Protestant clergy and with their concerns precedes and goes beyond her concerns with slavery, and for this reason too it is worthwhile to consider her attack on the clergy and especially her description of the camp-meeting in *Dred* somewhat separately from our discussion of her polemics about the patriarchal institution.

Not merely a fictional vehicle for religious or political argument, the camp-meeting recreates the religious life of that very large and expanding hinterland, only recently removed from primeval wilderness, through which the errant revivalists traveled in the decades from the 1820s on. This chapter is not documentary in the sense that many later chapters in the novel are, with their transcriptions of newspaper items, handbills, court cases, and the like. "The Camp-Meeting" is pure fiction, but fiction of a kind that transcends the limits of descriptive verisimilitude and allows us to experience the life of the time as, say, Dickens lets us know London. As a piece of historical realism, it is in itself a valuable document for those who would know what such a revival meeting was like, and, from the merely artistic point of view, it is valuable in realizing with vitality and truthfulness the whole sound and meaning of such a revival meeting, an experience which was central to the life of the newly-settled West.

The camp-meeting is a great affair for the whole region. The Gordon and Clayton families and their neighbors all go, as do all the slaves and servants, and tents and food enough are brought to provide for several days of praying and talking with the neighbors. The ministers of the different denominations in the vicinity gather to compete with each other for applause and converts. Booths are set up on the campground by whiskey

makers, slave-traders, slave-hunters, and peddlers of all sorts,
and, as the cleared area in the woods begins to fill up with
people, picnics are spread, tents erected, hymn singing begun in
intermittent groups, and general excitement begins to run high
in anticipation of the forensic battles and glorious conversions
ahead. A stand is built for the preachers, and presently the meeting is led off by a robust hymn, "Brethren don't you hear the
sound? The martial trumpet now is blowing." [15]

About noon the preacher adjourns the services and the crowd
disperses to tents for a picnic lunch and an appraisal of the
morning's clerical performances. Abijah Skinflint, proprietor of
the whiskey barrel, enjoys a good argument with a Methodist:

'I say,' [Abijah] said, 'Stringfellow put it into you Methodists
this morning! Hit the nail on the head, I thought!'

'Not a bit of it!' said the other contemptuously. 'Why, Elder
Baskum chawed him up completely! There wa'n't nothin' left of
him!'

'Well,' said Abijah, 'strange how folks will see things! Why it's
just as clar to me that all things is decreed! Why, that ar nails
everything up tight and handsome. It gives a fellow a kind of comfort to think on it. . . .'

'I don't like this tying up things so tight. . . . I go in for freedom
of the will. Free gospel, and free grace.'

. . . 'You strong electioners think you's among the elect!' said
one of the bystanders. 'You wouldn't be so crank about it, if you
didn't! Now, see here: if everything is decreed, how am I going
to help myself?'

'That ar is none of my lookout,' said Abijah.

Again Mrs. Stowe provides clever verbal parody as we hear these
two backwoodsmen neatly manipulate the stock phrases of
clerical debate. Their argument sounds more like a squabble at
a sporting match than anything else, and, in part, that is just
what it is: a camp-meeting has many functions, as Mrs. Stowe
well knows.

Elsewhere on the campground during the noon interval, a fight starts between Ben Dakin and his professional rival, Jim Stokes. Mrs. Stowe's description of Ben will serve for Stokes too, as will her comment on their common profession. She begins with a fine irony:

Ben was a mighty hunter; he had the best pack of dogs within thirty miles round; and his advertisements . . . detailed with great accuracy the precise terms on which he would hunt down and capture any man, woman, or child, escaping from service and labor in that country. Our readers must not necessarily suppose Ben to have been a monster for all this, when they recollect that, within a few years, both the great political parties of our Union solemnly pledged themselves . . . to accept a similar vocation; and as many of them were in good and regular standing in churches, and had ministers to preach sermons to the same effect.[16]

Mrs. Stowe caustically supposes that none of her readers will condemn the mighty hunter. This is not quite the same kind of polemical aside as we heard in *Uncle Tom's Cabin* concerning the brutality of the slave-trader whose degradation was forced upon him by the ruling classes who condoned, indeed required, his business; here Mrs. Stowe is saying that the brutalities of the small men whose trades were first created by the rulers of the system have finally returned to their source. The leaders of church and state are now as debased as the creatures they hired. After the beating of Sumner and the Pottawatomie massacre, it was not so easy to distinguish between the brutalities of the frontier and those of the Senate. Still, Mrs. Stowe hopes to humiliate those of her readers who still take pride in American principles. Hence she is especially scathing in her description of the "mighty hunter," once a heroic figure of pioneer courage, now a term which must include the hunter of men. For the reader who may have admired the mighty hunter of the old days, she offers the present bearer of the title for comparison.

A Georgia trader, who is also attending the revival, approaches Ben Dakin to say that one of his gang of slaves has made off into the Swamp during the morning meeting; the fight starts when Stokes interferes to claim, " 'Why, durn ye, his dogs ain't no breed 't all! Mine's the true grit, I can tell you; they's the true Florida blood-hounds! I's seen one of them ar dogs shake a nigger in his mouth like he'd been a sponge.' " This is the mighty hunter's boast in 1856.

No sooner have the members of the crowd around them laid their bets than the fight is interrupted by Father Bonnie, one of the heartier ministers: " 'let the nigger run; you can catch him fast enough when the meetings are over. You come here to 'tend to your salvation.' " After starting the group on an appropriate hymn, the minister turns to the trader, " 'you got a good cook in your lot, hey?' "

'Got a prime one,' said the trader; 'an A number one cook, and no mistake! Picked her up real cheap, and I'll let you have her for eight hundred dollars, being as you are a minister.'

'You must think the gospel a better trade than it is,' said Father Bonnie, 'if you think a minister can afford to pay at that figure!'

He offers seven hundred and fifty dollars, but the trader refuses, and Father Bonnie then walks away with the promise that he will think about it. Father Bonnie does not, as do some of the other brethren, attempt a biblical defense of slavery. He simply ignores the problem.

At the evening session the camp-meeting gets into full swing. The moon is so bright that it is decided to conduct the services by its light alone, and after the opening hymn the first preacher, none other than the seasoned revivalist Father Bonnie, takes as his text, "The heavens declare the glory of God. . . ." Mrs. Stowe's ear for the rhythms of revival preaching was trained, and excellent; to do justice to her rendering, not only of the preacher's idiom, but also of the whole structure and cadence of such a sermon, I must quote a fairly long passage from the opening section. This is, of course, an excellent document for the historian today.

'Oh, ye sinners! . . . look up at the moon, there, walking in her brightness, and think over your oaths, and your cursings, and your drinkings! Think over your backbitings, and your cheatings! think over your quarrelings and your fightings! How do they look to you now, with that blessed moon shining down on you? Don't you see the beauty of our Lord God upon her? Don't you see how the saints walk in white with the Lord, like her? I dare say some of you, now, have had a pious mother, or a pious wife, or a pious sister, that's gone to glory? and there they are walking with the Lord!—walking with the Lord, through the sky, and looking down on you, sinners, just as that moon looks down! And what does she see you doing, your wife, or your mother, or sister, that's in glory? Does she see all your swearings, and your drinkings, and your fightings, and your hankerings after money, and your horse-racings, and your cock-fightings? Oh, sinners, but you are a bad set! I tell you the Lord is looking now down on you, out of that moon! He is looking down in mercy! But, I tell you, he'll look down quite another way, one of these days! Oh, there'll be a time of wrath, by and by, if you don't repent! Oh, what a time there was at Sinai, years ago, when the voice of the trumpet waxed louder and louder, and the mountain was all of a smoke, and there were thunderings and lightenings, and the Lord descended on Sinai! That's nothing to what you'll see, by and by! No more moon looking down on you! No more stars, but the heavens shall pass away with a great noise, and the elements shall melt with fervent heat! Ah! did you ever see a fire in the woods? I have; and I've seen the fire on the prairies, and it rolled like a tempest, and men and horses and everything had to run before it. I have seen it roaring and crackling through the woods, and great trees shriveled in a minute like tinder! I have seen it flash over trees seventy-five and a hundred feet high, and in a minute they'd be standing pillars of fire, and the heavens were all ablaze, and the crackling and roaring was like the sea in a storm. There's a judgment-day for you!'

As the preacher mounts threat upon threat of the awful day at hand, the audience responds with tumultuous groans, cries, and applause which in turn arouse the preacher to ever fiercer urgency. At the highest pitch, he begins to call them to the stand: " 'Now is your time, sinners! Now is your time!' " "Multitudes rushed forward, groans and sobs were heard, as the speaker continued, with redoubled vehemence." The meeting is a huge success. " 'Brethren, . . . we are seeing a day from the Lord! We've got a glorious time. Oh, brethren, let us sing glory to the Lord! The Lord is coming among us!' "

Just at this moment of massive jubilation Dred makes his entrance into the novel. Concealed in the branches of a tree in back of the preaching stand, he booms out his message of vengeance. " 'Woe unto you that desire the day of the Lord!' "

'Hear, oh ye rebellious people! The Lord is against this nation! . . . 'The horseman lifteth up the sword and glittering spear! . . . There is no end of their corpses!—They are stumbling upon corpses! For, Behold, I am against thee, saith the Lord, and I will make thee utterly desolate!'

The explosive contrast between Fr. Bonnie's rabble-rousing calls to the crowd announcing the glorious coming of the Lord and Dred's apocalyptic cry of woe is a brilliant moment in the novel. The reader is made to experience, almost on his pulse, the frightening contrast between Bonnie's cynical histrionics and Dred's deadly prophecies. The effect is worth pages of argument saying that the churches no longer attend to the words they speak, that they have forgotten the language of the prophets and have taken to putting on a good show for the crowds, heedless of the wrath of God upon them and upon the souls they claim to save. The excitement of the sermon, far from moving its listeners to a more Christian life, has the effect of an escape into imagined glory; the result is that they forget the Lord, and forget their offenses before Him. Dred speaks as to the cities of Sodom and Gomorrah.

From this point in the novel to the end, Mrs. Stowe often reverts to a less artistic and more obvious mode of attack. Dred harangues the reader on behalf of the author in a way that often subordinates the artistic value to the polemical purpose of the story and makes fiction a mere vehicle for argument. This is not uniformly the case, but it is true of the second half of the novel to a depressing extent. Nonetheless, the chapter of the camp-meeting is a high artistic achievement and brings into focus the development of Mrs. Stowe's novelistic technique to this point. Scott is her progenitor as a novelist: but whereas she assumes Scott, she discovers Dickens; that is, she discovers how to turn descriptive background into historical realism.

*Uncle Tom's Cabin* uses the descriptive background of the historical romance not only to verify extravagances of plot and incident, as Scott does, but also to substantiate a moral argument. It exploits the conventions of the historical romance— the double stage, the use of dialect, the use of low life scenes— to strengthen the fictional narrative as well as to make the polemic more convincing. Finally, Mrs. Stowe's first novel also makes limited use of verbal and rhetorical satire.

The second novel extends the satirical range and sophistication of the first. The pictures of Aunt Nesbit and Mr. Jekyl and the several clerical portraits are drawn with a finer satirical edge than Mrs. Stowe had previously commanded. Milly is far more skillfully presented than the mothers in *Uncle Tom's Cabin* who appeal to much the same emotions. The sentimental pieties of little Eva and Tom are toned down in *Dred,* where more is said about Christian charity through Milly, or indirectly, through the dramatic hypocrisy of Fr. Bonnie than had been said bluntly by the author or her obvious spokesmen in *Uncle Tom's Cabin.* In these kinds of ways we can easily see Mrs. Stowe refining her craft and extending her control over fictional expression and meaning. And yet, *Dred* is a worse novel, and this is because Mrs. Stowe totally changed its tone and course in the middle. The result is not only that the earlier narrative is never completed satisfactorily; it is also that Mrs. Stowe seems finally to have given up the attempt to encompass her subject, as she saw it after the beating of Sumner and the Pottawatomie massacre, in any fictional terms whatever.

*Dred* has outstanding flaws and outstanding virtues. Certainly the two are connected in that many of the flaws result from her sudden perception of new and indeed tragic dimensions in a subject which she had begun by treating in the idiom of satirical romance. As regards the novel's flaws, it should be said that most of Mrs. Stowe's writing is spotty, partly for the reason that her talents lay more with doing a scene or imagining a situation such as Harry Gordon's than with constructing a plot or shaping a narrative form. Part of the trouble, too, is the simple fact that Mrs. Stowe did her writing in a hurried, haphazard fashion in odd moments between household and other preoccupations and that she never made time for revision.

The merits of *Dred* are, nonetheless, outstanding. First, there is a profound rightness in the conception of Harry Gordon's dilemma; it has stood the test of time. Further, *Dred* moves beyond pictorial verisimilitude into a kind of realistic writing the vitality and conviction of which transcend the conventions of the historical romance and the requirements of the historical chronicler in such a way that it is the energy and truthfulness of the art itself to which we assent. Despite the fact that *Dred* is a flawed novel, that it is structurally chaotic, and that it becomes extremely tedious in places towards the end, it does have moments, scenes, depths to which we can simply say, as it is always the aim of the artist to move us to say, yes, that is how life really is.

CHAPTER 4

# New England Then and Now: Children of the Morning

During the year 1859, in its second year of publication, *The Atlantic Monthly* extended its circulation and secured itself more firmly as a new literary magazine by the serial publication of Dr. Holmes's "The Autocrat of the Breakfast Table" and by the third novel of Harriet Beecher Stowe, who had by this time become very popular and widely admired in this country and in England. The novel, *The Minister's Wooing,* is the first of four novels about colonial New England which form, after *Uncle Tom's Cabin,* her most accomplished literary work.[1]

Her subject, however, was not new to her. Back in the early days in Cincinnati, before the great turbulence of *Uncle Tom's Cabin* had seized her, Mrs. Stowe had written several stories or "sketches" to earn a little money for her increasingly numerous family and to enjoy the company of a literary group in Cincinnati which called itself the Semi-Colon Club. These stories had been gathered into a book by Catharine Beecher who had written a short preface to the collection. As a title, the sisters chose "The Mayflower; or, sketches of scenes and characters among the descendants of the pilgrims." The book was brought out by *Harper's* in 1842.

In language and mood, and in the treatment of characteristic New England "types," the *Mayflower* stories are prophetic of their author's later work. The first sketch, originally called "Uncle

85

Lot" (the collection was revised by Mrs. Stowe in 1854 but not basically changed), concerns an outwardly dour but inwardly generous Connecticut Yankee. His own son, a pale, spiritual minister, dies young and Uncle Lot then takes to his heart a more dashing young man, James Benton, of whom he had formerly been suspicious and who loves his daughter. The plot, though sentimental, is lightly done, and the characterization of Uncle Lot is quite skillful. Already in this story the author's ear for Yankee idiom and cadence is excellent. Already too, Mrs. Stowe shows her skill in making events within her personal knowledge —the story is clearly based on Lyman Beecher's Uncle Lot Benton—ring true in fiction.

Another engaging story is the one called "Love Versus Law"; the antithesis of the title is a thematic foreshadowing in itself. Once again we have the sour Yankee farmer, Uncle Jaw, who speaks dialect. The cast includes Miss Silence Jones, an ornery old maid who first rails against going to a quilting at Deacon Enos Dudley's and then, finding that her pretty younger sister has made up her mind to go anyway, persuades herself that it is her duty to go too. Describing Uncle Jaw, Mrs. Stowe comments: "He was tall and hard-favored, with an expression of countenance much resembling a northeast rainstorm—a drizzling, settled sulkiness, that seemed to defy all prospect of clearing off, and to take comfort in its own disagreeableness." [2] This language, both blunt and humorously imaginative, reflects the New Englander's habitual wry awareness of the ill-favored climate and its effect on the regional character. The descriptive metaphor is, moreover, as frankly close to the natural facts as Emerson had required when he urged American writers to reject "the sere remains of foreign harvests," and to express themselves in plain American words. In many of the *Mayflower* sketches Mrs. Stowe suits her language to her subject in this way, to the great benefit of her often flimsy or trite plots.

Another anticipatory aspect of this collection is its apparently easy alternation between sentimental and anti-sentimental modes. The story called "The tea rose" is an example of the former. In it a pale, beautiful, spiritual woman named Florence L'Estrange gives a perfect rose to Mary Stephens, a seamstress whose mother is sick, because the Stephenses love flowers and are uplifted by their beauty. Presently a dark handsome gentleman, visiting the seamstress, sees the rose and eventually finds his true love, Florence; she had thought him dead, but "he had traced her, even as a hidden streamlet may be traced, by the freshness, the verdure of heart, which her deeds of kindness had left wherever she had passed." [3] Yet later, in the middle of a simple boy-girl story called "Cousin William," Mrs. Stowe allows herself this sardonic aside: "Now we know that people very seldom have stories written about them who have not sylph-like forms, and glorious eyes, or, at least, 'a certain inexpressible charm diffused over their whole person.'" [4]

Parenthetically this alternation between the sentimental and anti-sentimental modes is characteristic of a great deal of Mrs. Stowe's writing. A good illustration of it is this passage from the novel *Agnes of Sorrento*. Here both styles exist in the same paragraph. She begins in her factual, blunt manner.

Nothing can be more striking, in common Italian life, than the contrast between out-doors and in-doors. Without, all is fragrant and radiant; within, mouldy, dark, and damp. Except in the well-kept palaces of the great, houses in Italy are more like dens than habitations. . . .

Four lines later, she has lapsed into the rhapsodic,

The sun had sunk, but left the air full of diffused radiance, which trembled and vibrated over the thousand many-colored waves of the sea. The moon was riding in a broad zone of purple, low in the horizon, her silver forehead somewhat flushed in the general rosiness that seemed to penetrate and suffuse every object. [5]

Probably the main significance of the *Mayflower* collection for a study of the New England novels is Mrs. Stowe's tone, so early in her work, of didactic nostalgia, present even in those stories which tend toward slightly patronizing caricature of the old farmer or parson's wife. When Mrs. Stowe, then unhappily settled in Cincinnati we remember, writes in "Little Edward" of "New England, in the good old catechizing, church-going, school-going, orderly times," [6] it is clear that this setting is not only factual but also eulogistic. Mrs. Stowe does not entirely lament the passage of time; she does not by any means scorn the advantages of Progress, nor is her tone in the *Mayflower* stories or in the four New England novels mainly elegaic, as was true of later retrospective writers about New England. Mrs. Stowe is hearty rather than mournful. Nonetheless she makes it clear as early as 1842 that she feels great admiration for the old colonial society, and that what she admired in her forebears' way of life is no longer to be found in her own day.

Before analyzing the heart of the drama in the four major New England novels, the theological controversy, we will need to establish our point of view and that of their author. First, any or all of these novels has often been associated with the regionalism or Local Color writing of the post-Civil War period. Sarah Orne Jewett did, after all, consult Mrs. Stowe about the manuscript of *The Country Doctor,* which suggests that Miss Jewett recognized affinities between her own writing and Mrs. Stowe's New England stories. It is, therefore, proper for us to ask whether we should regard Mrs. Stowe's novels as being works of regional fiction. A second question, which calls for some digression, is that of Mrs. Stowe's religious convictions and concerns at this time and, thus, of her perspective on the theological issues which the novels treat at such great length. Finally, to what extent do these novels continue or develop Mrs. Stowe's practice of historical romance; and, what sort of history do they contain? These are all critical questions for the understanding of the New England novels.

In certain simple ways the New England novels may be considered prototypes of the regional fiction of the last two decades of the nineteenth century. The setting is more than just a backdrop for the action; it is itself the subject of the novels. The nostalgic effect of the good old days can be felt in all four, and the contrast is further made between the virtuous simplicity of the past and the less virtuous confusion of the present. To this general and rather vague extent, the novels anticipate the nostalgic mood of Jewett, Freeman, Aldrich, Garland, and others.

Yet when one compares Mrs. Stowe's novels with the work of later New England writers of the regional group, she seems, even superficially, very different. In part this is due to so simple a reason as that Mrs. Stowe's novels are distinctly set in the past whereas the stories of Miss Jewett or Mrs. Freeman are, more often than not, set in a present which seems anachronistic because it is so strangely close to the past. Moreover, the New England society we see in Mrs. Freeman's work is blighted; Miss Jewett's picture is more stylized, but often desolate. Mrs. Stowe's New England, by contrast, is full of color and action and self-confidence. In the work of the later women, the heroes and more numerous heroines are defined by their ability nobly to endure in a society which has been emasculated and made bleak by the course of time and change. In Mrs. Stowe's work, neither the population of old New England nor the reader or author of the present is shown to be isolated or bereft by history. Miss Jewett's haunting glimpse of Mrs. Todd as the embattled "Antigone alone on the Theban plain"[7] has no counterpart in the perspective of Mrs. Stowe.

Another rather simple reason for the difference between Mrs. Stowe's work and that of the younger women is that Mrs. Stowe, unlike most writers of the regional school, liked Progress. She thought modern improvements were a fine thing. The whole disenchantment with the industrial mêlée which so profoundly disturbed many writers toward the end of the century seems to have touched Mrs. Stowe hardly at all. Even less did the distress in some quarters over the polyglot clamor of the big influx of immigrants attract her concern. The original impulse to write a novel of New England life probably owes more to her return to the region of her birth after eighteen years exile in Cincinnati than it does to a desire to retreat from the public turbulence. Hence, there is no feeling, as there is in the later writers, of an imaginative escape into a remote locale free from foreign creeds and tongues and uncontaminated by the pollution of belching smokestacks. So little, indeed, does Mrs. Stowe share the distaste of many later writers for materialistic enterprise that she praises her colonial heroes for their respect for property.

. . . the sole reason why one set of colonists [those in New England] proved the seed of a great nation, and the other [the French in Canada] attained so very limited success, is the difference between the religions taught by the two.

The one was a religion of asceticism [the French]. . . . The other was the spirit of the Old Testament, in which material prosperity is always spoken of as the lawful reward of piety, in which marriage is an honor, and a numerous posterity a thing to be desired.

Admittedly, when Mrs. Stowe wrote this praise of the New England colonists in the year 1869, the full force of the postwar commercial expansion had not yet been felt. Nevertheless, she never conveys that sense of alienation from the postwar society common to so many writers a generation younger. Admittedly too, she points out that the colonists "superadded . . . the intense spiritualism of the New Testament," [8] thus controlling the material by a countervailing "spiritual" purpose. The combination constitutes another instance of their merit. Yet Mrs. Stowe simply did not feel the antagonism between herself and bustling modernity which one discovers in so much postwar literature. Certainly, characteristically, she had many complaints about the way things were done, and a great deal of practical advice to offer her contemporaries. It is the sense of a rupture between the artist and society that she does not have. In developing her New England theme in the late fifties and sixties, Mrs. Stowe is not turning her back on the national crisis; she is trying to meet it.

The national crisis as she sees it, before and after the war, is the loss of the old dignity and purpose of the colonial Calvinist society. The source of this dignity and purpose was faith—not the analyses of John Calvin or the doctrines of his followers, but the passionate commitment in the hearts and minds of men to carry out God's purposes in history and to submit to them in eternity. The doctrines of Calvinism were regarded by Mrs. Stowe as repugnant, "glacial." What she admired was the animating passion, the piety, the fervor of its adherents. In addition to this fervor of heart and mind, the Puritans had something else which Mrs. Stowe valued almost as highly and which she found had been lost in her own time, namely, the coherence of the Puritan community. The disorder and fragmentation in American society in the postwar period was only partly a consequence of the conflicts which slavery and the Civil War had engendered throughout the social fabric. The larger disorder, and in a sense she saw slavery and the war as a manifestation of this rather than as its source, was the fragmentation of the churches, of Christian society, and their loss of influence. She was as profoundly distressed as many Victorians, and more than most, to hear "the melancholy long withdrawing roar" of the tide of Christian faith and to behold the dark confusion it had left behind on the American strand. Had people forgotten Cotten Mather's opening sentence in the *Magnalia?*

I write of the *Wonders* of the CHRISTIAN RELIGION, flying from the Depravations of *Europe,* to the *American Strand:* And, assisted by the Holy Author of the *Religion,* I do, with all Conscience of *Truth,* required therein by Him, who is the *Truth* it self, Report the *Wonderful Displays* of His Infinite Power, Wisdom, Goodness, and Faithfulness, wherewith His Divine Providence hath *Irradiated* an *Indian Wilderness.*

The connection between Mather's "American Strand" and Arnold's "Dover Beach" is more than an accidental collocation of images, and so, for any American writing in the late 1850s when she began the saga of colonial New England, was Arnold's prophecy of the clash of ignorant armies. For Mrs. Stowe, the loss of faith is more than just a private agony for those whom

it afflicts; it is also a public calamity. With that loss, the old bonds are broken, the old order denied. "Things fall apart . . ." Like a good many others of her own and later generations, Mrs. Stowe anticipated the coming anarchy and tried to forestall it.

The New England novels can be seen as such an attempt. Although she could not herself accept Calvinist dogma, she found that it was their faith, and even their terrible theology, that made the earlier generations noble and their society coherent. "The hard old New England divines were the poets of metaphysical philosophy, who built systems in an artistic fervor, and felt self exhale from beneath them as they rose into the higher regions of thought." [9] It is the poetry of minds committed to the Christian faith, and not to the ends of private self-interest, that Mrs. Stowe wants to restore to her own time. It is their integrity, not only of private conscience but also in the social order, that Mrs. Stowe's novels recall. The lesson which the New England novels carry to their readers is the lesson of the example of a society "knit together" by a common faith and loyal to a higher, a God-given destiny.

What we have before us then is a representation of colonial society developed through four novels written over a period of almost twenty years and including the Civil War, a representation through which the author seeks to aid and admonish her contemporaries in the severe problems of their own time by interpreting to them the significance of their past. Mrs. Stowe's purposes in these novels are thus large and serious; her view of both past and present is wide; the uses to which she will put the novel are demanding. Both in their topical arguments and in the rendering of the controversies of the past, the novels shift and vary the focus of interest so that one cannot discuss them very quickly or neatly. At the outset of such a long and slightly indefinite critical inquiry, we can save ourselves some misunderstanding by turning briefly to several aspects of the author's personal relation to colonial Puritanism.

Since the New England novels are so largely about Puritanism, so knowledgable about and involved in the controversies of the Puritan churches, many readers have assumed that they were written by a Puritan. As I must repeatedly emphasize, this assumption is faulty. Mrs. Stowe did not accept the Puritan articles of faith. One reason for the persistent misunderstanding among her readers is that she is not altogether candid about her differences with the saints. Indeed, she makes it a virtue, in giving advice to her doubting son (pages 117–118), to conceal one's objections to the old faith. She advocates speaking only of those things in which one still does believe; she urges Charlie to do as she and her brother Henry Ward do, to keep up appearances in public and always give the impression of steadfast loyalty to the old catechism.

In addition to her own skillful efforts at concealment, there is another reason for our confusion, namely, that, although Mrs. Stowe rejected Puritan theology, she did adopt many of their habits of mind and much of their literary tradition. In this respect her debt to them is large and complex. It also often leads us to recognize similar connections between Puritan writing and the turns of mind and style of other American writers whose inheritance from the past is less direct. As I have already noted, people in this country have indulged themselves for too long in the misconception that extreme sentimentality, for instance the "literary-sentimental-pious" combination, is somewhat un-American and definitely un-Puritan.

Even in her argument with Edwards, Mrs. Stowe's emphasis is less on the theological than the psychological and social consequences of his teachings; she is more concerned with this world than the next. Mrs. Stowe attacks Edwards for rationalizing Calvinist doctrine and thus making it vulnerable to rationalist attack; she blames him for making Christianity itself unacceptable, indeed "agonizing," to large numbers of people and for causing dissension and schism within the churches. In this argument she is, as always, concerned with the unity and moral health of the faithful and with the immediate conversion of unbelievers. She is not nearly as worried as many people think she is, or think she ought to be, about salvation in the life hereafter. If men could be brought into the fold of Christ's church in this world and could be moved to recognize and reciprocate His love, then Mrs. Stowe would not doubt God's eventual mercy to them.

There is not time here fully to explore the dispute which dominated the Beecher household in 1822 when Catharine Beecher's fiancé, Alexander Metcalf Fisher, was shipwrecked off the coast of England and drowned, but much can be learned from the story of his possible damnation. At the time of his death, although Fisher had shown serious concern for the faith, he had not declared his belief. Catharine searched his diaries and papers and could find no unequivocal evidence of a commitment. Consequently, said Lyman Beecher, she could only hope for God's mercy to Fisher. There were no grounds on which he could even tentatively assure her of more than the possibility of divine clemency. That was not enough for Catharine. She "murmured." Lyman's letters to her at the time—she stayed for several months with Fisher's parents—far from revealing him as hardhearted and severe, are a model of sympathy and intelligent understanding. He is patient in his counsel to her, he is resourceful in keeping his arguments both rigorous and kind, he is full of grief for

her and of sympathy with her refusal to submit to the possibility
of Fisher's damnation. Yet Lyman did not prevail. Catharine
would not be comforted. She would deny every teaching of the
Christian religion for eighteen centuries rather than agree that
Fisher might be damned. Lyman told her that her misery and
defiance were natural, but they were wrong. She replied, in effect,
that in that case she would remain wrong. At length, he asked
her to return home to relieve her of the grief that daily association
with Fisher's belongings and with his parents kept strong.
Catharine decided to start a school, and Lyman not only sup-
ported the project but advised her not to be halfhearted about
it. She should make it a really good school. By 1824, Harriet had
joined her older sister at the Hartford Female Seminary where
the younger sister, then only 13, both studied and, soon after,
taught. Catharine devoted her life to the extension and improvement of higher education for women, and her work bore fruit
in her own time. She also, in due course, set down for the enlightenment of the general reader, her views on sin and salvation. In
*Common Sense Applied to Religion; or, The Bible and the People*
(1857) and *An Appeal to the People in Behalf of Their Rights as
Authorized Interpreters of the Bible* (1859), Catharine argues
not only that in cases of manifest good intention divine clemency
is to be assumed, but also that St. Augustine and the Fathers had
been quite wrong in foisting upon the world such gloomy doctrines as Original Sin. Both books are, needless to say, heretical.
It should also be said that Lyman Beecher himself had given some
ground in the intervening thirty years. He and Dr. Taylor of
New Haven were, in fact, leaders of the liberal revision of the
theology of Timothy Dwight.

In 1857, when her son Henry was drowned, Mrs. Stowe wrote
to Catharine of her certainty that God would be merciful. Like
Fisher, Henry had not shown proof of belief. It worried his
mother, but she refused, as her sister had done, to despair: that is,
she refused to believe that Henry might be damned. Granted, the

question may be Puritan, Would he be damned?, but the confident answer that he would not is not a Puritan answer. I have already said, in discussing the slavery novels, that Mrs. Stowe subscribes to, and urges upon the reader, both the revivalist belief that all men could seek their own salvation and the evangelical goal of establishing the Kingdom of God in America. This evangelical goal was a society every member of which was "in the fold"; hence a society redeemed. As Professor Niebuhr says, it was a millennial hope.[10] Mrs. Stowe shared it, as did her father within a very short time after he left Yale and as did his colleagues, most of his sons, and their colleagues. I emphasize Mrs. Stowe's evangelical position here for two reasons. It would be impossible to understand the theological controversy in the New England novels if one supposed that they were written by a rigorous Puritan. Second, one could not appreciate the point of the argument that the author is making to her readers. That argument, that American society needs to regain the fervor of heart and the integrity of a community, a nation, under God, is addressed to a Victorian audience. Mrs. Stowe is not asking them to adopt the five tenets of Calvinism. Rather, she is asking them to do as she has done, to disregard those dogmas which they find unacceptable but to remember the divine providence which had once irradiated the Indian wilderness and to dedicate themselves, as Lincoln would ask them to do, to bringing about a "new birth" for their society. Lincoln, who was two years older than Mrs. Stowe and who had lived in Illinois when she was in Ohio and had heard the same revivalist oratory that she had, also looked back in the traditional manner: "Fourscore and seven years ago . . ." He remembered the commitments of the past to noble ideals, he saw the Civil War as a "testing," he spoke of dedication, consecration, of high resolve to honor the ideals of the early republic and to renew this nation, under God. Mrs. Stowe and Lincoln spoke the same language. And of course, like Mrs. Stowe, Lincoln, in the Second Inaugural, spoke the language of Jeremiah.

Like Mrs. Stowe too, his adherence to the old way of speaking did not imply an agreement with the old dogma. For both, the connection is rhetorical, not theological; the old rhetoric serves a new argument, a plea for a new commitment to the nation's present and future integrity.

The matter of the language of the New England novels and of their adaptation of Puritan clerical and historical usage brings us to what I have called the literary, as distinct from the theological Puritanism of Mrs. Stowe. Since she writes both in and of this tradition, and since her borrowings are sometimes deliberate and elsewhere apparently unconscious, we confront here again, as often in her work, the problem of a writer so personally involved in her subject that her readers often cannot be sure what is historical fact, what is literary invention, and what is the author's own interested opinion. Moreover, since much of the Puritan language here is the language of argument, we must also be aware of the lessons these novels are addressing to the contemporary reader. An excellent example of the interplay of these factors is the following famous passage from *The Minister's Wooing*.

There is a ladder to heaven, whose base God has placed in human affections, tender instincts, symbolic feelings, sacraments of love, through which the soul rises higher and higher, refining as she goes, till she outgrows the human, and changes, as she rises, into the image of the divine. At the very top of this ladder, at the threshold of Paradise, blazes dazzling and crystalline that celestial grade where the soul knows self no more, having learned, through a long experience of devotion, how blest it is to lose herself in that eternal Love and Beauty of which all earthly fairness and grandeur are but the dim type, the distant shadow. This highest step, this saintly elevation, which but few selectest spirits ever on earth attain, to raise the soul to which the Eternal Father organized every relation of human existence and strung every cord of human love; for which this world is one long discipline, for which the soul's human education is constantly varied, for which it is now torn by sorrow, now flooded by joy; to which all its multiplied powers tend with upward hands of dumb and ignorant aspiration,—this Ultima Thule of virtue had been seized upon by our sage as the all of religion. He knocked out every round of the ladder but the highest, and then, pointing to its hopeless splendor, said to the world, 'Go up thither and be saved!' [11]

Mrs. Stowe frequently speaks of the 'poetry of ideas' in Puritan writing. As I have said, she often quarrels with the substance of the ideas; nonetheless she is profoundly moved by men who made their theological questions into a sublime poetry. In the above passage from *The Minister's Wooing,* she invests these ideas with their original eloquence and embodies them in the traditional metaphors of the Puritan plain style. She renders here the full force of the drama of these ideas and the power of the appeal of their grandeur to the poetic imagination; at the same time, she is using the Puritan figurative style to conduct her argument with the man who taught Hopkins to knock the rungs out of the ladder, namely Edwards. The plain style was originally fashioned for the purposes of exegesis and argument. She often adopts it, and often uses it to argue against the latter-day adherents of that "glacial" Puritan creed which it was first shaped to serve. The attack on Hopkins's theology here is made especially bitter by being phrased in that poetic language which ennobled, though it did not justify, the severity of the old doctrines.

Mrs. Stowe's inheritance from the colonial writers is manifest also in her descriptions. In *The Pearl of Orr's Island,* the second in the series but first conceived in 1852–53, she represents the wild bleak beauty of the Maine coast, and "the primitive and Biblical people of that lonely shore." The novel begins with a shipwreck just off the shore, followed by a funeral. The storm winds, though spent, still move the air and water.

When the singing was over, Zephaniah read to the accompaniment of wind and sea, the words of poetry made on old Hebrew shores, in the dim, gray dawn of the world:—

'The voice of the Lord is upon the waters; the God of Glory
thundereth; the Lord is upon many waters. The voice of the
Lord shaketh the wilderness. . . .'

How natural and home-born sounded this old piece of Oriental
poetry in the ears of the three! The wilderness of Kadesh, with
its great cedars, was doubtless Orr's Island, where even now the
goodly fellowship of black-winged trees were groaning and swaying,
and creaking as the breath of the Lord passed over them.[12]

Long before Cotton Mather elaborated on the analogy between
the Puritan community and the ancient nation of Israel, the first
colonists themselves had seen that providential pattern. For them
too, the language of the Old Testament rang with a peculiar
prophecy as they thought of their own flight across the sea and
beheld the wilderness they were chosen to inhabit. The four New
England novels frequently repeat and indeed emphasize this
traditional analogy. It is one of the more conspicuous aspects of
their literary Puritanism.

Of course, not all of the description is weighted with this kind
of symbolism. Much of it, in fact most, is done in Mrs. Stowe's
earlier and familiar manner, that of historical romance. Indeed, in
these novels the author is in the comfortable position of writing
about the past, the proper subject of historical fiction. Mrs. Stowe
continues here to make use of the verisimilitude of background,
minor character and incident that she had learned from Scott, as
well as to seek the more total and vital historical realism she
had achieved in parts of *Dred*. Her purpose throughout is to
recreate the life of New England in the colonial period as a complete historical experience, an experience which often and perhaps most profoundly she finds important in and of itself, beyond
its utility for her many-sided lessons and polemics.

Although the four New England novels were not designed as
a group, they have enough in common to lead us to consider
them as a loosely related tetralogy. There are a few instances of
the same character appearing in more than one novel, but the

plots are wholly separate and the four books would have nothing to do with each other were it not for the fact that all are set in colonial New England and that this historical setting is clearly essential to the events and characters of each; it is probably what the author cares most about. What happened, one suspects, is that Mrs. Stowe found herself more and more fascinated by her colonial subject, and found more, rather than less, to say about it as she wrote on.

The small differences in setting among the four novels help to clarify the major similarities. *The Minister's Wooing* takes place in a real city, Newport, and *The Pearl of Orr's Island* is also set in a real place, Orr's Island. The Oldtown of *Oldtown Folks* is a fictional place, although the identification of Oldtown with Natick, Massachusetts, where Calvin Stowe grew up, is unmistakable. *Poganuc People* is, in fact, about Litchfield, Connecticut. (There is also a town of Poquonock not far from Hartford.) Mrs. Stowe knew all four sites well and knew of each certain facts of colonial history. Hence, she has taken for all the novels an actual setting with a familiar past.

With respect to time, Mrs. Stowe's chronology is not specific. She rarely gives an exact date. Instead, all four settings are roughly located in the late colonial period, and are defined by such terms as "pre-railroad times," or "ante-railroad times,—the period when our own hard, rocky, sterile New England was a sort of half Hebrew theocracy, half ultra-democratic republic of little villages." [13] Mrs. Stowe is occasionally quite confusing and, in fact, ahistorical in her casual shifts backwards and forwards in time from what might be the seventeenth-century period to the era just before or even after the Revolution. The truth is that she wants simply the strongest possible cumulative effect of colonial life; even in *The Minister's Wooing,* which is the most specific of the four in both time and place, she will not say more than that "pre-railroad times" means "A.D. 17—," and that the scene is "the then small seaport town of Newport, at that time unconscious of its present fashion and fame." [14] Mrs. Stowe's emphasis as a historian is the contrast between Then and Now.

Although there is less specificity in chronology than one might expect to find in historical novels, the settings are verified and developed in descriptions of colonial houses, scenery, and custom. In these descriptions, Mrs. Stowe speaks as the serenely factual observer explaining how things were. For example, on the very first page of *The Minister's Wooing,* the author tells why one of her characters is known as "the Widow Scudder."

In New England settlements a custom has obtained, which is wholesome and touching, of ennobling the woman whom God has made desolate, by a sort of brevet rank which continually speaks for her as a claim on the respect and consideration of the community. The Widow Jones, or Brown, or Smith, is one of the fixed institutions of every New England village. [15]

In the Widow Scudder's house we are shown the old kitchen with its floor "of snowy boards sanded with whitest sand," and "the ancient fireplace stretching quite across one end"; the large kitchen also contains "a dresser, on which was displayed great store of shining pewter dishes and plates," and "a commodious wooden 'settee,' or settle, [which] offered repose to people too little accustomed to luxury to ask for a cushion." To be sure, Mrs. Stowe does not really maintain the cool factual tone; it is often interrupted with such apostrophes as, "Oh, that kitchen of the olden times, the old, clean, roomy New England kitchen!" [16] Or again, "With all our ceiled houses, let us not forget our grandmothers' kitchens!" The data are, however, sound, and the interjection of elated comparisons between Then and Now does not destroy, but really enhances, the effect of authenticity.

As in her earlier historical novels, the crowded physical detail of the setting—the descriptions of New England kitchens alone would make an impressive catalogue—is combined with a large array of minor characters to create a realistic context for the

action. Mrs. Stowe introduces a host of local New England types
—seamstresses, spinsters, parsons, farmers, grandmothers, and so
on—who play a small but useful role in the loose, often episodic,
narrative structure. They tend to fill out the historical picture
of colonial society and since they are drawn very closely after
Mrs. Stowe's relatives and acquaintances, to revive her sense of
historical reality after passages of romantic adventure or sentimental digression. As earlier, this veracious background also
sustains the reader's credulity by strengthening the force of an
often weak plot and makes improbable incidents convincing and
even exciting.

Miss Prissy, the town seamstress, figures in *The Minister's
Wooing* as a local celebrity whose arrival in the Scudder house
sends Mrs. Stowe into a verbose recollection of turning hems,
stitching ruffs on clerical sleeves, and the starching and retrim-
ming of bonnets for another year. She relaxes from her more
ambitious history into a narrative of housekeeping; between the
lines of Miss Prissy's gossip we are able to read an intimate
description of the daily life of a New England household in the
late eighteenth and early nineteenth centuries.

In *The Pearl of Orr's Island,* the Misses Roxy and Ruey Tooth-
acre give a similar flavor of down east speech and manners. In
*Oldtown Folks,* Mrs. Stowe works more seriously on her New
England characters and she presents a considerable variety of
interesting portraits, one of which is Sam Lawson, a wry, lazy,
jack-of-all-trades who is the narrator of some nicely told yarns
which Mrs. Stowe heard from her husband. Also in *Oldtown
Folks* is one Miss Minerva Randall, housekeeper to the school-
master, and known in the village as Nervy Randall. "There was
a sort of fishy quaintness about her that awakened grim ideas of
some unknown ocean product,—a wild and withered appearance,
like a wind-blown juniper on a sea promontory,—unsightly and
stunted, yet not, after all, commonplace or vulgar." [17] Nervy
Randall, appropriately, is from Maine. In *Oldtown Folks,* Mrs.

Stowe gives a much larger variety of colonial types than she does in the preceding two novels. There is, for instance, an extended scene in the house of some Boston friends of High Church and Tory sympathies, where toasts are given to the King and where well-mannered disapproval of the patriots dominates the conversation. There are also a few surviving Indians in Oldtown from the tribe to which John Eliot had preached, and there are, as in *The Minister's Wooing,* several Negroes.

As with such characters as Sam and Andy, the traders, and the St. Clare servants in *Uncle Tom's Cabin,* and with the preachers, and Aunt Nesbit in *Dred,* the company of town spinsters and Yankee farmers in the New England novels are indispensable to the texture of the composition. Taken together, their scenes form a continuous background against which the more sensational or sentimental episodes are played and within which they are contained in such a way that the dominant impression remains one of historical realism.

In thinking about the four New England novels as historical in the factual sense, it is interesting to notice in them Mrs. Stowe's old habit of footnoting and citing authorities for some of the episodes she thinks her readers might question. There is nothing comparable to *The Key to Uncle Tom's Cabin* or to the massive appendices of *Dred,* but she does see fit to defend herself against skeptics on several occasions. For example, in the preface to *Oldtown Folks,* after making the general statement that "some of those things in the story which may appear most romantic and like ficton are simple renderings and applications of facts," Mrs. Stowe has her narrator, who also signs the preface, remark: "Any one who may be curious enough to consult Rev. Elias Nason's book, called 'Sir Charles Henry Frankland, or Boston in the Colonial Times,' will there see a full description of the old manor-house which in this story is called the Dench House. It was by that name I always heard it spoken of in my boyhood." [18] Actually Mrs. Stowe's use of footnotes, documents and authorities is reminiscent of the New England minister's reliance on "proof-texts" to support his arguments and to dispel any suspicion of heresy. Again we have Mrs. Stowe the historical romancer simultaneously performing the task of providential historian in that she selects for her descriptive coloring data from the factual record.

In his *History of Plymouth Plantation* (1647), William Bradford keeps a factual record in accurate and thorough detail; and he faithfully points out the significance of the many events in his narrative to the divine design. It is no part of Bradford's intention to let his readers draw their own conclusions, nor did he choose to conceal his own biases. He is immensely scrupulous about the accuracy of his data, especially as these data are to him divine providences, but he is equally careful to leave no ambiguity in interpretation. It is important to remember Bradford's example in the combination of the documentary and the didactic writing of history since Mrs. Stowe's didacticism might otherwise seem at odds with her passion for authenticity. Well before the death of Mrs. Stowe in 1896, the two elements had come to seem contradictory in the minds of those historians to whom the ideal had become the disinterested, "scientific" study of the past. In the first two New England novels, as in her two slavery novels, Mrs. Stowe does not in the least question the didactic obligation of the historian.

In further comparing Mrs. Stowe to the colonial historians, however, we must take notice of a central difference between the slavery novels and these we are now considering, namely the difference in perspective. The first two are contemporary history; the second group treat of the past. The following famous passage from Bradford's *History* will clarify the important distinction. Bradford looks forward. He explains the significance to later generations of what his followers are doing in their first encounter with the wilderness. He is certain that some day the children of these fathers will look back to his time.

But here I cannot but stay and make a pause, and stand half amazed at this poor people's present condition; and so I think will the reader, too, when he well considers the same. Being thus passed the vast ocean, and a sea of troubles before in their preparation (as may be remembered by that which went before), they had now no friends to welcome them nor inns to entertain or refresh their weatherbeaten bodies; no houses or much less towns to repair to, to seek for succour. . . .

What could now sustain them but the Spirit of God and His grace? May not and ought not the children of these fathers rightly say: 'Our fathers were Englishmen which came over this great ocean, and were ready to perish in this wilderness; but they cried unto the Lord, and He heard their voice and looked on their adversity,' * etc.

\* Deuteronomy xxvi. 5, 7 [Bradford's note] [19]

The slavery novels are written by one who, like Bradford, anticipates the time when others will look back to the events to which she is a witness.[20] The New England novels are written by one of the children who does look back, as Bradford had anticipated, and who asks her own generation to remember the heroism of those who cried for the Lord's mercy in the wilderness. In so looking back, these novels have a retrospective rather than an anticipatory perspective, and this retrospective angle of vision is more like later New England historians, such as Cotton Mather, than it is like Bradford.

The restrospective stance of the New England novels was, if anything, more common among the colonial historians and pulpit orators than Bradford's own. Even by the time of the second generation, in the 1650s and early 60s, during the debates which finally resulted in the Half-Way Covenant (1662), men looked back to a nobler past, when piety had been fervent and compromise unnecessary, and took that very recent past as a standard for the present. In the later seventeenth century, men increasingly came to assume that the great era was in the past and the finest heroes were in their graves. In the *Magnalia*

*Christi Americana,* Cotton Mather comprehensively set down the great works of Christ in America in order that later generations might know and duly estimate that crucial period in the history of the human race when Christ's commonwealth had been founded by a saintly band on a new continent which God had reserved from the beginning of time for that very purpose. Mather tells his story from the moment when the saints first set foot on the American strand. The difference between him and Bradford might be defined by the fact that Mather's audience consists of the children, the descendants of the first settlers. Bradford imagines the time when others will look back. Mather is looking back.

Despite their agreement on the nature of history as God's providential plan for mankind, there is another slight difference, related to that of perspective, which is relevant to our discussion. Bradford admires his men for their piety and courage; he sees them as honored by God in their given task; but he does not see them as better men than their children will be. In the above passage, as elsewhere, Bradford is moved by the weakness of this tiny band in the huge and terrible wilderness. They are spared by God's mercy alone. They are scarcely, to him, epic heroes towering in virtue above lesser men. Yet this is just the way that Mather often represents the founding fathers. They loom up for Mather as mighty men, a race of giants, whose descendants are weak-kneed and faint-hearted by comparison. And in this respect, Mrs. Stowe is by no means always in agreement with Mather. She often tends to look back to the early days rather as Bradford saw them, as beginnings from which greater things would grow. She does, however, usually follow Mather in presenting the past as morally superior to her own day and thus an example to it, as in the following two instances.

In *The Minister's Wooing,* Mrs. Stowe makes much of the slave trade which came into the Newport harbor. She includes in the novel a merchant named Simeon Brown who has grown wealthy in this evil commerce and who has become a religious hypocrite in consequence. Through the character of Brown, she wishes to create a situation similar to that of her own contemporaries as she defines them in 1859. She wants to say that the evil of slavery existed Then as it does Now and that, in both instances, it is perpetuated by the corrupt rich who, whatever their pious claims and intentions, are morally ruined by the fact that they profit from slavery. She makes the same point in *Uncle Tom's Cabin* and *Dred*. In these first two novels, and especially in *Dred,* Mrs. Stowe tends, once she has identified the guilty trader, to shift the blame for his sins onto those who are responsible for correcting them, especially the clergy. The burden of her attack falls finally on the weakness and hypocrisy of those who fail to denounce slavery as unchristian. In *The Minister's Wooing,* the titular hero, Dr. Samuel Hopkins, exemplifies the courageous minister of colonial times who is bold where his successors are weak. To a congregation of well dressed, affluent "first families," Hopkins delivers an absolutely unequivocal tirade which concludes in the words of Jeremiah:

'If a bitter woe is pronounced on him "that buildeth his house by unrighteousness and his chambers by wrong," Jer. xxii 13,—to him "that buildeth a town with blood, and stablisheth a city by iniquity," Hab. ii 12,—to "the bloody city," Ezek. xxiv 6,—what a heavy, dreadful woe hangs over the heads of all those whose hands are defiled by the blood of the Africans, especially the inhabitants of this State and this town, who have had a distinguished share in this unrighteous and bloody commerce!' [21]

This is the way the clergy spoke in the old days; they were not the compromising intimidated ministers of the nineteenth century —such as those in *Dred*—but rather were themselves intimidators of the rich, the sinful, the weak-hearted. That, says Mrs. Stowe, is how it once was, and that, more than ever, is how it ought to be. The lesson of the past is here taught in the manner of the *Magnalia*.

Harriet Beecher Stowe, a somewhat bookish child, was a delighted reader of those biographies in the *Magnalia* where Mather portrays the heroic piety of John Eliot, missionary to the Indians at Natick, or the saintly humility of Thomas Shepard. Mather includes a whole section of biographies of the founders and early leaders of the Bay colony with the definite purpose of holding up these men as heroic models for the later generations to follow. Mrs. Stowe's fictional portrait of Hopkins is accurate enough to serve the same end as Mather's biographies, that of both informing and instructing later generations about the ancient virtues of the nobler men and more Godly society of an earlier time.

In *Oldtown Folks,* Mrs. Stowe gives another extended comparison between Then and Now, which also gives the palm of virtue to the past and makes it a model for her contemporaries. Fairly late in the novel she is discussing a school in the neighboring town of "Cloudland" to which the three children are sent.

For that simple, pastoral germ-state of society is a thing forever gone. Never again shall we see that union of perfect repose in regard to outward surroundings and outward life with that intense activity of the inward and intellectual world, that made New England, at this time, the vigorous, germinating seed-bed for all that has since been developed of politics, laws, letters, and theology, through New England to America, and through America to the world.[22]

Mrs. Stowe was never known for understatement. The lesson of the country academies, however, is not contained in this extravagant praise. It comes as an application of the ways of the past to the problems of the present, in this case, to the question of women's rights.

This question, like a great many others, was solved without discussion by the good sense of our Puritan ancestors, in throwing the country academies, where young men were fitted for college, open

alike to both sexes, and in making the work of education of such
dignity in the eyes of the community, that first-rate men were willing
to adopt it for life.[23]

A subsidiary lesson is also given to those who are resisting
Catharine Beecher's efforts to recruit able teachers for women's
higher education.

It should thus be clear that the four New England novels
owe a great debt to the colonial habit of instructing one's listeners in the pious example of their ancestors. It is also true, however, that Mrs. Stowe is regularly inconsistent about the relative
superiority of Past and Present in that she frequently suggests
that she admires the past for things she does not want for herself, that she is glad not to have to put up with. She is grateful
that she is not with Bradford in the howling wilderness. The
wooden bench in the kitchen in the days when people were too
unaccustomed to luxury to ask for a cushion is a typical instance
of the way in which the olden times are shown to have had a
noble simplicity which, though admirable, is also decidedly less
appealing to the author than her own cushioned comfort. This
ambivalence in Mrs. Stowe's homage to the past is particularly
nicely illustrated in the preface to *Oldtown Folks*. "My object,"
says Horace Holyoke of his forthcoming history,

is to interpret to the world the New England life and character
in that particular time of its history which may be called the
seminal period. I would endeavor to show you New England in its
*seed-bed*, before the hot suns of modern prograss had developed its
sprouting germs into the great treets of today.
New England has been to these United States what the Dorian
hive was to Greece. . . . [T]he seed-bed of New England was the
seed-bed of this great American Republic, and of all that is likely
to come of it.[24]

The business of interpreting to the world the seminal period of
New England's past is the standard subject of the providential

historian. Mrs. Stowe carries on the tradition, and yet no sooner has she made the extravagant claim that the New England colonists sired the mighty Republic of the mid-nineteenth century, than she implies, in her metaphor of the "sprouting germs" and the "great trees," that the contemporary scene has surpassed the achievements of the past. "Modern progress" has made the seeds grow and has brought numerous practical comforts to the descendants of these hardy colonial heroes. It is in the area of theology that these ambiguities are most pronounced because, to put it crudely, the very source and fountain of the grandeur of the past was, in Mrs. Stowe's view, the Puritans' austere religion, and in that she did not believe.

In introducing her hero in *The Minister's Wooing,* Mrs. Stowe makes a short explanatory apology to those readers who are expecting light ladies' fiction.

It is impossible to write a story of New England life and manners for a thoughtless, shallow-minded person. If we represent things as they are, their intensity, their depth, their unworldly gravity and earnestness must inevitably repel lighter spirits, as the reverse pole of the magnet drives off sticks and straws.

In no other country were the soul and the spiritual life ever such intense realities, and everything contemplated so much (to use a current New England phrase) 'in reference to eternity.' [25]

Of Hopkins's theology, she explains the fundamentals in a metaphor suggested by the Revolution:

The system of Dr. Hopkins was one that could have had its origin only in a soul at once reverential and logical. . . . And as a gallant soldier renounces life and personal aims in the cause of his king and country, and holds himself ready to be drafted for a forlorn hope, to be shot down, or help make a bridge of his mangled body, over which the more fortunate shall pass to victory and glory, so he regarded himself as devoted to King Eternal, ready in His hands to be used to illustrate and build up an Eternal Commonwealth, by either being sacrificed as a lost spirit or glorified as a redeemed one, ready to throw not merely his mortal life, but his immortality even, into the forlorn hope, to bridge with a never-dying soul the chasm over which white-robed victors should pass to a commonwealth of glory and splendor whose vastness should dwarf the misery of all the lost to an infinitesimal.[26]

Considering its brevity, this is an honest statement of Hopkins's teachings, and it is enriched by an occasional fidelity to the traditional language of the New England clergy who had for generations spoken of the Eternal Commonwealth as a particularly fitting definition of heaven. One hears, also, in this passage the language of 1859 when the soldiers of the Lord were again about to be called to battle, a coincidence which points a providential lesson.

In *Oldtown Folks,* Mrs. Stowe gives a long chapter to a discussion of Edward Bellamy, Hopkins's famous colleague in carrying forward to the next generation the teachings of their master, Jonathan Edwards. She quotes at length from "My Grandmother's Blue Book," which is Bellamy's celebrated "True Religion Delineated, and Distinguished From All Counterfeits." Having said that his grandmother was not unusually pious or bookish, but was rather typical of the average colonial woman in her study of Bellamy's treatise, Horace Holyoke reflects on the vigor and courage of every man and woman in those days.

They were a set of men and women brought up to *think,* . . . to wrestle and tug at the very severest problems. Utter self-renunciation, a sort of grand contempt for personal happiness when weighed with things greater and more valuable, was the fundamental principle of life in those days.[27]

Both Hopkins and Bellamy are presented as venerable historical figures, seen, even in *The Minister's Wooing,* at a deferential distance. The fictional parsons in the novels are viewed at closer quarters. They become central to the theological controversy.

In the village of Oldtown, there are three ministers of whom we are given full portraits, and in connection with whom Mrs. Stowe reminds her readers that, "In the little theocracy which the Pilgrims established in the wilderness, the ministry was the only order of nobility." [28] The first minister we meet, "in all the magnificence of his cocked hat and ample clerical wig," is the Rev. Mr. Lothrop, one of "a numerous class in the third generation of Massachusetts clergy, commonly called Arminian," who "came to regard the spiritual struggles and conflicts, the wrestlings and tears, the fastings and temptations of their ancestors with a secret skepticism,—to dwell on moralities, virtues, and decorums, rather than on those soul-stirring spiritual mysteries which still stood forth unquestioned and uncontradicted in their confessions of faith." The chilling portrait is continued by the information that "His Sunday sermons were well-written specimens of the purest and most elegant Addisonian English, and no mortal could find fault with a word that was in them, as they were sensible, rational, and religious, as far as they went." [29] He has, further, married a rich widow of good Boston lineage to soften the hardships of small town life.

The above sketch of Parson Lothrop sets the tone. Mrs. Stowe is not "preaching," to be sure, but the sarcasm, indeed the venom in her voice, would not be lost on any reader acquainted with New England theological warfare. Lothrop, the scholarly, the elegant gentleman subverts with his cowardly, secret skepticism the proud tradition he inherits. "He did not, like his great predecessor [John Eliot], lecture them [the Indians] on the original depravity of the heart, the need of a radical and thorough regeneration by the Holy Spirit of God, or the power of Jesus as a Saviour from sin, but he talked to them of the evil of drunkenness and lying and idleness, . . ." and when they remained unaffected by his hollow words, "he calmly expressed his conviction that they were children of the forest, a race destined to extinction with the progress of civilization but continued his labors for them with automatic precision." [30] What Mrs. Stowe cannot stand is Lothrop's bloodless, passionless, condescending ministerial character. She is not quarrelling with his doctrine, nor does she condemn him for his repudiation of the extreme Calvinist insistence on sin and election. The trouble with Lothrop, as Emerson more briefly put it, is that he is "corpse-cold," which is to say that he is not only emotionally cold but that also, as a minister of the Lord, he is utterly useless.

While Lothrop is a follower of the proto-Unitarian faction among the late eighteenth-century clergy, Dr. Moses Stern who, invariably, preaches the grim old dogmas in what he imagines to be the tradition of Edwards, represents the extreme orthodox position.

His Calvinism was of so severe and ultra a type, and his statements were so little qualified either by pity of human infirmity, or fear of human censure, or desire of human approbation, that he reminded one of some ancient prophet, freighted with a mission of woe and wrath, which he must always speak. . . .[31]

Somewhere between Lothrop and Stern is the Rev. Mr. Avery of whose preaching Mrs. Stowe relates that it was "made telling by a back force of burning enthusiasm." Avery's main theological interest is free agency; his style is *"manly,"* his doctrine, though loyal to the Calvinism he professes, is full of "cheerfulness and hope." He had "a passion for saving souls" and was determined "nobody should go there [to Hell] if he could help it." [32] Avery is a minister of the revivalist mold, energetic, optimistic, a saver of souls.

In the preface to *Oldtown Folks,* Mrs. Stowe shows her recognition of the demands of the newer "objective" role of the historian by describing her manner of writing as perfectly disinterested.

In doing this work, I have tried to make my mind as still and passive as a looking-glass, or a mountain lake, and then to give you merely the images reflected there.

She repeats her old claim that "my studies . . . [have been] . . . taken from real characters, real scenes, and real incidents." In 1869, however, she adds a new note:

In portraying the various characters which I have introduced, I have tried to maintain the part simply of a sympathetic spectator. . . . Though Calvinist, Arminian, High-Church Episcopalian, skeptic, and simple believer all speak in their turn, I merely listen, and endeavor to understand and faithfully represent the inner life of each. I myself am but the observer and reporter, seeing much, doubting much, questioning much, and believing with all my heart in only a very few things.[33]

Even giving her the benefit of every doubt, no reader of *Oldtown Folks* could avoid the conclusion that she is a more sympathetic spectator of some characters and opinions than of others. Among the ministers, her favorite is definitely Avery.

Like most of the New England ministers, Mr. Avery was a warm believer in the millennium. This millennium was the favorite recreation ground, solace, and pasture-land, where the New England ministry fed their hopes and courage. Men of large hearts and warm benevolence, their theology would have filled them with gloom, were it not for this overplus of joy and peace to which human society on earth was in their view tending.[34]

Avery's emotional energy and ebullient millennial optimism clearly define him as the best type of revivalist; in fact he sounds very much like Lyman Beecher.

One of the sources both of information and of inspiration about her colonial materials had been Mrs. Stowe's major role in the composition of Lyman Beecher's *Autobiography*. In 1854, under the general supervision of Charles Beecher, the seventy-nine-year-old patriarch was finally persuaded by his children to assist them in compiling a formal record of his life. Too weak to manage such a project himself, Beecher gladly responded to the questions of Charles, Harriet and Catharine, the three principal movers of the project, and while the other children were all solicited for reminiscences, Harriet took down her father's recollections as, after some initial proddings of his memory, they began vividly to flow. Thus, at the opening of her four-novel saga of colonial New England, Mrs. Stowe had been over much of the ground in her devoted study of her father's life, and although the dates in the novels are vague, it is evident that the first three at least are set roughly in the period of Lyman Beecher's youth and early career, extending backwards to the days he had heard described as a child (the days of the Revolution and immediately before) and extending forward into the time of Mrs. Stowe's own recollections. In addition to focusing her attention on the late colonial period, the study of her father's life led Mrs. Stowe into the fascinating subject of the theological warfare in which Lyman Beecher had been so enthusiastically engaged for most of his life. As a result, the daughter's story of colonial New England includes a great deal of theological discussion and anecdote. As might be expected, however, the combination of her own views with the recollections of an old man not fully in command of his mind makes for a presentation of theological systems and controversies which is occasionally inconsistent or inaccurate. Allowing, however, for a small margin of error, we can still credit Mrs. Stowe with a dramatically interesting and historically valid recreation of colonial life. The fact that she does not at all stay out of the argument, despite her prefatory disclaimer, only makes her more conspicuously a product of the past she describes.

It is important to be clear about the autobiographical aspect of the New England novels. With the important exception of a few episodes (for example, James Marvyn's supposed drowning), they are not autobiographical in the usual sense of recreating the events of the author's life. They do, like *Uncle Tom's Cabin* and *Dred,* draw heavily on Mrs. Stowe's personal knowledge, memory, and opinions; they in fact rely on the tremendous accumulation of stories and impressions of early New England which she had from her father, her husband, her friends, and from her own recollections. Mrs. Stowe writes from, and exploits, her personal experience, but she usually does not retell it.[35]

Thus, with respect to the ministers in *Oldtown Folks,* Lothrop, for instance, is not modeled on any particular person; he is rather a type of a certain clerical temperament and cast of mind which was indeed increasingly common in the second half of the eighteenth century, a type with whom Edwards himself did battle in the person of Charles Chauncy of Boston, and a type made increasingly bold toward the end of the century by the spread of Deism. By 1825, many of the ministers of Lothrop's persuasion officially and publicly formed themselves into the Unitarian Association after a long and bitter controversy within the Congregational brotherhood, a controversy which was not settled by this public regrouping. All his life, no matter what his hostility to Roman Catholics and High Church Episcopalians, not to mention right wing Calvinists of the Bangor or Andover groups, Lyman Beecher did steady service against the Unitarians. His animosity to these extreme liberals, despite his own liberal sympathies, is vehemently repeated by his daughter in 1881 in a letter to her only surviving son who has, naturally, gone into the ministry. The letter serves to show one of the ways in which her novels are personal without being autobiographical; it provides an unequivocal statement of the Beechers' position on Unitarianism, a position which remained constant through all the doctrinal shiftings of the members of that large and adaptable family. Mrs. Stowe writes to her son Charlie who is newly ordained and serving his first pastorate in Maine. I shall quote at some length from this letter because it gives, in addition to her views on Unitarian theology, such a characteristic picture of Mrs. Stowe's religious preoccupations.

When I was with you in Nov you told me that you believed the creed of your church & were disposed to preach a series of sermons upon it. Hardly more than a month passes & you write that you cán no more stay in the orthodox body & think of joining the Unitarians. . . .

I protest with all the energy of my heart & soul against your joining the camp of the Unitarians—for altho there are many good soldiers & servants of Christ in it yet *as a whole* it is a little band dissociated from the great body of Christ's church— Latin Greek Anglican & American. That you agree with conservative Unitarians is because conservative Unitarians are becoming every year more orthodox—in many cases coming out & joining them as Dr. Huntington & others. Then the *name* covers every form of dissent & unbelief down to that of men like Savage who believes no more in Christ than a Jewish Rabbi—I have heard most atrocious radicalism in E. Hale's pulpit—not from him but from br. ministers. Your constitutional danger is from sudden unadvised movements—which expose you to the imputations of changeableness. I always regretted that you did not finish your course at New Haven—your sudden change there however had the Bishop's order for its justification but it was a pity—& made necessary the finishing of your course in Germany & it is yet doubtful to me whether the scholarly advantages you gained there balance the lack of faith—the filling your head with rationalistic doubtings—whose bats wings every once & a while flap & flit about you when you are trying the simple old paths of child-like trust.

For you to go into a denomination of skeptics & rationalisers of whom scarce any two believe alike, would I think be *peculiarly* bad for you—who are altogether too much given to rationalistic dangers —& too little to faith. . . .

Look at Frothingham's case . . . how he preached himself out in N York & came to nothing & compare all these with the fruitful & successful ministries of yr Uncle Henry & Uncle Tom. They differed in many points with the reserved orthodoxy of their day— but they made no noise about it—they preached what they *sincerely did believe* & left what they were in doubt about to the further teachings of God's holy spirit. . . .

As to saying that you despise Liberal Orthodoxy for its slovenly inconsistency & its dishonesty—I cannot imagine what you mean. What I, and your Uncle Henry believe & teach is not either slovenly or inconsistent & we are neither of us dishonest. Your uncle is precisely the model I would hold up to you, of how a manly and honest man should guide himself in the ministry in an age when God is shedding new light on religion thro the development of his own natural laws in Science—What he could not conscientiously preach he let alone. He did not ridicule—he did not denounce he simply confined himself to teaching that of whose truth he was certain. . . . No man is recognized by more souls as a spiritual Father. Now if he had yielded to disgust—gone over to Unitarians —there would have been lots of scandal and bitter controversy—but no Plymouth Church.[36]

In sum, whatever her misgivings about the several parties within "the great body of Christ's Church—Latin Greek Anglican & American," she will maintain, as did her father before her, that the Unitarians are utterly beyond the pale of the Christian faith.

When it comes to Mrs. Stowe's arguments with those within the pale she is almost as fierce. It is here that we come to the central ambiguity of her theological history because her fiercest quarrel is with none other than the man whom she, like all New England believers of her generation, grew up to revere above all others, the sublime Jonathan Edwards.

In *The Minister's Wooing,* Samuel Hopkins is a boarder in the pious household of the Widow Scudder whose daughter, Mary, Hopkins has tutored in the study of Edwards's treatises. Mary is said to have mastered her subject, but in an unusual way. "Womanlike, she felt the subtile poetry of those sublime abstractions which dealt with such infinite and unknown quantities. . . ." Indeed, her teacher "was often amazed at the tread with which this fair young child walked through these high regions of abstract thought, often comprehending through an ethereal clearness of nature what he had laboriously and heavily reasoned out. . . ."[37] The implication is fairly clear that where Edwards and Hopkins have labored to climb, Mary Scudder has easily flown on the wings of her "ethereal nature." Moreover, the results of their efforts are inferior to her effortless ascent. After the description of Hopkins's doctrine quoted above, Mrs. Stowe goes on to say that "The only mistake made by the good man was that of supposing that the elaboration of theology was preaching the gospel. The gospel he was preaching constantly, by his pure, unworldly living. . . ." but in this, too, Mary goes him one better. She converts people, notably her young cousin, by her shining example. She even makes Hopkins himself feel a new inspiration. To these accomplishments I shall return, but first we must look at Mary's most unexpected conquest, Aaron Burr.

Burr is a character in this novel, the only historical novel ever written which holds Samuel Hopkins and Aaron Burr within the same cover. They are, as we might expect, opposites. Where Hopkins is all high-mindedness and unworldly piety, Burr is the sinister sophisticate, "the proverbial expression of the iron hand under the velvet glove." Burr is of course irresistibly attractive to women, while remaining himself utterly unmoved by any emotion whatever. In good melodramatic form, his victim is a Frenchwoman, Virginie de Frontignac. We are told that "Under all his gentle suavities there was a fixed, inflexible will, a calm self-restraint, and a composed philosophical measurement of others, that fitted him to bear despotic rule over an impulsive, unguarded nature."[38] Keeping in mind the terms of this indictment, we will now study the most important fact about Burr, namely that, as Mrs. Stowe loudly informs us, he is the grandson of Jonathan Edwards.

This genealogical fact is definitely not in the novel to serve the purpose of a Matherish tirade about the baseness of the younger generation. On the contrary, Edwards is the source of

Burr's trouble, which, it will be remembered from Lyman
Beecher's tirade against him in 1805, is assumed to be heinous
indeed. To appreciate the ways in which, according to Mrs.
Stowe, Edwards was responsible for his grandson's corruption,
it is necessary to examine the chapter entitled "Views of Divine
Government." Once again, Mrs. Stowe is explaining, in her
role of recording historian, the theology of eighteenth-century
New England. "The preaching of those times was animated by
an unflinching consistency which never shrank from carrying
an idea to its remotest logical verge. The sufferings of the lost
were not kept from view, but proclaimed with a terrible power."
She refers briefly to Hopkins's preaching, and then comes to her
main theme.

> The sermons preached by President Edwards on this subject are
> so terrific in their refined poetry of torture, that very few persons
> of quick sensibility could read them through without agony; and it
> is related that when, in those calm and tender tones which never
> rose to passionate enunciation, he read these discourses, the house
> was often filled with shrieks and wailings. . . .[39]

Just as the grandson conceals an inflexible will under gentle
suavities and with "calm self-restraint" takes the measurements
of others over whom he is able to "bear despotic rule," so once
did the grandfather read in "calm and tender tones," his "refined
poetry of torture" to sinners over whom he, more absolutely
than his grandson, exercised despotic rule. Mrs. Stowe is well
aware of the intellectual power of Edwards's mind, but she says
that in his calm, cold consistency he tortures and damns most
of the human race, and so mighty is his own will that he can
constrain himself to adore this God of wrath.

> But it is to be conceded that these systems, so admirable in
> relation to the energy, earnestness, and acuteness of their authors,
> when received as absolute truth, and as a basis of actual life, had,
> on minds of a certain class, the effect of a slow poison, producing

life habits of morbid action very different from any which ever
followed the simple reading of the Bible. They differ from the New
Testament as the living embrace of a friend does from his lifeless
body, mapped out under the knife of the anatomical demonstrator;
every nerve and muscle is there, but to a sensitive spirit there is the
very chill of death in the analysis.[40]

Thus Edwards, although perhaps heroic himself, so ignores the
temperament of others as to have the effect of a "slow poison,"
corrupting and killing instead of uplifting and renewing them.
Mrs. Stowe also insists that "a simple reading of the Bible"
would reveal the opposite of this intellectual system, this poetry
of torture. But the metaphor of the body "mapped out under the
knife of the anatomical demonstrator" is appropriate to Edwards not simply because it implies coldness of heart, but also
because it alludes to Edwards's precocious and lifelong study
of the most complex scientific concepts of his day, concepts which
did indeed affect his theology. The picture Mrs. Stowe points of
Edwards, although hostile, is not vague nor inaccurate.

Mrs. Stowe hates Edwards in much the same way many of
his contemporaries did, particularly those who pledged allegiance
to that permissive patriarch of the Connecticut Valley, Solomon
Stoddard. These people, who eventually had Edwards expelled
from his pulpit and from the town of Northampton, based their
grievance on Edwards's exclusion from church membership of
all who did not show convincing evidence of a new heart. Where
Stoddard and many after him worked to include as many as
possible in the fold, and to this end allowed church membership
fairly easily, Edwards insisted on including only the few best,
most saintly people into full membership. Controversies over the
qualifications for full church membership had been going on in
New England for almost a hundred years with the general trend
being to ease or modify some of the requirements, when Edwards reversed the compromising drift with a drastically severe
restoration of the first and highest standards. Much of the op-

position to Edwards in his own day came from people who were thus abruptly banished from the company of saints. Mrs. Stowe's complaint is less personal than this. To her mind, as to all evangelicals of the mid-nineteenth century, the proper relation between the church and society is that they should be coextensive. That is, for Mrs. Stowe, the ideal is to include everybody within the fold of Christ's church, and the minister should strive to attain this end. He should work day and night on the most hardened sinners, the worse reprobates, the blackest heathen. It will be remembered that Uncle Tom converts the two depraved lieutenants of Legree; this is a triumph of practical piety in the eyes of Mrs. Stowe. Edwards, she thinks, influences many people away from the church, not only by disqualifying them for membership, but by poisoning and torturing them until they flee in horror.

Thus it happened that while strong spirits walked, palm-crowned, with victorious hymns, along these sublime paths, feebler and more sensitive ones lay along the track, bleeding away in lifelong despair.[41]

As we have seen in *Uncle Tom's Cabin,* and as we shall see again and again in the later books, it is the reclamation of the bleeding and despairing in which Mrs. Stowe is most interested.

Hopkins, though a disciple of Edwards's theology, is presented in *The Minister's Wooing* as a model of gentle sensitivity towards the miserable slaves and the sinners of the community, and thus does not suffer from Edwards's coldness. And yet, it is Mary Scudder who excels in the minister's true calling. As might be expected, Burr, because he is such a hard-hearted cynic, is exactly the one Mrs. Stowe is most anxious to convert. He is a challenging subject because of his ancestry, and also because of the nature of his dilemma. In many ways he resembles Augustine St. Clare, and even Legree, in that he is subject to "those interior crises in which a man is convulsed with the struggle of two natures, the godlike and the demoniac, and from which he must pass out more wholly to the dominion of the one or the other." Like St. Clare's, only more so, Burr's mother had been a teacher and a model of the purest piety; like Legree, Burr had become more hardened in his flight from his own better nature. "Nobody knew the true better than Burr. He knew the godlike and the pure; he had felt its beauty and its force to the very depths of his being," [42] but by the force of his fierce will, he represses the emotions which prompt him to repent. He forces himself to live by the passionless logic of his skeptical ideas. At length, Mary Scudder, outraged by Burr's betrayal of Mme. de Frontignac's noble love, is moved to some "Plain Talk."

The scene takes place in the Scudder's parlor where Burr has come to call on the distraught Frenchwoman. After an introductory attack, and a skillful parry by Burr, Mary rises to biblical eloquence:

'Mr. Burr, you remember the rich man who had flocks and herds, but nothing would do for him but he must have the one little ewe lamb which was all his poor neighbor had. Thou art that man! You have stolen all the love she had to give,—all that she had to make a happy home; and you can never give her anything in return, without endangering her purity and her soul, and you know you could not . . . and if you die, as I fear you have lived, unreconciled to the God of your fathers, it will be in her heart to offer up her very soul for you, and to pray that God will impute all your sins to her, and give you heaven. Oh, I know this, because I have felt it in my own heart!' [43]

The climax is Burr's reaction to this speech.

Burr turned away, and stood looking through the window; tears were dropping silently, unchecked by the cold, hard pride which was the evil demon of his life. . . .
The diviner part of him was weeping, and the cold, proud demon was struggling to regain its lost ascendency.[44]

We must not let the demon's eventual victory confuse our estimate of Mary's accomplishment. She has made the ice-cold cynic
cry; that is, she has made the renegade grandson submit to his
own better nature and acknowledge the truth of Mary's doctrine of the holiness of love. She gains from him a recognition
which Hopkins, too much the disciple of Edwards's "poisonous"
theology, could never get of his buried sympathy with "true"
piety. By implication, Burr acknowledges his sin in rejecting
Mary's faith as a consequence of his rejection of his grandfather's reasoning. In gaining this tacit admission from the
weeping Burr, Mary has made an excellent beginning in bringing him back to the fold, a beginning, one suspects, which is
frustrated only by the historical facts of Burr's biography. In
later novels, Mrs. Stowe does not limit the scope of her heroines
in this awkward way.

To complete our picture of Mary Scudder, and of Mrs. Stowe's
dubious antagonism to Edwards in this novel, we must look at
one of the earlier scenes between Burr and Mary. From the beginning of their acquaintance, Mary is proof against the charms
of Burr in a way he has never seen among women. "What was
that secret poise, that calm, immutable center on which she
rested, that made her, in her rustic simplicity, so unapproach-
able and so strong?" The answer to this question is the finishing
touch on Mrs. Stowe's portrait of Edwards.

Burr remembered once finding in his grandfather's study, among
a mass of old letters, one in which that great man, in early youth,
described his future wife, then known to him only by distant report.
With his keen natural sense of everything fine and poetic, he had
been struck with this passage, as so beautifully expressing an ideal
womanhood, that he had in his earlier days copied it in his private
*recueil*.

'They say,' it ran, 'that there is a young lady who is beloved of
that Great Being who made and rules the world, and that there
are certain seasons in which this Great Being, in some way or other

invisible, comes to her and fills her mind with such exceeding sweet delight, that she hardly cares for anything except to meditate on him. . . .[45]

Following, Mrs. Stowe quotes a long passage from Edwards's beautiful appreciation of Sarah Pierpont. She is obviously very fond of this passage, and has, equally clearly, modeled her heroine on Edwards's ideal.

One can only conclude that Mrs. Stowe is herself involved in conflict. On one side, although she is in awe of his intellectual power, she hates the tyrannical Edwards and his cruel theology, while on the other side, she is enthralled by his ideal of pure, intense, intuitive piety and by the power of his passionate delight in the Creator and His Creation. In *Oldtown Folks,* where she gives a much larger and more comprehensive chronicle of colonial life than she had in the first of these novels, Mrs. Stowe returns to her quarrel with Edwards. Here she extends and elaborates the entire range of theological issues with which as a historian, as well as a believer, she is concerned, but it is hardly surprising to say at the outset that she does not, even after these more ambitious discursive attempts, resolve her problem or dispel her own disturbing attitude of bitterly angry admiration.

In *Oldtown Folks,* Mrs. Stowe introduces a character very similar to Burr in *The Minister's Wooing.* His name is Ellery Davenport; he makes his first appearance in the elegant Tory parlor in Boston where the children have been sent for Easter; he himself is a dashing young patriot, however, and, most important of all, he is said to be the grandson of Jonathan Edwards. With Ellery Davenport, Mrs. Stowe reopens the whole question of Burr's apostasy and of the psychology of that wickedness. Like Burr, Davenport is the soul of charm and debonair sophistication. When, on the first occasion we see him, church-going is mentioned, he ever so politely replies, " 'Mine is the religion of beauty, fair cousin.' " When accused of being a scoffer in this remark, he alarmingly responds, " 'What, I? because I believe in the beautiful? What is goodness but beauty? and what is sin but bad taste? I could prove it to you out of my grandfather Edwards's works, *passim,* and I think nobody in New England would dispute him.' " [46] One of the young Tory women assures them, in shocking tones, that Edwards " 'lived and died a stanch loyalist,—an aristocrat in the very marrow of his bones, as anybody may see.' " Repeating the same logic so mockingly attributed to Mr. Jekyl in *Dred,* the fictional grandson of Edwards continues, " 'The whole of his system rests on the undisputed right of big folks to eat up little folks in proportion to their bigness, and the Creator, being biggest of all, is dispensed from all obligation to seek anything but his own glory.' " [47]

One might suppose, thus far, that Mrs. Stowe was being careful to keep her attacks on Edwards in the hands of characters who are unmistakably suspect, but she takes the weapons into her own hands soon after this introductory scene. Speaking about Ellery Davenport again, she turns to a discussion of the old issue in the Calvinist churches of the standing of the children of the members. She quotes Cotton Mather at length in his authoritative defense of a lenient policy, and notes, correctly, how Edwards reversed the whole trend of New England practice in "casting out of the Church the children of the very saints and martyrs, who had come to this country for no other reason than to found a church." [48]

In the argument with Edwards, Mrs. Stowe is sometimes carelessly olympian.

It is remarkable that, in all the discussions of depravity inherited from Adam, it never seemed to occur to any theologian that there might also be a counter-working of the great law of descent. . . . Cotton Mather fearlessly says that *'the seed of the Church are born holy'* . . . certainly indicating that, in his day, a mild and genial spirit of hope breathed over the cradle of infancy and childhood.[49]

Since his day, alas, Edwards has prevailed and the church has been decimated; moreover, those whom he cast out of it

were the children for uncounted generations back of fathers and mothers nursed in the bosom of the Church, trained in habits of daily prayer, brought up to patience and self-sacrifice and self-denial as the very bread of their daily being, and lacking only this sixth supernatural sense, the want of which brought upon them a guilt so tremendous.[50]

To return to the grandson who is the product of Edwards's innovations and an example of whither they tend,

Ellery Davenport's feeling toward the Church and religion had all the bitterness of the disinherited son. . . . He had not been able entirely to rid himself of a belief in what he hated. The danger of all such violent recoils from the religion of one's childhood consists in this fact,—that the person is always secretly uncertain that he may not be opposing truth and virtue itself; he struggles confusedly with the faith of his mother, the prayers of his father, with whatever may be holy and noble in the profession of that faith from which he has broken away. . . .

Ellery Davenport was at war with himself, at war with the traditions of his ancestry . . . but he took perverse pleasure in making his [apostate] position good by brilliancy of wit and grace of manner which few could resist. . . .

. . . Such men are not, of course, villains; but, if they ever should happen to wish to become so, their nature gives them every facility.[51]

In studying this passage it is essential to remember that Mrs. Stowe assumes that Edwards's theology is in fact unacceptable to a great many sensitive spirits. The consequence to them of hearing sermons "so terrific in their refined poetry of torture, that very few persons of quick sensibility could read them through without agony" is that they are forced inevitably to reject the faith of their fathers; thereafter the guilty conflict within makes them, though not "of course" automatically, likely to be villains of the worst sort. We remember the downward path of Simon Legree, fleeing from the demons of his guilty conscience into ultimately maddening and self-destructive violence.

If the victim is not compelled to villainy and madness, he may be so profoundly demoralized as to be driven out of the church altogether, into the waiting arms of the Unitarians. Mrs. Stowe states, with her characteristic mixture of rightness and over-simplification, that the New England ministers

took their confession of faith just as the great body of Protestant reformers left it, and acted upon it as a practical foundation, without much further discussion, until the time of President Edwards. He was the first man who began the disintegrating process of applying rationalistic methods to the accepted doctrines of religion. . . . Little as he thought it, yet Waldo Emerson and Theodore Parker were the last results of the current set in motion by Jonathan Edwards.[52]

According to Mrs. Stowe, the reaction to Edwards was bound to come, not only because his doctrines were so agonizing, but also because they were so aristocratic. She argues that with the acceptance of republican government, the notion of divine, as well as secular, sovereignty as absolute lost its credibility to the majority of patriotic Americans. Following the Revolution, and especially following the demise of the Standing Order, the Protestant clergy had, in her view, to adapt itself to the new ways of thinking and thus maintain the essentials of the faith in the hearts of its republican listeners. This is what the revivalists—she does not use the term—did do. This is the example of Lyman Beecher, of Avery, and of her brother Henry, whose example she urges upon her son. To her mind, Edwards and his disputatious and rigid defenders have only ruined the whole prospect of continued Christian influence on the community at large by being so exclusive and inflexible. The result of their severities has been the nourishing of the Unitarian heresy; by being so rigorous in their cruel teachings, the Edwardseans have invited and made plausible "the moral argument against Calvinism." And after Channing, Waldo Emerson.

Hence, with respect to the relative merits of Then and Now, we are given a confusing picture. What went before Edwards and what he destroyed is nobler than the theology he fashioned and imposed. Cotton Mather and the seventeenth-century heroes of whom he writes are, together with the children of the saints, wrongly scorned in Edwards's new interpretations of Calvinism. Nevertheless, what came after Edwards, namely the Unitarians, is so appalling as to make him and his followers heroes and saints by comparison. And yet, if only Edwards had not intervened, loyal Calvinists like her father and brothers and like Avery might have provided those revisions of the old confession which were necessary to a newer day. These generous and sensible men could have spared themselves the cost of theological disputation (which Edwards had made so difficult) and poured their ebullient energies into the salvation of souls across the nation. No Unitarians need have raised their menacing rationalistic protest against rational doctrinal severities which need never, but for Edwards, have contaminated the good old faith.

So much for conjecture. Given the actual course of historical events, how does Mrs. Stowe finally think about the colonial society and how does she interpret its relation and lesson to her own day? The truth is that when she is not consciously occupied in her quarrel with Edwards and thus aware of certain distinctions between one period of the colonial past and another, she tends to refer to the whole one hundred and fifty-year period before the Revolution as a continuous, homogeneous society. In her anxiety over the dissipation and fragmentation of religious life in the nineteenth century, she finds herself imagining the colonial past as all one heroic situation. Thus, during a theological argument around the kitchen fire, Horace Holyoke recalls not the disagreements but the unifying fact that everyone in the community took it as a matter of course that religious issues were a vital personal concern in daily life. To the younger, more fashionable believers present in her kitchen, especially to Major Broad who observes that " 'Mr. Addison's religious writings . . . seem to me about the right thing,' " Holyoke's grandmother replies,

'I like good, strong, old-fashioned doctrine. I like such writers as Mr. Edwards and Dr. Bellamy and Dr. Hopkins. It's all very well, your essays on cheerfulness and resignation, and all that; but I want something that takes strong hold of you. . . .

Yes, my son, the Cambridge Platform. I ain't ashamed of it. It was made by men whose shoe-latchet we aren't worthy to unloose. I believe it,—every word on't.' [53]

Both they and their seventeenth-century predecessors taught the "good, strong" stuff; they are, to the grandmother, therefore equally worthy, and far nobler than the essayists of cheerful compromise.

In attacking the rationalizers, Mrs. Stowe's principal argument is that the emotional force has been bled out of the old dogmas as the dogmas themselves have been questioned, disputed and modified. She entirely agrees with Emerson that the chief trouble with Unitarianism is that it is "corpse-cold," and, while these two self-conscious descendants of the colonial Calvinists do not agree entirely on a desirable nineteenth-century alternative to the desolation wrought by the Unitarians, they are far closer to each other than Mrs. Stowe's rather contemptuous allusions to Emerson would imply. Both make passion, feeling, intuitive piety central.

Following the analysis by Perry Miller of Emerson's relation to Edwards and to the Calvinist past in New England,[54] we find Emerson trying to restore the emotional vitality of Edwards while accepting at the same time Channing's moral argument against Calvinist dogma. "Unitarianism," says Miller, "rolled away the heavy stone of dogma that had sealed up the mystical springs in the New England character." It "had stripped off the dogmas, and Emerson was free to celebrate purely and simply the presence of God in the soul and in nature." [55] The mystical and pantheistical impulses in Edwards's adoration of the creation in which God is immanent, controlled by his equally ardent insistence on the depravity of the soul and the separateness of God from the objects of his creation, result in a religion where dogma and passion are in tension. Gradually, the dogma is eroded by the liberalizing, rationalising tendencies which eventuate in Unitarianism; it is as if the prism of liberal theology had transmitted only the cold blue rays of defeated dogma and had deflected all the warmth and passion of the brilliant white light which radiated with such unbearable intensity from Edwards's original vision. Emerson's Transcendentalism, in Miller's view, is an effort to recapture the passionate fervor of Edwards and to redirect it towards a divinity identical with nature and with the mind of man. Mrs. Stowe's sentimental heroines convey a similar mysticism in their many rapturous visions of Christ and an analogous pantheism in their instinctive rapport with flowers and natural beauty. Anyone who has read many of her novels cannot but feel oppressed by the recurrence of mystical effusions of the heroine's "childlike faith" and by the inevitable descriptions of her "sunny," "golden," "cloudlike" movements. The fact that Mrs. Stowe clings to the orthodoxy which Emerson rejects makes less difference than one might expect in the language they invoke to convey those things which to them are holy.

A further element of congruence between the two also helps one to understand the rather complex attitude toward the New England past about which Harriet Beecher Stowe chose to write so much. In 1859, the year of the first of the New England novels, Emerson also had occasion to look back to the past with admiration. "Calvinism," he recalls,

> was still robust & effective on life & character in all the people who surrounded my childhood, & gave a deep religious tinge to manners & conversation. I doubt the race is now extinct, & certainly no sentiment has taken its place on the new generation,—none as pervasive & controlling. But they were a high tragic school, & found much of their own belief in the grander traits of the Greek mythology,—Nemesis, the Fates, & the Eumenides. . . .[56]

I suspect that Emerson supplies the Greek analogy rather than the Hebrew, which Mrs. Stowe prefers, because to his taste it was more appealing; Mrs. Stowe is closer to the past when she uses the Hebrew. The point is that Emerson too sees the early Calvinist society as heroic in the grand manner. He seems to say that their religious beliefs gave these people a point of view from which men and deeds, illuminated by the dramatic light of glory or damnation, were simplified and enlarged as each took its place in the battle between God and Satan. It is their theology which has given these people their heroic dimensions, and, thus, although he has rejected their articles of faith, Emerson does not fail to honor their example. It is this same combination which is the source of the contradictory elements one so often notices in Mrs. Stowe's history; in fact, she and Emerson are so much alike in their admiration for a past they do not wish to recover that Emerson sounds exactly like his younger contemporary when he looks "to that old religion which, in the childhood of most of us, still dwelt like a sabbath morning in the country of New England, teaching privation, self-denial and sorrow!" And here not only the religion of self-denial but also the lovely metaphor of the sabbath morning seems to reproduce, with Emerson's brilliant brevity, the whole impression of *The*

*Minister's Wooing.* The serenity, the courage, and the happiness born of conviction, however austere, give to the remembered scene a beauty that seems twice charmed when they recall, and many did recall, the awful severity of the faith from which it was expressed.

To repeat, if we compare Emerson's and Mrs. Stowe's alternatives to the old faith, we find that the main difference between them is that Emerson formally rejects Christian orthodoxy in favor of the intellectual system of Transcendentalism within which he found he could more honestly express the emotions he felt; whereas Mrs. Stowe formally remains within the sheltering limits of a very much modified orthodoxy in order to give form and force to many of the same feelings. Moreover both of them were aware, especially Mrs. Stowe was vitally aware, that Edwards himself had been engaged in an effort to restore the passionate and often mystical piety, and to some extent also the millennial fervor, which he found had been washed away from New England Calvinism by the gentlemanly revisionists of the late seventeenth and early eighteenth centuries. Edwards's insistence on a new heart in the true believer, and his definition of religious experience as originating in the religious affections make this apparent. His famous descriptions of his wife and of Phoebe Bartlett are classic statements of the view that to be truly touched by God is to be touched in the heart and soul in a way which is, to an observer, evidently emotional, spontaneous, irrational. Mrs. Stowe consciously models her young heroines on those in Edwards's *Personal Narrative.*

To call these heroines angelic is not extravagant. When Mary Scudder read from the Bible to her sorrowing friend Virginie de Frontignac, "her face grew solemnly transparent, as of an angel." When Mara, the heroine of Orr's Island, is dying, Mrs. Stowe speaks an aside on "the holy innocents who come into our households to smile with the smile of angels . . . whose life was like Christ's in that they were made, not for themselves, but to become bread to us." [57] This aside is virtually identical to Mrs. Stowe's interpretation of the death of little Eva: "It is as if heaven had an especial band of angels, whose office it was to sojourn for a season here, and endear to them the wayward human heart, that they might bear it upward with them in their homeward flight." [58]

The character of the angelic heroine is essentially the same wherever she appears in the writings of Harriet Beecher Stowe. She is young—usually between ten and twenty; she is beautiful; she is usually, even preternaturally, sensitive to the inner sorrows of others. Invariably, she is associated with nature in certain ways, particularly with flowers and sunshine and clouds. She is always a devoted Christian believer by instinct and intuitive goodness no matter what her official religious education has been. She is the best minister of the gospel in that she shows those who already count themselves among the faithful a higher, purer faith, and in that she reaches and often converts those remotest from the church—miserable slaves and sinister sophisticates alike. The following description of little Eva provides an excellent point of reference for angelic iconography:

. . . an airy and innocent playfulness seemed to flicker like the shadow of summer leaves over her childish face. . . . She was always in motion, . . . flying hither and thither, with an undulating and cloud-like tread. . . . Always dressed in white, she seemed to move like a shadow through all sorts of places, without contracting spot or stain . . . that visionary golden head, with its deep blue eyes, fleeted along.

A thousand times a day rough voices blessed her, and smiles of unwonted softness stole over hard faces. . . .

To [Uncle Tom] she seemed something almost divine; and whenever her golden head and deep blue eyes peered out upon him from behind some dusky cotton-bale, or looked down upon him over some ridge of packages, he half believed that he saw one of the angels stepped out of his New Testament.[59]

Inevitably, the angelic heroine is associated with the New Testament, although the heroism of the colonial society itself is typically defined by analogy to 'hebraic theocracy.'

When Mrs. Stowe was in Italy in 1859 she began a novel which, although it comes chronologically between *The Minister's Wooing* and *The Pearl of Orr's Island,* she set in Florence at the period of Savonarola. The novel is interesting for two characters, Agnes the angelic heroine, and Agostino Sarelli, a noble bandit of the mountains, proud and passionate, and a fierce opponent of the faith of his fathers who belonged to the Church of Rome. Sarelli is a familiar figure:

a man who lives in an eternal struggle of self-justification,—his reason forever going over and over with its plea before his regretful and never-satisfied heart, which was drawn every hour of the day by some chain of memory towards the faith whose visible administrators he detested with the whole force of his moral being . . . sometimes he felt wild impulses to tread down in riotous despair every fragment of a religious belief which seemed to live in his heart only to torture him.

And just as saintly Mary Scudder pierces the defensive "gallantry" of Aaron Burr, so Agnes melts the anger of Sarelli. "The first time he saw Agnes bending like a flower in the slanting evening sunbeams by the old gate of Sorrento . . . he felt himself struck to the heart by an influence he could not define." [60]

It is the influence of what Mrs. Stowe calls, in her letter to her doubting son, "the simple old paths of childlike trust." Although Agnes is a devout pupil at a convent school, she is not tormented as Sarelli is by the failings of the Church because, quite simply, she is unaware of them. She is by nature so innocent that she cannot be corrupted by worldliness in the Church or by the bitterness it has aroused in Sarelli. Agnes is a sweet innocent child who loves flowers and plays in the sunshine. Like little Eva and Mary Scudder, she approaches the victims of theological doubt and religious melancholy and dissolves their conflicts by an evangel of love.

In *The Minister's Wooing,* Mrs. Stowe apparently feels obliged to explain Mary Scudder's intimate friendship with the Catholic Mme. de Frontignac. And she does so with the greatest of ease. In a scene where Virginie has been telling Mary about her troubles with Burr, the Frenchwoman pauses to remark, " 'I cannot help feeling that some are real Christians who are not in the True Church. You are as true a saint as Saint Catharine.' " To which Mary replies, " 'All are one who love Christ . . . we are one in Him.' " Further on Mrs. Stowe says that

Mary queried in her heart, whether Dr. Hopkins would feel satisfied that she could bring this wanderer to the fold of Christ without undertaking to batter down the walls of her creed; and yet, [Mrs. Stowe answers Mary's question] there they were, the Catholic and the Puritan, each strong in her respective faith, yet melting together in that embrace of love and sorrow, joined in the great communion of suffering.[61]

Where Edwards excludes from the fold all but a few saintly Calvinists, Mrs. Stowe points the way toward inclusion of even Catholics if they are prepared to be "melted together" in one all-embracing fold.

Mara, or the Pearl of Orr's Island, is a further development of the angelic heroine in the Emersonian directions of pantheism and mysticism. As with the others, only more so, she is not a product of her environment or training; her special gifts are innate.

It is common for people who write treatises on education to give forth their rules and theories with a self-satisfied air, as if a human being were a thing to be made up, like a batch of bread, out of a given number of materials combined by an infallible recipe.[62]

Such authors may do well enough on the average child, but they ignore the special few. In noticing the special grace of Tina

Percival, the angel of *Oldtown Folks,* Mrs. Stowe reiterates her view that "there are persons, in fact, who seem to grow almost wholly from within, and on whom the teachings, the doctrines, and the opinions of those around them produce little or no impression." A favored metaphor for such persons is that they grow up "as a fair white lily grows up out of the bed of meadow muck . . . side by side with weeds." [63]

Possibly the angel does enter the world under some special providence. Since Mrs. Stowe has rejected Edwards's belief in election and divine grace, she simply makes her heroines born pure. To heighten the effect of a special origin, distinct from the influences of the prosaic society in which they move, both Mara and Tina are given mysterious, even exotic biographies. Mara is born on the night when her father is lost in the howling tempest just as his ship is entering harbor. Her mother, Naomi, dies in childbirth. Mara is adopted by Naomi's elderly parents, Captain Pennel and his wife, and the good captain forsakes the sea to wait upon his pearl of great price. Tina and her brother Harry suddenly appear in Oldtown with their sickly, dark-eyed mother who is dying after wandering the earth because her husband, originally of the English gentry but a victim of drunken ruin, has abandoned her. Tina's real name is Eglantine Percival. She is blonde, and even at the age of seven "the delicate polished skin and the finely moulded limbs, all indicated that she was one who ought to have been among the jewels, rather than among the potsherds of this mortal life." [64] Tina and Harry are adopted by an ornery Yankee farmer and his sister.

Thus, from the outset the child is set apart, mysterious, somewhat otherworldly. This solitude is itself an environmental influence which nurtures the special sensibility within. As a child, Mara is a lonely wanderer on the island coast where "the sense of wild seclusion reaches . . . the highest degree." She is also a dreamer; and her dreams come true, when, shortly after she has dreamed of a little boy playmate, a second shipwreck leaves in its wake a beautiful Spanish-looking boy found lying among the rocks in the arms of his dead mother. The boy is called Moses by the Pennels, and the story of his parents is even more romantic than that of Mara's. Moses is the son of a Spanish woman named Dolores, whose own beautiful mother died when she was young and whose father, Don José Mendoza, married her to a brutal Cuban planter, Señor Don Guzman de Cardona. Moses learns this story from a neighbor, the reticent minister Theophilus Sewell who had, as a young man, been a tutor to the children of Mendoza in St. Augustine, Florida, and had fallen in love with Dolores. Their attempted elopement was frustrated by the father, but Sewell has recognized her by a bracelet she wore at the time of the shipwreck, a bracelet with a locket containing a lock of her mother's hair! Sewell has also discovered that Moses may well be heir to a large fortune in Cuba. It is also within the knowledge of Sewell that Dolores's husband had been so cruel to his slaves that they had revolted against him, which is why the family had taken the ship for Boston.

The story of Dolores is, however, only an embellishment to the central romantic fantasy in the novel, namely the story of Mara and Moses. Mara is a sentimental heroine, but with a difference. She is as good as Mary Scudder, but not as goody-goody; she is as angelic, but not as ministerial, and she makes no converts, properly speaking. She is as otherworldly as Mary, but not as habitually pious. Moreover, Mara is a real mystic, where Mary is merely sensitive. Mara's dramatic entry into the world in the midst of the tempest, and especially her mysterious dream picturing the little boy being offered by his mother to be her playmate, mark her as spiritually gifted from the beginning. She is contrasted to a more ordinary child, Sally Kittredge, who romps and stitches sheets and gets punished and is only fairly pretty. Mara paints the flowers and berries that she collects, she reads history and poetry, and one day when she is seven she finds a torn copy of *The Tempest* in the Pennels' attic. She is especially fond of the play, and inquires of Captain Kittredge, who is a habitual spinner of fantastic yarns about mermaids and oriental adventure, if the story be true. Unwilling to deny any of his own fables, he says this one is probably true too, though being a theatrical piece is suspect among orthodox folk. Shortly after this first discovery of an "enchanted island" in *The Tempest,* Mara and Moses take a boat to Eagle's Island off Harpswell Bay where their adventures are also fantasy play. Later when Moses whittles a small ship, Mara suggests that he call it the Ariel; that evening she reads *The Tempest* aloud to Moses while he is at work, wondering why he does not show any recognition of his own past in the line, "full fathom five thy father lies."

Some six years later, Moses gets entangled with some smugglers who are operating off Orr's Island in defiance of Jefferson's embargo. One night Mara hears Moses get out of bed and leave the house, and she follows him. Mrs. Stowe describes the terrain as one approaches Orr's Island from Great Island:

The sense of wild seclusion reaches here the highest degree; and one crosses the bridge with a feeling as if genii might have built it, and one might be going over it to fairy-land. From the bridge the path rises on to a high granite ridge, which runs from one end of the island to the other, and has been called the Devil's Back. . . .

By the side of this ridge of granite is a deep, narrow chasm, running a mile and a half or two miles parallel with the road, and veiled by the darkest and most solemn shadows of the primeval forest. Here scream the jays and the eagles, and fish-hawks make their nests undisturbed; and the tide rises and falls under black branches of evergreen. . . .[65]

The smuggler's ship is moored in the cove at the foot of the ravine, and it is to this spot that Moses is led by his "tempters," in the middle of the night. Several men are already there with a fire, ready to begin the feast of clams and punch. Mara, hovering on the ledge above, finds herself watching a furious debauch in which Moses drinks with the rest. The whole episode has the most tangential relation to the story, but it does serve to continue the mood of the outlandish and the fantastic. Mara's response is not at all to lecture Moses on temperance, although she is moved to horror by the scene. She loves him in silence and sorrow, since he apparently does not love her. Eventually, he declares himself, and after a proper scene of sighs and blushes, they walk outdoors and look out at the ocean. Moses tells her the tale of his life, which he has just learned from Sewell:

'You see, Mara, that it was intended that you should be my fate,' he ended; 'so the winds and waves took me up and carried me to the lonely island where the magic princess dwelt.'
'You are Prince Ferdinand,' said Mara.
'And you are Miranda,' said he.

Mara, however, is still very much the angel. "Ah!" she said with fervor, "how plainly we can see that our heavenly Father has been guiding our way! How good He is,—and how we must try to live for Him,—both of us." He frowns, and avows that he is "a child of this world," [66] and that he does not really believe these other things.

From this point on, the novel shifts direction. Mara is discovered to have consumption, and Mrs. Stowe embarks on that favorite Victorian subject, the death of the beautiful child. Henceforth Mara continually speaks in religious language, and the author lingers over her uplifting words. Yet even here, when she is treated so similarly to the other angelic heroines—"Mara had been all her days a child of the woods; her delicate life had grown up in them like one of their own cool shade flowers" [67]— the theme is given a cast of fantasy. The closer she comes to death, of course, the more "spiritual" does she sound, but at the climactic moment Mara does not become preachy in the manner of little Eva, but lapses instead into a clairvoyant trance.

Gradually her eyelids fell, and she dropped into that kind of half-waking doze, when the outer senses are at rest, and the mind is all the more calm and clear for their repose. In such hours a spiritual clairvoyance often seems to lift for a while the whole stifling cloud that lies like a confusing mist over the problem of life, and the soul has sudden glimpses of things unutterable which lie beyond.[68]

Later, Sally Kittredge comes into the room, and Mara describes to her her vision.

'Well, then, I lay on the bed, and the wind drew in from the sea and just lifted the window-curtain, and I could see the sea shining and hear the waves making a pleasant little dash, and then my head seemed to swim. I thought I was walking out by the pleasant shore, and everything seemed so strangely beautiful. . . .

Then it seemed to be not by our sea-shore that this was happening, but by the Sea of Galilee, just as it tells about it in the Bible, and there were fishermen mending their nets, and men sitting counting their money, and I saw Jesus come walking along, and heard him say to this one and that one, "Leave all and follow me," and it seemed that the moment he spoke they did it. . . .'

The dream vision tells about how Jesus asked her to follow, and she felt pain because she could not; finally she does, " 'and I woke then, so happy, so sure of God's love.' " [69]

Though identical in its message to deathbed scenes in her other novels, Mrs. Stowe makes this one much more elaborate; she also continues in it the elements of mystery, mysticism and fantasy which have been so important in the earlier parts of the novel. Even in her frequent allusions to the Bible, she is more apt in this novel to quote fables and parables than, as in *Dred* or *The Minister's Wooing,* prophetic injunctions of wrath.

After the death of their mother, Tina and Harry Percival are assigned by the village to the care of old "Crab" Smith and his sister Miss Asphyxia, a grizzly couple devoted to whipping and austerity in the name of pious duty, and of whom Mrs. Stowe can only say that they are "as ignorant of the blind agony of mingled shame, wrath, sense of degradation, and burning for revenge, which had been excited by [their] measures, as the icy east wind of Boston flats is of the stinging and shivering it causes in its course. Is it the wind's fault if your nose is frozen?" [70] "Glacial" Calvinism again.

Naturally, Tina and Harry run away. By the time Miss Sphxy starts after them, the children, who have had a long head start, are sporting in a field and pretending to be Hansel and Gretel. They spend the day, which Mrs. Stowe calls "a day in fairy-land," climbing over and under fences, stopping to exclaim over the glories of the red and yellow leaves, caressing the flowers and mosses at their feet. We are not surprised to learn that "the children were both endowed with an organization exquisitely susceptible to beauty, and the flowers seemed to intoxicate them with their variety and brilliancy." [71]

After their escape, the children are adopted in Oldtown, Harry by Horace Holyoke's family and Tina by Miss Mehitable Rossiter, an intelligent, sensitive spinster. One night Tina repeats a hymn her mother taught her, concluding with the line "What a Friend we have above." "The child had entered so earnestly, so passionately even, into the spirit of the words she had been repeating, that she seemed to Miss Mehitable to be transfigured into an angel messenger, sent to inspire faith in God's love in a darkened, despairing soul." [72] After this event Miss Mehitable writes a letter to her brother about her experience, which she specifically calls a "conversion." She tells about the coming of Tina as a blessed relief from her long loneliness and misery, caused, we infer, from the mysterious disappearance of their younger sister Emily, whose full story we learn much later. Emily's disaster, says Mehitable, was produced by the effect on her "highly nervous, wildly excitable" temperament of "that glacial, gloomy, religious training in Uncle Farnsworth's family."

Emily's was a nature that would break before it would bow. Nothing could have subdued her but love,—and love she never heard. These appalling doctrines were presented with such logical clearness, and apparently so established from the Scriptures, that, unable to distinguish between the word of God and the cruel deductions of human logic, she trod both under foot in defiant despair. Then came in the French literature. . . . Rousseau and Voltaire charmed her, and took her into a new world. She has probably gone to France for liberty, with no protection but her own virgin nature. Are we at once to infer the worst, when we know so little? I, for one, shall love her and trust in her to the end. . . .[73]

Blighted by "these appalling doctrines," Emily has gone off to Europe and doubtless fallen prey to romantic adventure. Miss Mehitable, on the other hand, has endured the long winter and now found a new faith through Tina's prayer.

When I laid my little Tina down to sleep to-night, I came down here to think over this strange, new thought,—that I, even I, in my joyless old age, my poverty, my perplexities, my loneliness, am no longer alone! I am beloved. There is One who does love me,—the One Friend, whose love, like the sunshine, can be the portion of each individual of the human race, without exhaustion. This is the great mystery of faith, which I am determined from this hour to keep whole and undefiled.[74]

Miss Mehitable's brother Jonathan, himself a skeptical victim of "glacial" Calvinism, acknowledges in his reply to her letter that "That throb of protecting, all-embracing love which thrilled through your heart for this child taught you more of God than father's whole library." [75]

In passing, we may say that Mrs. Stowe's sentimental heroine has affinities with Lucy Gray. Rarely does one hear, as above, a direct echo of Wordsworth, but the whole conception of these girls, all of whom "dwelt among untrodden ways," and all of whom draw mystical inspiration from fields and sunshine and flowers, derives in part from Wordsworth's very strong influence on American writers. Wordsworth's celebration of childhood and of the wisdom of the impulse from the vernal wood was often imitated by those who did not follow his development of the philosophic mind. Yet just as it would be foolish to ignore his influence on Mrs. Stowe's sentimental iconography, so it would be a mistake to overestimate it. Her imagination was deeply affected by his writing and by his presence on the American literary scene. No one in this country, at least after 1830, could write about a natural child without responding to his work. Nevertheless, in the case of Mrs. Stowe, a strange case in that she was so little interested in literature, Wordsworth's influence must be said to be a matter of indefinite literary climate and not of direct impression. For direct literary influence from nineteenth century English authors we must turn to Scott, to Dickens, and, above all, to Byron.

The fourth and last New England novel, written when Mrs. Stowe was seventy-three, is hardly a novel at all but rather a fictional memoir of her childhood years in Litchfield. It differs from the first three novels in being more autobiographical and more elegiac and in its comparatively thinner background picture of colonial life. Where *The Minister's Wooing* and especially *Oldtown Folks* give an extensive realistic representation of colonial characters and life, *Poganuc People* tends to be a highly simplified, almost lyric recreation of personal experience, distilled by distance, yet intimate in mood.

The novel opens in "a large, roomy, clean New England kitchen of some sixty years ago." [76] The house is the local parsonage belonging to the Rev. Dr. Cushing, father of ten children of whom Dolly is the youngest. The scene is unmistakably Litchfield, and Cushing is engaged, as the novel opens, in the defense of the Standing Order against the encroachments of the Episcopalians whom he anathematizes as corrupt tools of the Jeffersonian democrats. Cushing is very much like Lyman Beecher, vigorous, learned, and enormously warmhearted and resilient. No sooner has the Standing Order gone down to defeat than Cushing, in the words of the author's father, declares it "the best thing that ever happened to old Connecticut," [77] for now the clergy may forget politics and renew itself in its true calling, the preaching of the gospel and the saving of souls:

there was laid upon his soul a yearning desire to bring every one of his flock to a living, conscious union with God. . . . More especially now, since the late political revolution had swept away the ancient prescriptive defenses of religion and morals . . . had the doctor felt that the clergy must make up in moral influence what had passed away of legal restraints.[78]

Envigorated by defeat, he has seen a new day dawning. "With all his soul he was seeking a revival of religion; a deep, pathetic earnestness made itself felt in his preaching and prayers. . . ." [79] It was in this mood that Lyman Beecher and many of his brethren had set out to preach a freer, more impassioned evangel both in New England and in the newly settled West.

Dolly is the author as she would like to remember herself, a solitary, sensitive child who reads, in the seclusion of the attic, *The Arabian Nights* and the almost equally wonderful tales of old New England in Mather's *Magnalia*. The other children of the family are very shadowy in the novel. Like the other angelic heroines, Dolly has grown up in a "sphere of loneliness" which has nurtured her special sensibility. Like the others, she is a dreamer, an idealist, even a visionary child.[80]

As the novel advances, it happens that Mary Higgins, the wife of a particularly recalcitrant farmer in the neighborhood, develops tuberculosis; once again Mrs. Stowe finds herself writing about an uplifting death, and it should be said that she does a much more skillful account of this "affecting" theme here than elsewhere. Mary Higgins is "a silent, prayerful woman" whose passionate religious devotion reminds Mrs. Stowe once again of Sarah Pierpont. "The philosophic pen of President Edwards has set before us one such inner record, in the history of the wife whose saintly patience and unworldly elevation enabled him to bear the reverses" [81] of his life. Her sickness also recalls the death of Mrs. Stowe's mother, Roxana Foote Beecher, and of Roxana's sister, Mary Hubbard; the deathbed scene, the best Mrs. Stowe ever did, does convey the essence of the Puritans' rapt vision of "a triumphant death." Even the funeral is well done. After the burial Cushing, "a true soul-physician . . . forbore to address even a word to Zeph Higgins; he left him to the inward ministration of a higher power." Deacon Peasley, however, with whom Zeph had had a bitter quarrel, "was inwardly shocked to see that no special attempt had been made to 'improve the dispensation' to Zeph's spiritual state." Wherefore Peasley pursues his quarrel. " 'Well, my friend . . . I trust this affliction may be sanctified to you.' " [82] Needless to say, Zeph is further than ever from being reconciled to his grief. The exchange is a nice realistic touch in the funeral scene.

Following close upon the death of Mary Higgins there is a general "revival of religion" in the village; many people are moved to renew their commitment to the faith and Dr. Cushing labors night and day to bring in the lost and despairing. His efforts are rewarded with virtually all but Zeph, whom he admits he has been unable to approach. Zeph himself is torn between a defiant bitterness over the loss of his wife and a sore knowledge that defiance is useless and he ought to submit himself to the Lord. As so often happens, it is with these last, hardest, proudest sinners that the angel proves her powers. After the others have left a prayer meeting one evening, a meeting during the course of which Zeph has publicly confessed that " 'I ain't resigned— not a grain . . . my heart's hard and wicked. . . . I ain't a Christian, and I can't be, and I shall go to hell at last, and sarve me right!' " Dolly stays behind in the empty room with her father and mother. Then "suddenly, as if sent by an irresistible impulse," she steps up to the forlorn Zeph: " 'Oh, why do you say that you cannot be a Christian? Don't you know that Christ loves you?'" Zeph is amazed. "The words thrilled through his soul with a strange, new power; he opened his eyes and looked astonished into the little earnest, pleading face." Dolly insists, "'he loves us all. He died for us. . . . Oh, believe it. . . . Only trust Him. Please say you will!'"

Zeph looked at the little face earnestly, in a softened, wondering way. A tear slowly stole down his hard cheek.
'Thank'e, dear child,' he said.
'You will believe it?'
'I'll try.'
'You will trust Him?'
Zeph paused a moment, then rose up with a new and different expression in his face, and said in a subdued and earnest voice, '*I will.*'
'Amen!' said the doctor, who stood listening; and he silently grasped the old man's hand.[83]

This scene is the perfect type and essence of the angel's heroism. Learning from, but surpassing her father by virtue of her childish "earnestness," the angel articulates the gospel of love in its purest emotional terms. She shows that there are no hopeless cases, that even the toughest and proudest can be brought into the all-encompassing fold. As "irresistibly" moved by God's power within her as was the author of *Uncle Tom's Cabin,* Dolly pleads for the cause of millennial union, the dissolution of doubts and quarrels in the blissful effulgence of Christian love. This is the angel's vision, and with all the force of her own desire Mrs. Stowe makes her heroine's dream come true.

As a continuation and conclusion to the saga of early New England, *Poganuc People* is beautifully simplified and distilled. A great deal of the occasional and secondary incident and personality which had been used to extend the historical verisimilitude of the earlier novels is omitted or condensed, leaving the central events clear and uncluttered. The Fourth of July celebra-

tion, Election Day 1819, Thanksgiving and Christmas, a tea
party of the village gentry, some scenes with fashionable Boston
cousins and family expeditions to gather huckleberries and
chestnuts give a feeling of the true rhythm and color and meanings of life in a village such as Litchfield in those years. In its
very simplification, the novel carries a conviction the others lack.

In *Poganuc People,* the chronicle of New England reaches its
ultimate statement in the descriptions of the place itself; in fact,
place and time are defined together, as in the coming of spring:

Long after the bluebird that had sung the first promise had gone
back into his own celestial ether, the promise that he sang was
fulfilled. Like those sweet, foreseeing spirits, that on high, bare treetops of human thought pour forth songs of hope in advance of their
age and time, our bluebird was gifted with the sure spirit of
prophecy; and though the winds were angry and loud, though snows
lay piled and deep for long weeks after, though ice and frost and
hail armed themselves in embattled forces, yet the sun behind them
all kept shining and shining, every day longer and longer, every day
drawing nearer and nearer, till the snows passed away like a bad
dream, and the brooks woke up and began to laugh and gurgle, and
the ice went out of the ponds. Then the pussywillows threw out
their soft catkins, and the ferns came up with their woolly hoods
on, like prudent old housemothers, looking to see if it was yet time
to unroll their tender greens, and the white blossoms of the shad
blow and the tremulous tags of the birches and alders shook themselves gayly out in the woods.[84]

So strong is Mrs. Stowe's love of the place itself that even her
final elegy expresses the serenity of a past not really lost but
only out of sight to mortal eyes, continuous, eternal.

Generation passeth, generation cometh, saith the wise man, but
the earth abideth forever. The hills of Poganuc are still beautiful
in their summer woodland dress. The Poganuc River still winds at
their feet with gentle murmur. The lake, in its steel-blue girdle of
pines, still reflects the heavens as a mirror; its silent forest shores are

full of life and wooded beauty. The elms that overarch the streets of
the central village have spread their branches wider, and form a
beautiful walk where other feet than those we wot of are treading.
As other daisies have sprung in the meadows, and other bobolinks
and bluebirds sing in the treetops, so other men and women have
replaced those here written of, and the story of life still goes on from
day to day among the POGANUC PEOPLE.[85]

*Poganuc People* does not include extensive theological controversy. Except for such episodes as Dolly's conversion of Zeph
Higgins, which alludes to the whole problem of the churches
in speaking to men whom Edwards did so much to antagonize,
Mrs. Stowe does not reopen the debate with Edwards or instruct
her readers directly on theological issues. The success of the
novel lies in its serenity, in its poetic recreation of the life of
Litchfield, rather than in heated polemics. The source of that
serenity is Mrs. Stowe's ability, in this final novel of the New
England past, to give the essence of its way of life and cast of
mind, to beautifully crystallize its mood and meaning.

When it does allude to the provocative subject of theology and
the New England clergy, this novel speaks eloquently. Mrs.
Stowe refers with equal truthfulness to the primary concern of
the Puritan clergy with eschatology and to her own generation's
efforts to realize in America the millennial kingdom of God
when she writes:

The millennium was ever the star of hope in the eyes of the
New England clergy; their faces were set eastward, towards the
dawn of that day, and the cheerfulness of those anticipations illuminated the hard tenets of their theology with a rosy glow. They
were children of the morning.[86]

In this juxtaposition of the seventeenth-century eschatological
theme with the millennial language of the nineteenth-century
revivalists, Mrs. Stowe points the way she hopes her readers
can take towards the recovery of their heroic past and the recon-

ciliation of its older theology with the needs and sensibility of
her own time. She implies that one can heal the breach which
was opened in the old faith by the rationalists, both those who
rationalistically defended Calvinism as Edwards did, and those
who rationalistically attacked it as the Unitarians were still
doing. She appeals here to the old strain of piety for which the
Puritans so valued St. Augustine, and which had remained the
highest Christian virtue, not only to them, but also to Edwards
and to nineteenth-century evangelical believers like herself.

Again and again in the New England novels, Mrs. Stowe
praises the poetic fervor of the old clergy. By the time *Poganuc
People* is written, it is almost as if she had given up lecturing
the mid-century Protestant churches on their irresponsibility and
moral flaccidity over slavery and had turned instead to a dramatic
recreation of the whole soul and splendor of the earlier period,
as if by painting it large enough and bright enough, she could
command the emulation of her contemporaries.

Finally, and perhaps of greatest significance, Mrs. Stowe expresses, in the passage above, an appeal to her readers to renew
the old vision in language which belongs not only to the colonial
clergy and to the revivalists but which belongs to the Romantic
writers as well. It recalls Thoreau's "constant expectation of the
dawn" and Emerson's haunting "sabbath morning." It is the
language of the poets of natural innocence and joy. In this lovely
blending of historical fact with Romantic language, we hear the
hope that the exalted prophecies of long ago may once again
stir the hearts of the nation which grew from that seed. In a
phrase that applies equally well to the saints of the past and to
the angelic heroines who attempt to revive the old piety in
Victorian hearts, Mrs. Stowe invites us to be "children of the
morning."

# CHAPTER 5

# The Taste of the Angels

While intermittently pursuing her saga of colonial New England during the war years, Mrs. Stowe busied herself with the building and furnishing of her new house in Hartford, Connecticut, and with the preoccupations attendant upon her becoming, in the words of one of her biographers, "America's first female journalist." With respect to the war which Lincoln allegedly said she started, she followed the news attentively, attended the flag-raising of the Andover volunteers, visited her son Fred with the Union Army on several occasions, and wrote a number of newspaper pieces on war subjects. Given her passionate involvement with the issues of the Civil War, however, one is, at least at first, amazed at how little she had to say about it at the time, and at how much she wrote instead on mundane, even trivial, domestic subjects in the tone of the hearty and familiar family counsellor. What she did write about the war, however, makes very clear what it meant to her.

It was God's war, the final coming of the Almighty wrath, the cleansing of the sins of a nation which had dishonored its covenant. Even after almost four years of terrible battles and after the injury of her son Fred at Gettysburg she was still able to speak of the war as a "chastening." In January of 1865 she explains to her readers:

151

The great affliction that has come upon our country is so evidently the purifying chastening of a Father, rather than the avenging anger of a Destroyer, that all hearts may submit themselves in a solemn and holy calm still to bear the burning that shall make us clean from dross and bring us forth to a higher national life.[1]

Seeing the war as a holy war she is almost callous to the suffering of the soldiers. When she does think of them it is again in the language of religious exaltation. Her piece called "The Noble Army of Martyrs" includes an atrocity story typical of the kind current on both sides with respect to treatment of prisoners. It concerns one Walter Raymond, aged sixteen, who is "robbed of clothing, of money, of the soldier's best friend, his sheltering blanket,—herded in shivering nakedness on the bare ground, . . . fed on a pint of corn-and-cobmeal per day, with some slight addition of molasses or rancid meat, . . ." She pictures him as the victim of "slow, lingering tortures" which she says "it was the infernal policy of the Rebel government" to inflict. But Walter is a model Christian martyr. "Through all his terrible privations, even the lingering pains of slow starvation, Walter preserved his steady simplicity, his faith in God, and unswerving fidelity to the cause for which he was suffering." There follows a violent emotional tirade phrased in exactly the same terms as, ten years before, she had used to anticipate these events.

And is there to be no retribution for a cruelty so vast, so aggravated, so cowardly and base? And if there is retribution, on whose head should it fall? Shall we seize and hang the poor, ignorant, stupid, imbruted semi-barbarians who were set as jailers to keep these hells of torment and inflict these insults and cruelties? or shall we punish the educated, intelligent chiefs who were the head and brain of the iniquity?[2]

The most remarkable aspect of Mrs. Stowe's attitude toward the war is that it never changed. It was neither modified by events nor blurred by the passage of time. During the period of

Reconstruction she continued to invoke the traditional language of the covenant and the ideas about democracy and independence which she had first expounded in the fifties. In a passage from "A Family Talk on Reconstruction," one of the "Chimney-Corner" series, she summarizes her view of the war and her concern for the postwar society:

> This war, these sufferings, these sacrifices, ought to make every American man and woman look on himself and herself as belonging to a royal priesthood, a peculiar people. The blood of our slain ought to be a gulf, wide and deep as the Atlantic, dividing us from the opinions and practices of countries whose government and society are founded on other and antagonistic ideas. Democratic republicanism has never yet been perfectly worked out either in this or any other country. It is a splendid edifice, half built, deformed by rude scaffolding, noisy with the clink of trowels, blinding the eyes with the dust of lime, and endangering our heads with falling brick.[3]

Her enthusiasm for the holiness of the cause betrays Mrs. Stowe into such excesses as the figure of a royal priesthood, but most of all it prompts her to recall the traditional notion of the peculiar people, separated morally as well as physically from European decadence. Like the Puritans, Mrs. Stowe imagines that the New World society is to be a model of righteous government for Europeans to emulate, and for this model she picks a characteristic nineteenth-century image of building and progress. Thus the war takes its place in the providential pattern wherein we are to read after Mather the further great works of Christ in America.

Aside from its intrinsic interest to a general study of Mrs. Stowe's life and work, this remarkable consistency is noteworthy in that it marks a difference between her and many of her literary contemporaries. The war did not interrupt Mrs. Stowe's literary career. Her four-volume saga of colonial New England life continued and, in fact, reached new heights after the war with the completion of *Oldtown Folks*. Moreover, as the postwar scene presented new ideas and social situations, these were easily accommodated to the fictional purposes of a writer whose own convictions remained essentially secure. To writers perhaps more sensitive to their environment, but also far less firmly related to such hardy habits of mind as those developed by the New England clergy, the events of the war caused strange ruptures in their careers. Emerson, only eight years older than Mrs. Stowe, became repetitious, and produced nothing after the war to equal what he had done before. Hawthorne, seven years older, can be seen struggling in his late unfinished romances with the literary idiom he had previously brought to perfection but which failed him completely in the end. His humorously weird contrivances and gothic devices simply lost the power they once had to convey moral truth; they became for him hollow tricks, meaningless old toys.[4] Similarly with Melville's haunting silence after the war one senses dislocation of belief so profound as to forbid even the old defiance. Whitman, like Melville eight years younger than Mrs. Stowe, did recover, largely through treating the war, in *Drum Taps,* as a holy war which had brought us to great sacrifices and given us Christ-like heroes; like Mrs. Stowe he chose to look at the postwar scene as "noisy with the clink of trowels and falling bricks" which were building a strengthened democratic society. Yet even Whitman never soared as high again as he had in the grand original "Song of Myself."

That the war had a profoundly disturbing, even permanently disordering effect on the thought and writing of all four of these more famous contemporaries is beyond question. That it did not have a similar effect on Mrs. Stowe is probably due to the fact that Mrs. Stowe saw the war as divinely ordained, an inspired effort to restore the rightness of the nation's onward course. Perhaps because she never changed her mind about the war she was simply impervious to the common doubt and despair. Actually for Mrs. Stowe the war strengthened rather than weakened her old convictions; the wrath of the Almighty did descend on the wicked nation just as the prophets—herself among them—had foreseen. Even the unprecedented horrors of the first "modern" war and the sickening bitterness of the fratricidal slaughter could be seen by her as justified in the glorious cause of the Christian soldiers. Again, as in *Uncle Tom's Cabin,* she spoke of the separation of families, the sufferings of mothers parted from their sons, but in the holy war these sufferings became ennobled, the sacrifices of the good and true to redeem their country.

In late April of 1864 Mrs. Stowe moved her family and possessions from Andover to the large and still unfinished house in Hartford. Two of her sisters were already living in that city, and she had herself, some forty years before, spent eleven years there teaching in her sister Catharine's Hartford Female Seminary. Mary Perkins, the second oldest of the Beecher girls and the only one of Lyman Beecher's eleven children who never entered public life, was a wise and gentle woman to whom the more excitable and often feuding younger sisters could appeal; her husband Thomas Perkins had frequently advised Mrs. Stowe on business matters. Isabella Hooker, the youngest daughter and the child of Lyman's second wife, also lived in Hartford where her husband, John Hooker the sixth, was a lawyer. Isabella was a fiercely opinionated, energetic woman and later a vehement supporter of the more radical wing of the Suffrage movement led by Victoria Woodhull and Tennessee Claflin, the two flamboyant militants who, seven years later, were the first to publish the story of Henry Ward Beecher's adulterous liaison with Mrs. Tilton. Isabella varied the traditional Beecher vision of the millennium by imagining it a matriarchy, and it is rumored that one New Year's Eve she stayed up waiting for the angel to descend and pronounce her the president of the new dispensation.

In 1864, however, before Henry Ward was in the headlines and Isabella clearly mad, and while the righteous war still went on, the Stowes moved into the Hartford house in high spirits. Mrs. Stowe had by this time become accustomed to the role of famous author and European traveller, and was anxious to set up housekeeping in style, a rather costly style in fact. To pay the bills she began two series of magazine articles, the first called "Men of Our Times," for the *Watchman & Reflector* and a second one for the *Atlantic* which she called "House and Home Papers."

The "House and Home Papers" and their sequel "The Chimney-Corner," also written for the *Atlantic,* are the most interesting and coherent of a large bulk of journalistic pieces the earliest of which began to appear in the *Western Monthly Magazine,* the Cincinnati *Journal,* and the Cincinnati *Chronicle* during her years in Ohio. Her association with the *National Era* which serialized *Uncle Tom's Cabin* came next, and immediately after that a New York paper, the *Independent,* for which Henry Ward was doing a popular series of "Star" papers, signed Mrs. Stowe as a regular contributor. In their announcement of her advent to the staff, the editors optimistically promised "frequent and perhaps weekly contributions." Further they foresaw that

These contributions will be of a miscellaneous description, embracing every variety of incident, of subject, and of character, from the "Mayflower" to "Uncle Tom's Cabin:" sometimes an essay, sometimes a story, sometimes a graphic picture of home life or a sketch of the olden time. . . .[5]

The editorial emphasis on miscellany was a fair prediction of Mrs. Stowe's contribution to the *Independent.* The two *Atlantic* series, however, both in the magazine and between hard covers, showed by their immense popularity how sensitive Mrs. Stowe was to the perplexities and aspirations of American housewives. As shown by her collaboration with her sister Catharine on the *American Woman's Home,* Mrs. Stowe knew precisely what middle class homemakers wanted and needed to know and how to present it to them in casual, greatly detailed and readily useful form. She was not the first or the only one in this period to concern herself with the popular arts, household decoration and fashion, but she was one of the more canny, as well as prolific, advisers to middle class taste and pretension.[6]

Perhaps this is the time to remind ourselves that, in treating Mrs. Stowe's work as worthy of serious critical attention, this study is necessarily selective and must ignore a large part of her total output. She was a terrific potboiler, one of those lucky people who confidently assume, and in her case often rightly, that their least passing observation on any subject from religious dogma to the latest curiosity in the shop window will be eagerly, even gratefully, received by the reading public. For the most part this considerable quantity of Mrs. Stowe's writing has little or no literary interest.

In the early postwar years, in addition to her various journalistic enterprises, Mrs. Stowe wrote three novels which also dealt with home, the woman question, fashion, women's education and the complexities of that division in family life, so well recorded in *The Rise of Silas Lapham*, that set the man in charge of his business and the woman and her educated daughters in charge of Culture. Since these novels deal so extensively with the same issues as the domestic journalism, I shall include the novels in this chapter, following the discussion of the *Atlantic* essays.

The essays date from 1863. They were thus begun before the end of the war and continued after it was over. The three novels are slightly later: *Pink and White Tyranny* and *My Wife and I* were both published in 1871; the sequel to the latter, *We and Our Neighbors,* appeared in 1873. Thus it should be borne in mind that the period of Mrs. Stowe's main output on social and domestic questions, as I am somewhat vaguely referring to them, is roughly 1863–1873 and overlaps in time the period of her work on the New England novels. Mrs. Stowe had not by any means abandoned her interest in the colonial era while she was at work on the more immediate public issues of her own day. *Oldtown Folks* itself includes extensive asides on the subjects of contemporary debate, such as the education of women. It is largely a matter of convenience, rather than to show a development from one theme to another, that I have chosen to discuss the domestic journalism and novels of manners of the middle to late sixties and early seventies separately from the ongoing saga of colonial New England.

In the domestic journalism, as well as in the three novels, Mrs. Stowe is to be heard, as of old, speaking to the public issues of the day. Her foremost concern is with what she and her contemporaries called the woman question, in reality a whole Pandora's boxful of questions dealing with everything from cooking and fashion to the vote, women's education, and, of course, women's influence on the religious training of their children, the public men of the future. Mrs. Stowe's arguments in the long course of these journalistic discussions focus on moral issues, or often they make the issues into moral ones. Thus, once again, Mrs. Stowe's social and political polemics are an extension of her religious concerns. What is finally at stake, when she is talking about interior décor as well as about the religious nurture of the young, is the moral order of American society.

Mrs. Stowe fears this moral order is threatened. She had been saying as much in the New England novels. In the popular journalism of this period, however, her arguments and assumptions show that, like many Victorians, she had come to define morality by secular criteria. She had, of course, from the outset in *Uncle Tom's Cabin* made secular voices the oracles of religious truth—the self-denying mothers, the angelic heroines. After the war she moved even farther away from doctrinal squabbles in the direction of pious feeling. In this movement she came to rest her conceptions of morality on aesthetic rather than theological grounds. Religious life itself, in her writing, becomes more and more a matter of feeling and a response to beauty and less and less a concern for the kind of intellectual propositions about the nature of God and man that are expressed in doctrinal statements. Such a shift is entirely in keeping with her lifelong distrust of rationalizers—Edwards, Channing, anyone who disrupted the faithful and divided the churches by angry debates on points of doctrine—and with her constant appeals to let love dissolve the doubts and suspicions that set North against South, black against white, Protestant against Catholic, and the various Calvinist factions against each other. Mrs. Stowe's domestic journalism preaches a practical piety, an applied Christianity; the reader is taught how to make cooking and home decoration express and even instill religious feeling, and the distractions of dogmatic subtlety are pointedly ignored. Not that she was ever a systematic moralist; as I have said, even in *Uncle Tom's Cabin,* which retains the framework of Christian ethics and makes its appeal to the conscience of the readers, North and South, who have been nurtured in the evangelical tradition, Mrs. Stowe rests her case against slavery finally on the violence it does to the feelings of both its victims and its defenders. The suffering of the mothers in the novel is the measure of slavery's offense against God. The remedy the novel proposes for social ills—the dissolution of conflict in Christian, typified by family, love—also clearly presupposes that the society as a whole is capable of responding to the appeal to its Christian conscience. Moreover, the passionate response to the book, whether in anger or in sympathy, shows that this appeal hit its mark.

In the postwar period, apparently, one could not speak to a large readership in these terms. People did not share a common evangelical commitment which one could invoke. By the mid-60s and early 70s, one could no longer assume a general acceptance of Christianity. Indeed, Mrs. Stowe herself no longer felt comfortable with the old revivalist style. She was no more inclined to come forth again with a ringing call to return to the nation's covenant or an impassioned summons to the millennial union of perfect love than her readers were to listen to such old-fashioned piety.

Mrs. Stowe's postwar polemics on the subjects of home and the woman question advise the combination of comfort and gentility with virtue. This question was important in the early part of the period when, with the rising profits of business expansion after the war, Americans developed a ravenous appetite for all those things we might glibly identify by the word Culture: French fashions and cooking, the dancing masters and pastry cooks of Uptown, as Henry James refers to them in the preface to *Daisy Miller;* elaborate houses, later even palaces filled with the objects of European art and wealth. This was the beginning of the era of the collectors and it should be remembered that it was not only Frick and Mellon and Mrs. Jack Gardner, but also large numbers of affluent middle class tourists who were increasingly determined to know about, and where possible to possess, the treasures of the old world. Mrs. Stowe was wholeheartedly in sympathy with the stirrings of this inquisitive and acquisitive impulse, but she also wanted to see to it that her contemporaries tempered their pursuit of happiness by a regard for goodness. How then shall she define goodness, given the fact that she and her contemporaries no longer wish to do so in the old theological terms? How shall she persuade her readers to adhere to a moral order?

She does not resort, as Arnold did in "Dover Beach," simply to private loyalty or personal integrity. Although it is true to say that Mrs. Stowe comes to define morality by aesthetic criteria, as Arnold himself eventually came to rest the moral order on an aesthetic basis when he chose to replace the priest with the poet and the authority of the church with that of the wisdom of the inspired poet/prophet, it is important to understand their differing methods. To the question of how to ensure a moral order in Victorian society, Mrs. Stowe, in effect, argues that Christianity can still do this if we rightly understand it. Rightly to understand the old faith is, first, to ignore doctrinal controversy. Second and crucial is to stress and rely upon sentiment, the response to beauty, poetry, harmony—aesthetic qualities in art, religious art in particular, and in nature—which stimulate uplifting emotions, the love of God and a feeling of reverence.

In her letter of advice to young Charlie over his dangerous liking for the Unitarians, Mrs. Stowe had held up her brother, Henry Ward Beecher, as a model clergyman. Uncle Henry's strength lay in his silence on all matters of doubt or controversy and in his exemplary tact in confining his preaching to "those things of which he felt certain." The articulation of Mrs. Stowe's own convictions can be followed in the New England novels through the sentimental heroines' formulation of Christian piety as well as through Mrs. Stowe's author's comments on them and her asides about Hopkins, Edwards and New England theology. A good statement of the faith Mrs. Stowe created for herself to supersede Calvinist doctrine is her account, in the same letter to Charlie, of those things of which she says Henry Ward Beecher was certain.

He never said any thing about Adam's fall one way or the other—but preached Christ as the Savior from Sin—as the Friend—Comforter & Guide. He preached the certain punishment of sin here & hereafter. The need of God's Holy Spirit—God's willingness to give it. Prayer—& its answer. The Bible—& its inspirations & how to use it. All thro the earlier part of his ministry his steps were dogged by those who said he was not orthodox but he devoted himself to persuading men to become Christians—Above all and constantly he preached Christ his life on earth—his throne in Heaven & God blessed his preaching to the salvation & comfort of thousands of souls. No man is recognized by more souls as a spiritual Father. Now if he had yielded to disgust—gone over to the Unitarians—there would have been lots of scandal a bitter controversy—but no Plymouth Church.[7]

The important thing is for everyone to be within the fold of Christ's church, and to the extent that the several feuding Calvinist factions have dispersed the great body of loyal Christians and set them to excluding each other they have done a great disservice to the Christian religion. Mrs. Stowe grants in this letter to her son that the temptation to excessive liberalism exists, but as she sees it, "in an age when God is shedding new light on religion thro the development of his own natural laws in Science," it is the business of the faithful to give thanks for the new light and to hold fast to the central faith.

It is commonly supposed that in 1864 Mrs. Stowe rejected Calvinism and joined the Episcopal church. This is not true. Never in her adult life had she embraced the five tenets of Calvinism; never had she believed the doctrine of the Cambridge Platform whose makers she so admired. After her adolescent years with Catharine at the Hartford Female Seminary she had moved into the orbit of the freewheeling revivalist preaching of the West. Two years after she had returned to the East she became famous and began visiting the Catholic churches of Europe to which she responded surprisingly sympathetically. And all this time she had been evolving a highly emotional creed of her own, a creed which focused on Christ the "friend," the "comforter," the shining example of "self-sacrificing love." Her orientation was secular rather than ecclesiastical. Instead of doctrinal subtleties, instead even of salvation in the sense that Edwards used the word, Mrs. Stowe's piety led her to concern herself with redemption of drunkards, with Christian love rather than selfish hate between black and white, and with the lifting of the burdens of the oppressed everywhere. As to her "joining" the Episcopal church in Hartford, it is simply known that she bought a pew and attended services with her twin daughters.[8]

From Mrs. Stowe's letters to members of her family at this time one can see exactly what her attitude was toward the Episcopalianism of her daughters. To Hattie in 1862 she writes that the Episcopal church "suits your temperament better than our denomination," namely hers and Calvin Stowe's. "I shall sometimes go with you," she writes, "always to the sacrament because I find that service is more beneficial to me than ours." Most important, "I have long long [?] looked on you as a true Christian." That is always the basic thing for Mrs. Stowe. She even goes so far as to tell Hattie that "in my heart & belief I am an Episcopalian—& if ever I leave —————— [word illegible] here I shall freely unite with that church whither I should be happy to have all my children go." [9] This letter was written two years before the move to Hartford, at the time when the twins, Hattie and Eliza, joined the Episcopal church. In another letter, to her sisters Catharine and Mary, she comments on her son Fred's confirmation:

What a comfort it is to have all my children united in religious sympathy. I have never ceased to bless the day when the girls were confirmed—It has been to them that personal education & progression which they & I hoped for—and I see every year how the services & prayers gain on them more & more. [10]

In other words, the denomination, as long as it is not Unitarian, matters not at all. This is because the main differences between the large Protestant denominations in this country at that time, namely differences of doctrine and of polity, were inessential to Mrs. Stowe's conception of Christian piety. This conception was both sentimental and practical. It combined fervor for the benevolence of Christ with the pursuit of daily virtue and wholesome living. Mrs. Stowe's writings—novels, poems, hymns, sketches, letters—are filled with rhapsodic passages about the love and goodness of Christ whom, in turning away from the severities of Edwardsean Calvinism, she makes the focus of worship, another reason for her hostility to the Unitarians. The crux of religious experience for Mrs. Stowe is this intense feeling for the divine, an emotion which exalts the spirit in private and which unites the individual with all those who acknowledge it within the one shelter of the fold of Christ. Mrs. Stowe's brother Henry, the celebrated pastor of Plymouth Church, went so far in rising above doctrinal subtlety that he was able, having been finally acquitted of the charge of adultery after a four-year public scandal and sensational trial, to soar to new rhetorical heights in the preaching of his favorite subject, "the gospel of love." Admittedly, Henry Ward had the dullest mind in the family. Still, Harriet noticed no irony.

Finally, however, it should be said that the evangelical notion of the all-encompassing Christian fold within which denominational differences would be dissolved and doctrinal disputes resolved by love had nothing in common with the Anglican doctrine of catholicity. The millennial Kingdom preached by the revivalists was to be realized in the hearts of their listeners, not in the churches. Revivalism sought ultimately to obviate the need for a church of any denomination. It wanted to supersede worldly, institutional, as well as logical and rational definitions. It sought to propel its adherents directly into an emotional unity co-existent with society and within which a church would be obsolete.

The Episcopal church in this country, although autonomous in polity, had, since shortly after the Revolution, reaffirmed its fellowship in the Anglican Communion and was hence committed to certain traditions, liturgical and doctrinal, which concerned universality. Particularly since the Oxford movement of the 1840s, Episcopalians, as well as other Anglicans, had specifically embraced the idea of the catholic (although not the Roman Catholic) nature of their church. In her explicit statements during and after the period of the change from attending a Congregational or Presbyterian church to attending an Episcopalian one, Mrs. Stowe invariably rejoices that her children are in the fold. She finds the Episcopal service "uplifting" and "beautiful."

Moreover, her natural suspicion of rationality in religion would make it all the more unlikely that she might do anything so apparently logical as to join a church which made it an articulate point of doctrine that there was and always had been only "one catholic and apostolic church."

Although Mrs. Stowe did not make any dogmatic connection between her own all-embracing, millennial idealism and the Episcopalian concept of catholicity, she certainly did respond to the Episcopalian aesthetic emphasis quite explicitly. Her essays of the "House and Home" and "Chimney-Corner" series concur exactly in point of time with her move to Hartford and to the Episcopal church. What the Oxford movement called "the beauty of holiness" had become increasingly important in Anglican thought and in the services of the Episcopal churches and it is to this aspect of Episcopalianism that she always refers in her letters. Similarly, in *Agnes of Sorrento* and elsewhere in discussing the Roman Catholic church, she praises the "poetry" of the liturgy and the "beauty" or "harmony" of the church interior and its ornaments. Mrs. Stowe even has Dolly Cushing remark at the beginning of *Poganuc People* that she is attracted to the Episcopal church, which is observing Christmas as the Congregationalists are not, by the flowers and evergreens with which they decorate the church building for the occasion. It is warm and lovely and moving, whereas the Congregational church of Dr. Cushing is cold and austere.

When T. S. Eliot, commenting on his conversion to Catholicism, explained that he did not tolerate the dogma for the sake of the sentiment, but rather that he put up with the sentiment for the sake of the dogma, he was contrasting himself to those Victorians, including those Victorian New Englanders from whom he was descended, who had done precisely the reverse. Mrs. Stowe tolerated the Anglican dogma for the sake of the sentiment, for the feeling of being uplifted by the beauty of the music and the flowers and by the poetry of the ritual.

In so doing, she makes clear in her own life a transition from her original emphasis on religious sentiment in the context of early nineteenth-century revivalism to a postwar religious sentiment which responded to the ornamental symbols of Anglican and Roman Catholic worship. The reason that she could so easily shift from the Congregational to the Episcopal church is that she had always trusted sentiment, religious feeling and its expression, as the essence of Christian piety. Thus, when she felt herself responding to the beauty of Anglican holiness, she trusted the feeling within. Had it been the Anglican dogma or catechism to which she had been asked to assent, she might never have felt so comfortable. It was because the Episcopal service held more of the things which evoked religious sentiment that she found, as she wrote to her daughter, the service "more beneficial to me than ours." Because religious sentiment, this response of the feelings to that which is beautiful and holy, is usually not aroused by doctrinal debate or exegesis, but rather almost always by music, flowers, painting, ritual, in short, the aesthetic aspect of a church service, Mrs. Stowe tends to experience the faith itself in aesthetic terms. It is for this reason that she readily defines private and also public or social morality in the language of aesthetics.

If the first step in the process which eventually led to the aesthetic or secular morality was the substitution of sentiment for dogma as the essence of Christian belief—a step taken by the early nineteenth-century evangelical clergy—the second step was the discovery, ingenuous and indeed inevitable, that religious sentiment could be evoked outside the church as fully as inside it. When she was spending the winters at her cottage in Mandarin, Florida, Mrs. Stowe would often write to her children that she had passed a Sunday morning beneath the oaks in her back yard, delighted by the scent of orange blossoms, repeating prayers to herself and humming hymns. She reports that these mornings were "beneficial"; indeed the response of the heart, and of the senses, to beauty and harmony proves to be quite as moving in the home as in the church.

For Mrs. Stowe herself there was no conflict between church and home. To feel stirred by religious affections everywhere in the world was, on the contrary, to feel how pervasive was God's bounty to men. The sentimental response to the sunny morning does not replace the response to the church service. She was not herself a pagan. The extension of piety and good works to the secular sphere was entirely natural and did not induce in her an indifference to the transcendent divinity. Yet Mrs. Stowe had, as I have said, profoundly shared the experience of Arnold and others who grieved over the loss of faith in their society. She responded to the challenge of defining a moral order for a society which had lost its faith by formulating a secularized gospel in which she hoped to preserve Christian piety by locating its temple in the home.

At this point, one might well object that it is unnecessary to explain a notion of piety whose chief focus was the Christian home by introducing a discussion of aesthetics. After all, Horace Bushnell, the foremost American Protestant theologian of his generation, had made Christian nurture in the home central to his theology. Is it really necessary to talk about Arnold, and as I shall do later, about Ruskin, when one need look no further afield than Dr. Bushnell of Hartford for a thorough exposition of the sanctity of home?

One of the most baffling facts of Mrs. Stowe's life is her apparently complete unawareness of Bushnell. Not only was she always involved with the life of the New England clergy and theological debate, but she was also a resident of Hartford, where Bushnell lived, for forty years. None of her biographers, including Wilson, mentions Bushnell. The only direct reference she ever made to him was the remark, in a letter describing a party she had gone to in Hartford, that participating in a game of charades there had been one "Dr. Bushnell." [11] The fact that she calls him "doctor" indicates that she is probably speaking of the theologian, but even this is inference. Her silence about Bushnell is so conspicuous that one is tempted to regard it as some sort of clue, like Holmes's famous hint to Watson about the dog in the night. Bushnell was even born in Litchfield, only a year later than Catharine Beecher.

Reading "House and Home Papers" and the "Chimney-Corner" for the first time one is convinced that the author could not have come so close to the idea of Christian nurture without meaning to. The psychological argument that the child will form the habits of faith and piety in the Christian home and therefore not require in later life either rational persuasion or the "technical experience," as Bushnell calls it, of conversion sounds just like him. Bushnell pleads, in *Christian Nurture* for "those humble, daily, hourly duties, where the spirit we breathe shall be a perpetual element of power and love, bathing the life of childhood." "What is the true idea of Christian education?" asks Bushnell. *"That the child is to grow up a Christian, and never know himself as being otherwise."* [12] This sounds like a statement of Mrs. Stowe's program, and since it was written fifteen years before her articles, one might well conclude that she was, admittedly or not, following in Bushnell's footsteps. The fact is she was not.

In the first place, Bushnell was not sympathetic to revivalism or revivalist theology. Temperamentally as well as intellectually, he was at odds with the style of Lyman Beecher. Bushnell was opposed to the proposition "that the child is to grow up in sin, to be converted after he comes to a mature age"; [13] this, he says, is what those who put so much emphasis on conversion condone. There is evidence that Bushnell, especially as a young man, felt an obligation to seek to attract crowds of converts and to stir people, as the revivalists seemed to him to be doing, to reawakened faith and commitment to the church. Nevertheless, he was unhappy in the role of emotional champion of the Lord and soon satisfied himself that he could fulfill his ministry more successfully in other ways.[14]

One of these ways was as a scholar and theologian, and it is here that he departs most radically from the eclectic liberal theology as well as from the giddy ecumenical enthusiasm of revivalism. Eventually, Bushnell attacked the very things Mrs. Stowe most heartily cherished. Somewhat in the tradition of a latter-day Edwards, Bushnell undertook to defend the essentials of orthodox Calvinism. Specifically, he insists on Original Sin. He therefore denies that Christian education is the cultivation of innate good in the child: "there is no so unreasonable assumption, none so wide of all just philosophy, as that which proposes to form a child to virtue, by simply educing or drawing out what is in him. The growth of Christian virtue is no vegetable process, no mere onward development." [15] Mrs. Stowe does not believe in Original Sin. She is not as bold as to say so, although Catharine Beecher attacked not only the doctrine itself but also St. Augustine for having made it so influential.[16] Harriet, as she says in her letters, prefers to say nothing about those things in which she disbelieves; nonetheless, it is perfectly clear that she accepts the revivalist implication that one can have a hand in one's own salvation and in that of society. Likewise, she rejects the doctrine of election in favor of the evangelical ideal of an all-encompassing unity in Christ. Christian nurture in the home is for Bushnell part of the participation of society, in its organic and historical relations, in the redemptive work of God. It is not, as for Mrs. Stowe, the source of virtue, a new focus for the work of redemption, personal and social, when the Calvinist dependence on divine agency has been replaced by liberal notions of "ability."

Similarly, when it comes to Bushnell's discussion of the supernatural, it is clear that he is thinking in far more orthodox terms than Mrs. Stowe would admit. Where she does give credence to supernatural powers, she tends to be drawn towards certain aspects of spiritualism, or mystical visions. Where Bushnell insists that these powers combat and overcome depravity, she rejects both his question and his answer. Her brand of Christianity was altogether more worldly, more naturalistic, and more secular than was Bushnell's: hence, we are led to believe, her absolute silence concerning the most searching Protestant theologian of her generation. That Mrs. Stowe lived away from Hartford during the thirty years of Bushnell's most active writing and preaching is important too, but the Beechers kept in touch, even in Cincinnati, with remoter outposts than Hartford, and one strongly suspects that they were aware of, and deliberately ignored, the man whose thought constituted the most forceful critique of their day on what they themselves were doing.

As for Mrs. Stowe's commitment to spiritualism, it was fairly superficial. Like so many others who had accepted a liberalized, worldly faith, a religion concerned with immediate results both material and emotional, spiritualism appealed to an imagination which found itself denied the great mysteries of the old dogma. Yet for Mrs. Stowe the main reasons for her interest in the subject were personal. First, Calvin Stowe had been subject ever since childhood to impressive hallucinations and visions. He was constantly undergoing extraordinary visitations from creatures real and unreal, dead and alive. Both he and his wife believed that these were supernatural happenings of some sort; thus, when spiritual encounters became a subject of popular discussion, the Stowes were not only interested, they were old hands. Second, their son Henry, a sophomore at Dartmouth, was drowned in the Connecticut River near Hanover just before Mrs. Stowe returned home from her trip abroad in 1857. This was the greatest tragedy of her life. When, a year later, she recreated the event in *The Minister's Wooing* in the scene where Mrs. Marvyn hears news that her son James has been drowned at sea, Mrs. Stowe describes the force of that grief as driving the mother to the verge of madness. It is one of the most moving scenes she ever wrote. Her real interest in spiritualism was in the possibility of somehow reaching Henry. Even in her attempts to persuade her friends and some of her correspondents of the possible merits of the subject, Mrs. Stowe argued the case in such a way as to prompt the skeptical George Eliot to the response, "Your view as to the cause of that 'great wave of spiritualism' which is rushing over America, namely, that it is a sort of Rachel-cry of bereavement towards the invisible existence of the loved ones, is deeply affecting." [17] One can only agree with George Eliot that it is deeply affecting. It is very little more. Spiritualism never replaced or even altered for Mrs. Stowe her Christian belief.

Having examined above the grounds of Mrs. Stowe's social morality in the mid-sixties, I should like to pause and illustrate from the *Atlantic* articles themselves how she conducts these arguments and what her tone and immediate purpose are in several of them. It is, to most of us, a long way from the care of indoor plants to the essentials of a moral order in society. Yet Mrs. Stowe does go that distance. Some of this journalistic advice is quite comic to a modern reader, and much of it is tedious, but perhaps we smile and yawn because the arguments are so familiar. The symbolism of home as Mrs. Stowe defines it has, for better or worse, endured.

In one of her *Atlantic* pieces, "The Economy of the Beautiful," Mrs. Stowe tells the parable of Phillip and John, two recently married young men who buy two identical houses and who move in the same social circle. Phillip is rich and furnishes his house with fashionable imported finery—carpets, fancy wallpaper, elegant chairs and tables. John is poor and thus unable to afford these fashionable trappings. Since he cannot buy heavy draperies, his windows transmit floods of sunlight and he has chosen to decorate the window seats with plants and flowers. On the walls he has hung copies of paintings or lithographs, and he arranges the rest of the parlor to "harmonize" with these elements. Clearly his results are superior in Mrs. Stowe's opinion to those of his rich neighbor. She calls Phillip's parlor "cold" and "confused" while she admires John's for its warmth, modesty and aesthetic unity. Further, she emphasizes the virtues of "our good American things," which she says are often superior to imported finery and are, in general, of better quality than the fashion-conscious reader supposes.

As regards dress, Mrs. Stowe laments that all fashion emanates from France where morals are "at the very lowest ebb" and fashion is dictated by courtesans, "women who can never have the name of wife." She is scandalized that American women have so lost their heads that, "lest these Circes of society should carry all before them, and enchant every husband, brother, and lover, the staid and lawful Penelopes leave the hearth and home to follow in their triumphal march and imitate their arts." Mrs. Stowe is angry. "The love of dress and glitter and fashion is getting to be a morbid, unhealthy epidemic, which really eats away the nobleness and purity of women." [18] This is not only a matter of personal virtue and personal thrift, but of general social concern, and it affects the extravagant and corrupt fashions of men as well as those of women. "There is enough money spent in smoking, drinking, and over-eating to give every family in the community a good library, to hang everybody's parlor walls with lovely pictures, . . . to furnish every dwelling with ample bathing and warming accommodations, even down to the dwellings of the poor; and in the millennium I believe this is the way things are to be." [19]

The parlor ought not to be "too fine for the ordinary accidents, haps and mishaps of reasonably well-trained children." There are several reasons for this. The first is that the well designed parlor's "beauty and its order gradually form in the little mind a love of beauty and order, and the insensible carefulness of regard." [20] This is part of the educational purpose of home. A more far-reaching reason for the accommodation of children to the parlor is that they may otherwise resort to flight and "run the city streets, and

hang around the railroad depots or docks." [21] In the city streets
they would meet the usual vices associated with them, but from
the railroad depots and docks a boy might easily have left home
for good to try his fortune in the West, as so many disgruntled
New England emigrants were then doing.

In connection with her instructions on interior décor, Mrs.
Stowe repeatedly contrasts the "cold," "correct" parlor to the
warm, cheerful one. The cold one repels people, both visitors and
members of the family; whereas, the warm rooms always connote
affectionate families and comfort. The import of this distinction
is further evident in her commendations of those natural decora-
tive elements, sunshine, plants, and flowers. The avuncular narrator of the "House and Home" series, Chris Crowfield, explains
the connection between beautiful flowers and virtuous sentiments:

'I can tell you what your mother puts into her plants,' said I,—
'just what she has put into her children, and all her other home-
things,—her *heart*. She loves them; she lives in them; she has in
herself a plant-life and a plant-sympathy. She feels for them as if
she herself were a plant; she anticipates their wants,—always remembers them without an effort, and so the care flows to them
daily and hourly. She hardly knows when she does the things that
make them grow, but she gives them a minute a hundred times
a day. She moves this nearer the glass,—draws that back,—detects
some thief of a worm on one,—digs at the root of another, to see
why it droops,—washes these leaves and sprinkles those,—waters,
and refrains from watering, all with the habitual care of love.' [22]

Thus, the presence of healthy plants in the parlor connotes a
special quality of soul in the inhabitants of the house, the quality
of devoted loving care of a woman for her child, the quality
which makes mothers emblems of pure Christian charity.

A further analogue between the domestic scene and the higher
life is defined in the paper on "Home Religion," where the
reader is urged to practice regular family Bible reading and
prayer. "The little one thus learns that his father has a Father

in heaven, and that the earthly life he is living is only a sacrament and emblem,—a type of the eternal life which infolds it, and of more lasting relations there." [23] Thus, the child is educated in knowledge of, and a right relation to, eternal truth by his childhood experience in the home. The metaphor of God as a father to his children is made literal by Mrs. Stowe who argues that the child will come to know God by understanding the relation between his own father and himself and then, when he gets older, translating this into a higher key. Similarly, the "self-sacrificing love" of the mother becomes an emblem to the child of the same quality in Christ.

At this point, having returned to the religious preoccupation which underlies Mrs. Stowe's commentaries on the home and women's place in it, it is time to say that, all along, Mrs. Stowe has been lecturing on 'the taste of the angels.' As Ruskin had said, "What we *like* determines what we are, and is the sign of what we are; and to teach taste is inevitably to form character." It is on the basis of this proposition that we can understand the efficacy in the home made beautiful by plants, harmonious colors in the parlor and appropriate pictures on the walls of a moral influence on the characters of the children. The love of natural beauty which lies behind the mother's success as a grower of plants, the love of health and harmony reflected in the objects of the décor, will condition the children to love the moral good which these objects reflect. In acquiring a taste for the good, the children will become good; moral education, even religious faith, begin at home, at least in the beautiful home.

Mrs. Stowe's interest in the relation between beauty and goodness, however, goes farther than questions of dress and decoration. Ruskin's famous dictum, "Taste is not only a part and an index of morality;—it is the ONLY morality," is echoed by Mrs. Stowe in a letter to her husband in which she reports that she has been reading the novels of Eugène Sue. Mrs. Stowe makes the Ruskinian distinction between cleverness and moral merit in a work of art. The novels of Eugène Sue "are powerful but *stiflingly* devoid of 'moral principle'—Their atmosphere like the air of a forcing house at 90—or so—tho full of luscious blossoms & fruit makes you stagger & pant for air—not the first discernment of any boundaries between right & wrong in them—talented—so much the worse!" [24] In "Traffic" Ruskin tells the Yorkshiremen the same thing.

I don't mean by 'good,' clever—or learned—or difficult in the doing. Take a picture by Teniers, of sots quarreling over their dice; it is an entirely clever picture; so clever that nothing in its kind has ever been done to equal it; but it is also an entirely base and evil picture. It is an expression of delight in the prolonged contemplation of a vile thing, and delight in that is an 'unmannered,' or 'immoral' quality. It is 'bad taste' in the profoundest sense—it is the taste of the devils. On the other hand, a picture of Titian's, or a Greek statue, or a Greek coin, or a Turner landscape, expresses delight in the perpetual contemplation of a good and perfect thing. That is an entirely moral quality—it is the taste of the angels. [25]

Ruskin concludes his argument in this passage in a way which, turning as it does on the word "love," clarifies some of the meanings Mrs. Stowe too attaches to that word. Speaking of the "taste of the angels," Ruskin continues,

And all delight in fine art, and all love of it, resolve themselves into simple love of that which deserves love. That deserving is the quality which we call 'loveliness'—. . . . What we *like* determines what we *are,* and is the sign of what we are; and to teach taste is inevitably to form character. [26]

The subjects we have been discussing thus far—the matter of good taste in dress and home decoration and the influence of beauty and harmony in the home on the moral character of the children—are, of course, very much a part of the woman question. One of the arguments put forward by advocates of women's suffrage was that women ought to be "liberated" from the degrading conditions of housework. Women confined to the home became drudges. Mrs. Stowe considers housework anything but degrading; on the contrary, it is exalted. Some people also argued that woman was a delicate creature whose proper role was the creation of elegance—fine dress, needlepoint, —and the attention to Culture. Mrs. Stowe replies that "America is the only country where . . . there is a class of women who may be described as *ladies* who do their own work." [27]

We have heard much lately of the restricted sphere of woman. . . . It may be true that there are many women far too great, too wise, too high, for mere housekeeping. But where is the woman in any way too great, or too high, or too wise, to spend herself in creating a home? What can any woman make diviner, higher, better?

To this rhetorical question the answer is:

From such homes go forth all heroisms, all inspirations, all great deeds. Such mothers and such homes have made heroes and martyrs, faithful unto death, who have given their precious lives to us during these three years of our agony! [28]

"Such mothers" are those truly consecrated to their domestic calling.

On the question of the vote for women, Mrs. Stowe observed: "The woman question of our day, as I understand it, is this: Shall MOTHERHOOD ever be felt in the public administration of the affairs of state?" "The state," she asserted, "is nothing more nor less than a collection of families, and what would be good or bad for the individual family would be good or bad for the state." [29] Mrs. Stowe's sister, Catharine Beecher, so scorned the suffragettes' hostility to women's true role in the home and in school that she opposed even giving women the vote. She thought it would make them abandon their true calling and become "masculine." Harriet, although she agreed with everything Catharine said about the sacredness of women's role in the home and in schools, did not consider the vote a menace. As far as she could see, "a state is but an association of families . . . and there is no reason why sister, wife, and mother should be more powerless in the state than in the home." [30] Her main interest was to bring about a correct appreciation of women's role in both spheres; after all, if people could be brought to see the true dignity of home and mother, they would be glad enough to honor the woman's voice in public affairs. She hoped to show that all the clamor over the vote, as a necessary first step to greater freedom for women, was misguided. Women already had a great many opportunities if only they knew it. They need not choose between the life of a pale flower and the way of raucous political agitation; they might instead pursue their tastes and talents in any one of a number of suitable and useful professions and spare themselves the indignities of battle. Above all, they could live up to their "calling"—she also called it their "profession"—in the home.

Once again, we can turn to Ruskin for clarification of Mrs. Stowe's many statements about the religious significance of "home."

64. Now, you feel, as I say this to you—I know you feel—as if I were trying to take away the honour of your churches. Not so; I am trying to prove to you the honour of your houses and your hills; not that the Church is not sacred—but that the whole Earth is. I would have you feel what careless, what constant, what infectious sin there is in all modes of thought, whereby in calling your churches only 'holy,' you call your hearths and homes 'profane'; and have separated yourselves from the heathen by casting all your household gods to the ground, instead of recognizing, in the places of their many and feeble Lares, the presence of your One and Mighty Lord and Lar. [31]

The passage is a perfect statement of Mrs. Stowe's own views on the sanctity of home. She resisted, as Ruskin does here, the inference "that the Church is not sacred"; she insisted as he does that "the whole Earth is." Mrs. Stowe maintained her own loyalty to the faith, yet it is not hard to understand why others might gradually take her arguments to mean that their One and Mighty Lord and Lar required no further honor or obedience than was offered up in the daily rites of the affectionate, earnest, beautiful home. In order to rescue the moral order of American society from the threat of the declining influence of the churches and clergy and from the prospect of an atheistic worldliness, Mrs. Stowe sought to shore up the faith by emphasizing the sanctity of home. It was not her intention to create a new faith, but rather to renew the old. Yet in retrospect, we can probably say that it was the new emphasis on the harmony and beauty of home and on the beautiful sentiments of family love that led eventually in a secular direction. Ironically, Mrs. Stowe gave comfort to those for whom churchgoing was to become increasingly a matter of social decorum, and for whom the business of life was business and the beauties and comforts of home needed and held no religious significance whatever.

Turning from the *Atlantic* essays to the three social novels of this period, one asks whether Mrs. Stowe began these novels simply in order more persuasively to accomplish the purposes of the essays. This is very likely the case. Mrs. Stowe had never questioned the suitability of the novel to the purposes of propaganda. The novel's highest service was to show real life, be it the patriarchal institution or the heroic colonial society. To give pleasure was not the point; the novelist ought to give true enlightenment, to record real life and to instruct the reader about its meaning. In turning now to the novel as a more spacious and dramatic vehicle than the essay for carrying her message to her public, Mrs. Stowe was acting true to character.

The essays themselves have a fictional form. They are presented as recollections and reports by the friendly Chris Crowfield of conversations and events among his own family and acquaintances. The first of the three novels, *Pink and White Tyranny,* is the other side of the coin, a novel always on the verge of turning into a lecture. *Pink and White Tyranny* is unsuccessful because it is so similar to the "House and Home" and "Chimney-Corner" articles. Whole scenes will consist of nothing but edifying conversations on the role of women or home decoration. These subjects recur in the other two social novels, but they are handled more skillfully there and do not arrest or obliterate the movement of the story. *Pink and White Tyranny* is in itself something of a halfway house between the domestic "lectures" (as she occasionally called them) of the "House and Home" and "Chimney-Corner" and the form of *My Wife and I* and *We and Our Neighbors,* novels which can properly be said to belong to the genre of social fiction.

My use of the terms "social fiction" and "novel of manners" or "social novel" does not rest on any theoretical or critical definition but simply refers to the kind of novel which became so prominent in this country in the latter part of the nineteenth century and of which the chief practitioners were Howells and James and later writers such as Edith Wharton. One thinks of Mrs. Stowe's friend Dr. Holmes, of DeForest, and of others of the period. I will take Howells as the measure of the type, but will refer more to his actual practice than to his critical theory.

The distinguishing feature of the social novel is its subject matter. Although the novel as a form has usually been taken to be the literary genre preeminently concerned with society, especially middle class society, the social novel or novel of manners specifically directs its attention to the situations and customs, thoughts and styles of ordinary middle class people. Typically, such a novel is set in a city or town, or if in the country then on the estates of city-dwellers. It is set in parlors and clubs, normally private places of one sort or another, although it could and did, as Howells proved despite James's later doubts about the accessibility to the artist of life Downtown, enter the offices of businessmen and represent them at their mysterious work. The central characters are typically decent, middle class people engaged in trade or the professions. The stance of the author is that of the chronicler of "real life."

For Howells the real was the common, the usual, the daily or routine affairs of ordinary men and women. Mrs. Stowe, although she had neither the wish nor the self-restraint to confine the events in her novels to these affairs, always acknowledged that they were, indeed, reality. She indulged herself and her audience in sentimental extravagance and romantic adventure, but she always knew the difference between these things and how most people really lived. Not infrequently, as in the aside on St. Clare's unhappy romance quoted earlier, she quite pointedly emphasized the difference. As we have seen, too, she was given to sardonic comparisons between the way things happened in novels, or the way people liked to imagine life, and the way things really happened. Thus she readily, although not deliberately, as there is no direct evidence that she read Howells or thought about his views, sympathized with the realistic mode as he understood it. She assumed that "novels are to be considered true pictures of real life." [32]

There are two interesting, perhaps remarkable, things about the way Mrs. Stowe conceived and represented the real life of the postwar commercial society in fiction. One is her grasp, before Howells portrayed it or James analyzed it, of the pattern I have already mentioned, the separation of the 'worlds' of Uptown and Downtown not only geographically but, more important, culturally and psychologically. This separation proved to be fundamental to later novelists' understanding of American life in the later nineteenth century. The sphere of Culture, Uptown, tended to be dominated by women; the men associated with it were often regarded as 'effeminate.' Commerce, the province of men and the sphere of what James called the "serious male interest," was supposedly beyond the pale for women and when they did enter it, as they began doing in the latter part of the century, working women were identified as tough, aggressive, 'masculine,' even, frequently, unmarriageable. The stresses which this division between business and Culture wrought in the family are particularly characteristic of the pattern, and often the focus of much of the novelist's interest, as they were of Howells's in *Silas Lapham*. In thus anticipating a pattern so basic to the novelist's later and continuing understanding of the reality she sought to portray in these two novels, Mrs. Stowe repeats the accomplishment of *Dred;* she shows a power of imagination to articulate the underlying or essential drama at the heart of that part of real life she has chosen to represent in fiction.

*My Wife and I,* which is much the best of Mrs. Stowe's social fiction, invites comparison with *The Rise of Silas Lapham* in several ways. First, Mr. Van Arsdel is very much like Howells's hero.

Mr. Van Arsdel was . . . a simple, quiet, silent man, not knowing or caring a bodle about any of the wonders of art and luxury with which his womankind have surrounded him, and not pretending in the least to comprehend them; but quietly indulgent to the tastes and whims of wife and daughters, of whose superior culture he is secretly not a little proud. In Wall Street Mr. Van Arsdel held up his head, and found much to say; his air was Napoleonic; in short, *there* his foot was on his native heath. But in his own house, among Cuyps, and Frères, and Rembrandts, and Fra Angelicos, with a set of polyglot daughters who spake with tongues, he walked softly, and expressed himself with humility, like a sensible man.[33]

We need not question too closely the probability of his having a collection of Rembrandts, or Fra Angelicos either; we may also make allowances for Van Arsdel's supposed total indifference to his wife and daughters. What is striking is the presentation of the honest, energetic businessman, full of vigor and confidence downtown and of slightly awkward demeanor amidst the refinements and Culture of the women's world uptown. It is exactly the antithesis James defines in the preface to *Daisy Miller,* and the one which Howells portrays in the life of Silas Lapham.

Again, like Lapham, Mr. Van Arsdel is originally from the country, in fact from New Hampshire. "Mr. Van Arsdel, like many of our merchant princes, had come from a rural district, and an early experience of the hard and frugal life of a farm." [34] Mrs. Stowe is doubtless right that, in the postwar era as the population was shifting in increasing numbers from agriculture to business and industry, such a biography was fairly typical. For her, as for Howells, however, the combination has an ethical significance. The businessman is untutored in the ways of commercial chicanery; his head is high, his hands are clean, and his soul is innocent of the corruptions of the Gilded Age. Moreover, like Howells, Mrs. Stowe has her businessman fail at the end of the book. He is not given any role in his own misfortune, which is simply the result of the workings of the mysterious stock market, much less is he given any moral dilemma as is Lapham. It is nevertheless interesting that Mrs. Stowe also feels more comfortable with her businessman when she can have him rise above his loss. James too preferred to cleanse his businessmen by removing them from the countinghouse.

Mr. Van Arsdel's daughters resemble Lapham's too. The daughter Eva is like Irene, sweet, pretty, demure and exactly the young lady that the society generally, and potential suitors particularly, seemed to require. Ida Van Arsdel, like Penelope Lapham, is a bluestocking, intellectual and independent and noticeably less pretty than her sister. Ida shows the hand of her creator, however, in being a crusader. In a letter to a former teacher, Mrs. Courtney, Ida declares, " '. . . I mean to do something worthy of a Christian woman before I die, and to open a path through which weaker women shall walk out of this morass of fashion-slavery and subjection where they flounder now.' " Ida is also conspicuously high-minded about religion. She will not succumb to the blandishments of churches which she thinks have become too worldly, and hence unChristian. For her part, as she writes to Mrs. Courtney, " 'I shall keep the spirit of Christ, though I wander from the letter' " [35] and Mrs. Stowe was now quite willing to concede that this might be the better way.

Mrs. Stowe's concern with the state of American Christianity was a lifelong preoccupation and does set her apart from other novelists. She never seems to have found conversational polemics on the controversial subjects of the day out of place in a novel, and these social novels are all well stocked with topical opinions and arguments. In Howells and James such matters are often implicit, but Mrs. Stowe had no qualms about speaking directly to her readers.

By and large, the position on social issues in *My Wife and I* and *We and Our Neighbors* repeats or expands that of the *Atlantic* articles. On the woman question particularly, we are given the familiar arguments. As a result of the failure of the society, including women, to recognize the sanctity of home and the proper role of women therein as the authors and models of virtue and moral strength, women feel undervalued and patronized. Consequently they take to "fashion-slavery" in defense of their femininity against the attacks of those who say they are, or ought to be, like men. These women should be made to see the true nobility of their function and influence in the home. Replying to her husband's praise of her domestic furnishings, Eva Van Arsdel, now married to the narrator, Harry Henderson, says,

'And that is what I call woman's genius. To make life beautiful; to keep down and out of sight the hard, dry, prosaic side, and keep up the poetry—that is my idea of our "mission." I think woman ought to be what Hawthorne calls "the Artist of the Beautiful." ' [36]

There is also a good deal of talk about prostitution in *My Wife and I* and *We and Our Neighbors*. This is another way in which society is said to injure woman by failing to recognize her true role and denying her self-respect. Especially in *We and Our Neighbors,* much time is given to discussion of brothels and to the situation of a fallen young woman who is rescued from prostitution by Eva and Harry Henderson. The rescue is carried out on the assumption that the trouble with this girl is that she is demoralized and hence allows herself to be exploited; the remedy is to show her their own happy home and to demonstrate to her, and to the reader, the dignity of her own appointed "profession" in the home. It might be said, as it has been of her attitude toward the Negroes in *Uncle Tom's Cabin,*[37] that Mrs. Stowe is herself excessively patronizing towards the victims of prostitution and intemperance in her social novels. This judgment is not altogether fair. True, she weeps for them and melodramatically pictures them as helpless wretches. And yet she genuinely pities these people, whom she considers victims of society's misunderstanding and abuse, and she honestly believes that they can be "redeemed" and made over into happy, prosperous middle class citizens. Her contempt here, as elsewhere, is always reserved for the educated influential groups whom she thinks responsible, either directly or by neglect, for the loss of these despairing souls from the Kingdom of God.

It must be said that some of the commentary on topical issues in these two books is strictly personal and arises from private grievances which troubled Mrs. Stowe at the time. First, the attack on the Suffrage movement, although it rehearses the old complaint that its leaders deny women's true calling in the home, runs into venomous caricature in *My Wife and I* in the character of Miss Audacia Dangyereyes, who marches into Harry Henderson's quiet office one day and pounces on him: " 'Now, look here, bub!' " she says to the tender young journalist.

'. . . I'm just a-going to prove to you, in five minutes, that you've been writing about what you don't know anything about. . . . Well, here comes a woman to your room who *takes* her rights, practically, and does just what a man would do. I claim my right to smoke if I please, and to drink if I please; and to come up into your room and make you a call, and have a good time with you, if I please, and tell you that I like your looks, as I do. . . .

I don't stand on ceremony. Just look on me as another fellow.' [38]

Miss Dangyereyes is definitely a spiteful portrait of Miss Victoria Woodhull from whom, together with such of her colleagues as Mrs. Stanton, who is similarly parodied in the character of Mrs. Stella Cerulean in the same novel, Mrs. Stowe had much to fear in 1871 on behalf of her brother Henry Ward Beecher. The author does what she can in these two novels, especially the first, to destroy the reputation of those women, notably Miss Woodhull, on whose authority the reading public had recently been informed of the adulterous guilt of Henry Ward Beecher.

In addition to such direct assaults on their credibility, Mrs. Stowe tried to vitiate the effect of their story by repeated attacks on the credibility of the public press itself. In the words of Jim Fellows, a sophisticated and cynical friend of Henderson,

'we want to sell our papers, and these folks want hot hash with their breakfast every morning, and somebody has got to be served up. . . . I tell you, now, what this great American people wants is a semi-occasional row about something, no matter what; a murder, or a revival, or a great preacher. . . .' [39]

The attack on the scandal-mongering of the press is, however, as much in self-defense as it is a protest against the mistreatment of her brother. *My Wife and I* follows by one year the famous journalistic adventure of Mrs. Stowe herself in publishing first an article and then her notorious book on the subject of Byron's incest. From the first appearance of the article in '69, the vilification of Mrs. Stowe in the press, English and American, had been terrific. Two years later she was still fighting back when she had

Mr. Bolton, himself a seasoned newspaperman, inform young Henderson that

'English criticism has generally been unappreciative and brutal; it has dissected butterflies and humming-birds with mallet and cleaver —witness the review that murdered Keats, and witness in the letters of Charlotte Brontë the perplexity into which sensitive, conscientious genius was thrown by obstreperous, conflicting criticism.' [40]

The merits of the Byron controversy will be discussed in the next chapter. Here, it is necessary only to point out that among the general range of opinions on public questions in the social novels, one finds views that stem from the author's private quarrels. That Mrs. Stowe did not hesitate to include remarks of this kind is further evidence that her writing was always highly personal, and had been so from the beginning, and that she never felt artistically compromised or embarrassed on this account.

Indeed, some of her best moments also originate in personal experience. For example, her treatment of Bolton's alcoholism in *My Wife and I* is a far cry from the shrill speeches on temperance one is apt to find in her earlier writing, and the reason is that her son Fred, apparently as a result of a shell wound in the head at the Battle of Gettysburg, had become an alcoholic. The family said and even wrote very little on the subject, but the evidence seems clear that, perhaps partly for its benefits as an anesthetic, Fred was often ill from overdrinking. Mrs. Stowe's sympathy for him becomes Bolton's eloquence in his own defense. The chapter called "A New Opening" includes a letter from Bolton to Harry Henderson in which Bolton describes his past life and his struggle with alcoholism in terms that are both subtle and moving. As in the account in *The Minister's Wooing* of Mrs. Marvyn's desperate grief at the news of the death of her son by drowning, Mrs. Stowe's personal experience could give her fiction moments of great emotional force and psychological truthfulness. Indeed, one might argue that the rigorous self-discipline of Howells or James in this respect, and the consequent absence in their work of this kind of directly spoken personal passion, was not always an unmixed blessing or a clear victory for art.

In considering Mrs. Stowe's handling of the city setting—the scenes in trolleys, in Central Park, in the drawing rooms or on the country lawns of the Van Arsdels and their friends—one is tempted to say that the main difference between her presentation and that of her more accomplished successors is Mrs. Stowe's relatively complete lack of artistic self-consciousness. Without, as it were, a moment's hesitation, she will do up a great country weekend, beginning with a ferry trip up the Hudson and including an elaborate croquet match on the lawn as if it were a matter of course for the novelist to go where she pleased. Similarly, she thinks nothing of stepping into the office of Henderson or Bolton and of discussing the affairs of men in the mysterious realm of commerce. James's term "naif" is more apt than ever when applied to Mrs. Stowe's social novels, especially when one compares them to James's own diffidence; yet one might say that she often makes up in the vitality of the sheer realized scene itself what she loses in formal subtlety and by her lack of awareness of a novelist's complex limitations.

The second and, to me, more interesting way in which Mrs. Stowe's social novels show a remarkably profound understanding of the 'real life' they describe is in their delineation of the character who later becomes the observer or center-of-consciousness in the story. Here Mrs. Stowe, without much experience in the genre of social fiction, makes an important innovation. She seems somehow to know that the form, and also perhaps the subject itself, demand such a character. Mrs. Stowe makes him a simple first-person narrator, but this superficial difference need not obscure the essential similarity between Harry Henderson and, for example, March in *A Hazard of New Fortunes* or Strether in *The Ambassadors*.

Mrs. Stowe had used first-person narration intermittently since *The Mayflower* of 1845, but all of her main work before the war was written in the third person. Christopher Crowfield is really the first important example of the first-person narrator in her work, and Horace Holyoke of *Oldtown Folks* is the most important before Henderson. In some ways they are quite similar. *Oldtown Folks* is told by Holyoke as an old man looking back on events and passions in a mood of retrospective good humor. He makes it quite clear that he is no longer emotionally sensitive to the passions of past moments. His tone is like that of father recollecting for his children's curiosity the people and dramas of long ago. In *Oldtown Folks* we are not constantly brought back to the fireside scene and so the presence of the old man is often lost in the story he is telling, but we are reminded of the narrator's point of view often enough to make it truly affect our attitude toward the story as a whole. In the intervening two years between *Oldtown Folks* and *My Wife and I,* the fatherly aspect of the first-person narrator faded considerably. Harry Henderson is a much younger man than Crowfield or Holyoke, but, like them, he is detached. So important is this emotional distance between the narrator and the events he describes that when, in the happy ending of *My Wife and I,* Henderson marries Eva Van Arsdel, he forfeits his role. *We and Our Neighbors* is told in the third person.

Henderson, like Crowfield or Holyoke, is presented as the pseudonymous author in *My Wife and I,* yet like his predecessors he is exposed by Mrs. Stowe who put her own name on the title page. Evidently there is no question of a real pseudonym intended to conceal the true identity of the author. The whole arrangement is only a somewhat clumsy shift permitting Mrs. Stowe to introduce a new kind of character into her work and, thus, an element of awkwardness, since the role of the first-person narrator is essentially as demanding as is that of March or Strether. All three have free access to the inner circles of the society about them, yet none is a member of these circles. Each originates from in or around Boston—Henderson describes himself as "a plain Yankee boy from the mountains of New Hampshire, and at present a citizen of New York"—and each finds himself in a more or less strange metropolis, Paris or New York, which impresses him with its glamor and with a certain sinister complexity. All three are thus both observers and interpreters of the scene to which, from a simpler past, they have come.

The device of the first-person narrator is crude only in that the importance of this figure is to provide a single detached, yet informed, sensibility through whom the story is unified and interpreted. As Howells and James later discovered, the observer's experience could quite as easily be reported by the author as by himself. The former method is just as convincing, and it would seem to allow the author greater freedom to manage the shadings of his characters' responses to one another and to control the plot itself. James was especially adamant about the formal disadvantages of the first-person technique. Nevertheless, despite Mrs. Stowe's cruder conception and clumsier treatment of the observer figure, she had found, by the time of her second social novel, that he was a pivotal character, necessary to the genre and to the fictional realization of the subject.

It is an interesting fact that the figure of the detached observer, who participates in the action of the story but does not belong to—is not born in or identified with—the society where that action takes place, who is in a sense not only the spokesman for the author but also the author's emissary to the scene of events, is peculiar if not unique to the American social novel. As Lionel Trilling says in his essay on the *Princess Casamassima,* the figure of 'the young man from the provinces' removed to the metropolis is thoroughly familiar in nineteenth-century European novels. Trilling cites the work of Stendhal, Balzac, Flaubert, Dickens, Tolstoi and Dostoevski.[41] But the figure of the

observer, who both involves himself in the action and inter-
prets it to the reader, the figure, that is, of whom Harry Henderson is the prototype and Strether the celebrated archetype, is
not to be found in European novels. This particular blend is
peculiar to the American novel.

Why, one can only speculate. As so often in inquiries about
the novel, the most provocative and most thorough analyses are
to be heard from Henry James. In the Preface to *Daisy Miller,*
and speaking of course of the postwar period, James argues
that the great problem for the American novelist lies in the dis-
sonances and divisions within American society—especially those
between the separate and contrasting worlds of Uptown and
Downtown—and in the inaccessibility to the artist of the vital
center of American postwar enterprise, Downtown. London or
Paris may have been mysterious to James, but New York was a
complete enigma. Debarred from "the office," the artist was then
restricted to "the salon" where the Uptown women were busy
with French chefs and dancing masters and where, the artist
uneasily remarked, nothing important ever happened. James
describes the hopeful novelist as Micawber, fixed on a coign of
vantage from which, cock his head which way he will, he cannot observe the truth about the commercial society around him.

The feeling of being estranged, and thus apart from a particularly unintelligible spectacle of human life, need not be
defined only in terms of the frustrating confrontation with
Downtown or the world of business. It could equally well apply
to the feeling, which would of course be shared by the immigrants themselves, of hearing and seeing the tremendous number and variety of foreign immigrants who poured into the
American coastal cities after the Civil War. It could apply to
the country boy coming to work in the town as well. In every
case, although one part of the total scene might be familiar
and some people might be like oneself, many, and perhaps the
majority, would be strangers, not in the sense of being unknown

but more because one felt they could not be known. In other words, when Harry Henderson referred to New York as "the world of observers and observed" he was not unduly self-conscious or metaphorical.

The position of the observer, in, but not of, the society around him, is also that of the traveller abroad. Indeed, he may feel more natural in the role when he is abroad. Here again historical fact supports the literary impression. Henry James and Henry Adams, who knew himself an observer from outside even in Boston, were not the only travellers abroad in the postwar decades. Mrs. Stowe well knew that the audience for whom she wrote the *Atlantic* articles was filled with people who either had been or were anxious to see Europe for themselves. Increasingly in this period, the American tourist was to be seen, and observed, in the cathedrals, museums, shops and resorts of the Old World.

Thus, wherever he went at home or abroad in the latter nineteenth century, the American was likely to find himself an observer of a somewhat alien scene. The stance was historically and psychologically true to his experience. It was a stance, too, which the artist may have found not only natural, but even necessary. Gone were the days when the great spectacle of American diversity was a splendid manifestation of our expansive destiny. It was all too appallingly true. We really were divided, by the war, and by the events of the postwar decades. We were not merely diverse; we were actually different from each other in a hundred ways. The novelist who set himself to write about this society needed to be cautious and subtle and serious. He needed, moreover, the figure of the observer and interpreter, not only to express his own relation to the society around him, but also to give artistic unity to his work. The first-person narrator is not only an intermediary between the reader and the world of the novel; he is also a unifying thread, binding together the several scenes and characters he visits into a single fictional action. Henderson is an integrating figure.

For James, the first-person technique was still too loose and too weak to accomplish a satisfactory formal unity. For his more demanding purposes it was not enough to follow in the footsteps of a single observer. One had to enter his mind. This was because what was needed was not only, or even primarily, a relationship between the outward parts of his experience. One needed intellectual and imaginative coherence; one needed the integrity of a single, comprehending sensibility. Certainly Mrs. Stowe's conception of the novel was far less sophisticated. It is all the more surprising, really, that she should have recognized the importance of the observer, that she should, however casually, have invented him.

In conclusion, I should like not only to admit, but even to emphasize the obvious: postwar American society held for Mrs. Stowe no very great significance, and her writings about it, both the essays and the novels, hold for the reader of her work today no very great fascination. The truth is that the polemics, although they show the interesting and significant shift from evangelical to genteel, cultivated sentiment and from revivalist theology to virtually none at all, are not as eloquent as were Mrs. Stowe's arguments against slavery or her dramatic recreation of heroic colonial New England. The social novels, from the merely artistic point of view, are not impressive. The observer figure is interesting to see in this early, more or less prototypical form, to students of the history of literary ideas, but certainly Howells and James and Henry Adams were the ones that made significant artistic use of the observer. Thus, while a study of Mrs. Stowe as a writer of fiction and of history must include this part of her work, the conclusion one tends to draw from an examination such as I have undertaken in this chapter is that Mrs. Stowe was not deeply stirred by the manners or even the morals of the postwar parlor or office and that she was not moved by the woman question as she had been earlier by slavery, and as she continued to be by the heroic New England past.

There was, however, one subject that did engage Mrs. Stowe during this period as fully and passionately as she had ever been moved before and that subject was the disclosure to her by her friend Lady Byron of Lord Byron's relationship—the two women called it incest—to his half sister, Augusta Leigh. All Mrs. Stowe's appreciation for genteel goodness and benevolence found focus in her admiration for Lady Byron. Moreover, all Mrs. Stowe's much older and deeper concern for the victims of "glacial" Calvinism and political oppression saw, and had always seen in Byron, a profoundly kindred spirit. With her article for the *Atlantic* in 1869 on the subject of Byron's incest and consequent "moral monstrosity," Mrs. Stowe was again inspired, possessed by a vision, embarked on a literary errand for the Lord.

CHAPTER 6

# Byron

Late in the summer of 1869, *Macmillan's Magazine* in England and the *Atlantic* here published an article by Harriet Beecher Stowe entitled "The True Story of Lady Byron's Life." By indirect but nevertheless unmistakable implication, it gave to the world for the first time the story of Byron's incestuous relationship with his half-sister, Augusta Leigh. One year later, in 1870, Mrs. Stowe retold the story at length, with copious documentation and appendices, in her book, *Lady Byron Vindicated*.

One might well wonder what moved Mrs. Stowe to write the story. Her immediate motive in the writing of the article was to rectify the outrage done to the memory of Lady Byron by the memoir, published earlier in the summer, of Byron's well-known mistress, the Countess Guiccioli.[1] The portrait in *My Recollections of Lord Byron* of the sensitive genius hounded into exile and an early grave by the unfeeling selfishness of his wife, although scarcely a fresh picture by the year 1869, seems to have struck Lady Byron's American friend with the force of a diabolic visitation. Once again the scribe of the Lord felt herself summoned to take up her pen in a holy cause. No amount of caution from husband, publisher, or friends could dissuade her from setting the truth upon the ledger of history. Mrs. Stowe forbade dispute over the rightness of publishing the story to such an extent that, in commenting on the manuscript which she had sent him, Oliver Wendell Holmes was obliged to use the utmost tact in persuading her to modify even her most egregious statements. He writes with a courtesy the more generous for its desperate purpose: "In an argument it is as well not to make an unnecessary assertion. . . . An argument should avoid superlatives. They *look* as if the writer was given to overstatement." He cites several examples from the manuscript and proposes specific revisions, masking what can only have been his horror in the language of the detached critic and legal advisor, but finally he permits himself to remark, "Favored among women you are to be chosen by both sexes as worthy to hold their hearts in your hand and turn them inside out!" [2] Friendship could go no farther.

In retrospect, one marvels at Mrs. Stowe's audacity, despite the claims of injury upon the memory of a dead friend. The Guiccioli book contained nothing either new or at all sensational to which such an answer might be appropriate. Nonetheless, it is instructive to consider the merits of Mrs. Stowe's professed motives. She considered the *Recollections* an offense by an aging, obscene courtesan against a woman who was not only her own friend, but a Lady, a wronged wife and mother, a woman of sublime benevolence. It is entirely false to suppose that Mrs. Stowe wrote out of a desire to boast of her friendship with Lady Byron. Certainly she was proud of it, and saved the letters she had from Lady Byron, and doubtless cherished the appreciative response of her American listeners when the great name was spoken. Yet Mrs. Stowe was a very famous woman in 1869, admired as an author both here and abroad, and accustomed by her three trips to the Continent to the acquaintance and to some extent the confidence of people of title and fame. She was herself a celebrity. Ironically, it was the story of Lady Byron which destroyed her public reputation. Although Mrs. Stowe was not deterred by the risk of provoking a controversy, she had anticipated only a mild outcry. When a fury against her broke out in the press, it merely increased her zeal. After a slight hesitation in the hope the storm would abate, she set to work on the book-length account.

In Mrs. Stowe's eyes, the outrage against Lady Byron had been more than personal calumny. It had been an attack on all the ideals she most dearly loved. One has only to notice the way in which she speaks of Lady Byron to observe that, for Mrs. Stowe, all the virtues of home, pure womanhood, self-sacrificing motherhood, and charity to the down-trodden clustered about the image of her friend. One strongly suspects that the two women were in fact kindred spirits in righteousness.

The method of *Lady Byron Vindicated* is to elaborate and contrast two moral portraits, those of Byron and his wife. Sec-ondarily, the book contrasts the portrait of Lady Byron as Mrs. Stowe knew her to be with the picture painted of her by Byron's friends. Similarly, although not so categorically distinct, two portraits of Byron are presented, that of the suffering genius and that of the "moral monster." Following Mrs. Stowe's stated object in telling the story, we shall consider Lady Byron first.

To her enemies, Lady Byron is "a moral Clytemnestra." To Mrs. Stowe, she is a "saint," martyred by the man who, with all the cunning of his genius, defends himself by the claim that her heartless goodness martyred him. It is an issue between angels and devils, with the devils putting on the cloak of innocence in order to slander the truly innocent, and the angel suffering in silence rather than take justified revenge against those who in-sist that her virtue is a cruel sham. The angels and devils shall both be revealed in their true colors at the Last Judgment. In the meanwhile, Truth shall not fail of a defender. "And, first, why have I made this disclosure at all? *To this I answer briefly, because I considered it my duty to make it.*" [3]

She had not always so considered it. Mrs. Stowe first met Lady Byron in 1853. They had liked each other and corresponded. When Mrs. Stowe returned to England in the summer of 1856, she saw her friend again; this time she found her ill and bed-ridden, urging visits to the sickroom.

'I *will* be indebted to you for our meeting, as I am barely able to leave my room. It is not a time for small personalities, if they could ever exist with *you;* and, dressed or undressed, I shall hope to see you after two o'clock.' [4]

Wilson further relates that "During the August days following, their intimacy grew like a yeast-culture in a warm medium." [5] Eventually, in early November, came the great day of confidence. Mrs. Stowe and her sister Mary Perkins had been to lunch with Lady Byron. Leaving Mary with two other guests, Lady Byron invited Harriet to a private conference which lasted into the early evening and in the course of which Lady Byron told the story of her separation from Lord Byron. I quote Wilson's account.

When she came to the "true cause" of her separation from Lord Byron, Lady Byron did not mince words. She used the word *incest*. Harriet thought her friend was going to faint after she said this, but Harriet herself did not feel faint. She had heard the story before— from Mrs. Follen. . . .[6]

Lady Byron was not, she told Harriet, exposing the details of her married life with Lord Byron for the mere purpose of imparting scandalous information. She wanted Harriet's advice. Some publishers were about to bring out a cheap edition of the poet's works and in the promotion meant to revive the old story of Byron's having been driven to exile and death by the cold, mercenary heart of his wife. Should that wife keep silent any longer? . . . Then, too, Lady Byron believed that repentance and regeneration continued after death. Could Lord Byron's soul ever find peace, unless the great injustice were righted? [7]

At first Mrs. Stowe wanted to see her friend vindicated, and perhaps Byron's soul saved, at once, but her sister Mary, to whom she repeated the story that night, was so strongly against publishing that, six weeks later, she wrote to Lady Byron urging restraint, or rather, delay. " 'I would say, then, Leave all with some discreet friends, who, after *both* have passed from earth, shall say what was due to *justice.' "* [8] Wilson is careful to mention that Lady Byron did not appoint Harriet Beecher Stowe to the station of "discreet friend" in the case. Apparently, she did not reply to this piece of advice at all.

In the article in the *Atlantic* Mrs. Stowe made no reference to her confidential interview with Lady Byron or to the fact that she had heard the story from so intimate a source. Even now it is difficult to understand either the article or the book without knowledge of the close friendship between the two women and of the particular fact that Mrs. Stowe had heard the incest story from Lady Byron herself. We must also remember that Mrs. Stowe never doubted the veracity of her friend's account, nor did she consider whether, forty years later, Lady Byron might not have nurtured and distorted the unhappy incidents leading to her separation from Byron. Mrs. Stowe was absolutely certain, and on good grounds, that the story was true. Moreover, she seems to have expected that some day, when both had died, it would be publicly told. In 1869 her immediate motive for publishing was the conspiracy of silence, as she imagined it, to which those of Lady Byron's English friends, who should more properly have been the ones to speak out against la Guiccioli, had committed themselves. She fully expected cries of scandal to be raised against her, but we may imagine what the author of *Uncle Tom's Cabin* might have thought on that score: the louder the cries, the more truly had the book hit its mark and the more heroic a service had its author performed. These, then, are the circumstances of the publication of Mrs. Stowe's article and of *Lady Byron Vindicated*. The causes lie deeper.

The *Recollections* of the despised Guiccioli had befouled the memory of the purest of women—"a slug on the petals of a damask rose!" [9] in Wilson's sympathetic words. And it is the woman question with which Mrs. Stowe begins. Byron and his iconoclastic partisans, among them the poet Thomas Moore to whom Byron left his memoirs, blasphemed against women. "For Lady Byron, Moore had simply the respect that a commoner has for a lady of rank, and a good deal of the feeling that seems to underlie all English literature,—that it is no matter what becomes of the woman when the man's story is to be told." [10] Indeed, "one would suppose that the usual moral laws that regulate English family life had been specially repealed in his favor." [11] As a result, "Literature has never yet seen the instance of a person, of Lady Byron's rank in life, placed before the world in a position more humiliating to womanly dignity, or wounding to womanly delicacy." [12] Never has such treatment been so wholly undeserved.

Mrs. Stowe next turns to the true nobility of Lady Byron, in whose defense she quotes from an article in the *Atlantic* by Harriet Martineau. After her separation from Byron, writes Miss Martineau,

'Her life, thenceforth, was one of unremitting bounty to society, administered with as much skill and prudence as benevolence. She lived in retirement, changing her abode frequently; partly for the benefit of her child's education and the promotion of her benevolent schemes, and partly from a restlessness which was one of the few signs of injury received from the spoiling of associations with *home*. . . . Years ago, it was said far and wide that Lady Byron was doing more good than anybody else in England; and it was difficult to imagine how anybody could do more. . . . She has sent out tribes of boys and girls into life fit to do their part there with skill and credit and comfort. Perhaps it is a still more important consideration, that scores of teachers and trainers have been led into their vocation, and duly prepared for it, by what they saw and learned in her schools.' [13]

Miss Martineau here provides an exact inventory of the virtues which Mrs. Stowe repeatedly extolls in her own "House and

Home" and "Chimney-Corner" articles. Mrs. Stowe had discovered these virtues herself in Lady Byron. In defending the
wronged woman, she was defending the whole system of moral
models and axioms which she long and urgently advocated not
only in these pieces but elsewhere in her writing as well. What
particularly enraged her about Byron and his supporters was
not merely that they ignored these virtues but that they ridi-
culed them. The attack on Mrs. Grundy hit no one more squarely
than it did Mrs. Stowe.

Considering the impeccable virtue of Lady Byron's character
and benevolent deeds and the unthinkable wickedness of Byron's
mockery of that goodness, Mrs. Stowe confidently invites the
reader to choose between the two. "We have simply to ask the
reader whether a life like this was not the best, the noblest answer
that a woman could make to a doubting world." [14] Unfortunately,
Mrs. Stowe never understood what those doubts were in every
case. She was unaware that people might willingly acknowledge
the pious virtues of Lady Byron and yet doubt the ultimate moral
merit of these virtues. She supposed that only a mind depraved
to a rare and exquisite degree could harbor such doubts. Her
book would banish them forever from rational minds.

She was, however, aware of the dangers of silence, and she
paused over the difficulties Lady Byron might have created for
herself in refusing to give complete court testimony towards a
divorce, and in her subsequent refusals, even after Byron's death,
to speak publicly in her own defense.

All this time, she lost sympathy daily by being silent. The world will
embrace those who court it; it will patronize those who seek its
favor; it will make parties for those who seek to make parties: but
for the often accused who do not speak, who make no confidants
and no parties, the world soon loses sympathy.[15]

The world is easily duped by sensation-mongers. The virtuous
often suffer for their delicacy in refusing to inflame scandal by

replying to it. The innocent often prefer to take blame upon themselves if protest would injure another. Silence is imprudent, yet considered in this light it is not, as some may suppose, a cloak for guilt, a sign of fear of exposure; rather it is the sign of true selflessness. Moreover, should anyone attempt to speak out in defense of the silent sufferer, that person too will invite scorn and persecution. In *Lady Byron Vindicated,* Mrs. Stowe, still sore from the abuse her *Atlantic* article brought upon her, defined her own role as champion of despised virtue and bearer of bad news to Byron's deluded but adoring public as "the severest act of self-sacrifice that one friend can perform for another, and the most solemn and difficult tribute to justice that a human being can be called upon to render." [16] Mrs. Stowe had always loved a martyr. In 1870 she felt the mantle clinging to her own shoulders.

As Mrs. Stowe was writing the vindication of her noble friend across the seas, events in Brooklyn were bringing the cause of scandalous calumny against the innocent nearer to home. It was in 1870 that the stirrings of rumor first became audible in New York that Henry Ward Beecher, the famous pastor of Plymouth Church, had been guilty of an adulterous liaison with one of his parishioners, the wife of his good friend Theodore Tilton. Mrs. Stowe's favorite brother was alarmed to the point of considering suicide.[17] The news had reached the ears of some of the most prominent leaders of the woman's Suffrage movement against which and even against whom both Henry Ward and Harriet had publicly spoken. The most dangerous were Victoria Woodhull and Tennessee Claflin, but there were also Mrs. Stanton and Susan B. Anthony to fear, women of known courage who had known grievances against Henry Ward Beecher and his sister.[18] As it happened, these ugly rumors, mounting to sensational public charges and extended private intrigue, festered for half a decade before Henry Ward was finally brought to court on a charge of adultery. Nevertheless, it is certain that Mrs. Stowe was aware of her brother's distress almost from the first. It is also certain that she believed in his innocence until her dying day. Throughout the years of his ordeal, Mrs. Stowe considered her dearest brother the victim of vile slander. She considered him a blessed martyr, a description to which of course he agreed. Although the Beecher-Tilton controversy has no direct relation to Mrs. Stowe's quarrel with Byron, we may simply assume that, coming to her attention when it did, it heightened her dedication to the cause of a person of such rare nobility of soul and purity of heart that he or she was incomprehensible to a wicked world and hence persecuted by it. Both Henry Ward Beecher and Lady Byron were called frauds, Henry Ward for violating the seventh commandment and Lady Byron for concealing beneath the semblance of Christian charity an inhuman coldness and cruelty.

Thus, in addition to her doubtless sincere distress over the Guiccioli book, Mrs. Stowe's passionate defense of Lady Byron owed a great deal to her devotion to the principles for which this woman stood. Moreover, the perception of a deeply kindred sympathy was not all on the part of Mrs. Stowe. Lady Byron recognized their common convictions to such an extent that, speaking of Byron on that famous afternoon when she confided the true cause of the separation, she said to Mrs. Stowe, "'I think *you* could have understood him.'" [19] Be that as it may, the two women understood him in much the same way.

Among the many descriptions of Lady Byron in the *Atlantic* article there is a statement which fits its author almost as well as its subject: "Lady Byron, though slight and almost infantine in her bodily presence, had the soul, not only of an angelic woman, but of a strong, reasoning man." [20] Mrs. Stowe was physically very small, and despite her Victorian reticences on many occasions, her voice often carried with it a bluntness and aggressive, argumentative toughness that seems quite masculine. The word "angelic" was taken as the highest flattery by both women. Not least of their shared attributes is that they both fell in love with Byron.

The poet was read and honored in the Beecher household during his lifetime and mourned at his death. When Lyman Beecher heard the news from Missolonghi he exclaimed, " 'Byron is dead—*gone!* . . . Oh, I'm sorry. I did hope he would live to do something for Christ. What a harp he might have swept!' " Beecher sees a mighty force, gone awry. " 'Oh, if Byron could only have talked with Taylor and me, it might have got him out of his troubles!' " [21] As events had unfolded, however, Byron's superior capacity had perhaps resulted in blacker damnation. Beecher preached a sermon the next Sunday in which he took especial care to point this lesson to the poet's admirers. On this occasion Mrs. Stowe's father " 'began with an account of Byron, his genius, wonderful gifts, and then went on to his want of virtue, and his want of true religion, and finally described a lost soul, and the spirit of Byron going off, wandering in the blackness of darkness forever!' " [22] Mrs. Stowe was thirteen years old when she heard these words. They did not make her love Byron the less.

Indeed, Byron is the single greatest literary and imaginative influence on the writings of Harriet Beecher Stowe, and this despite her very considerable debt to Scott and, somewhat less, to Dickens. The importance to us of Byron's importance for her is to suggest a general corrective to our way of looking at the major literature of Mrs. Stowe's generation. We have always acknowledged the popularity of Byron in this country in the nineteenth century, but we have tended to consider Wordsworth the most important of the English Romantic poets for American writers. Because Wordsworth made Nature central, and because not only our writers of the first rank—Emerson, Thoreau, Whitman—but also American political orators moved by the mythology of "Nature's Nation" and "Manifest Destiny" concentrated so heavily on Nature, we have concluded that

Wordsworth was the virtual progenitor of American Romanticism, much as Locke was of the Constitution. The centrality of Byron for Mrs. Stowe raises the question of his significance for her major literary contemporaries as well, a question to which some tentative answers can be given by reflecting on the reasons for, or sources of, Byron's interest for Mrs. Stowe.

In some ways the Byronic elements in Mrs. Stowe's writing are thoroughly commonplace, and perhaps more common to what we now regard as popular (that is, inferior) fiction than to the work of her 'great' contemporaries. One of the figures most often imitated from Byron at this time was the dashing young man, a figure who comes mainly from the early tales and of whom one could take as prototype this description of Lara:

> Light was his form, and darkly delicate
> That brow whereon his native sun had sate,
> But had not marr'd, though in his beams he grew,
> The cheek where oft the unbidden blush shone through;
> Yet not such blush as mounts when health would show
> All the heart's hue in that delighted glow;
> But 'twas a hectic tint of secret care
> That for a burning moment fever'd there;
> And the wild sparkle of his eye seem'd caught
> From high, and lighten'd with electric thought,
> Though its black orb those long, low lashes' fringe
> Had temper'd with a melancholy tinge.[23]
>
> Canto I, xxvi

Both Harry Percival in *Oldtown Folks* and James Marvyn in *The Minister's Wooing* are conspicuous examples of this youthful romantic figure as Mrs. Stowe draws him. She describes James Marvyn as having a "fine athletic figure . . . a sort of easy, dashing, and confident air . . . a high forehead shaded by rings of the blackest hair, a keen, dark eye, a firm and determined mouth, gave the impression of one who had engaged to do battle with life, not only with a will, but with shrewdness and ability." [24] Harry Percival is similar in appearance, and more definitely melancholy of soul. Moses Pennel in *The Pearl of Orr's Island* is the same sort of beautiful, sensitive, finely adventurous young man.

Although it is applied to a different context, one cannot overlook the passage from *Childe Harold's Pilgrimage* which precedes chapter thirty-five of *Uncle Tom's Cabin*. The chapter deals with the susceptibility of Legree to Cassy's psychic torments, a susceptibility which originates in Legree's hypersensitivity to the stings of his own guilty conscience.

> And slight, withal, may be the things that bring
> Back on the heart the weight which it would fling
> Aside forever; it may be a sound,
> A flower, the wind, the ocean, which shall wound,—
> Striking the electric chain wherewith we're darkly bound. [25]
>
> Canto IV, xxiii

It is precisely in this chapter that Sambo delivers to Legree the piece of paper from around Tom's neck, and in which Legree, on seeing the lock of Eva's hair, is reminded of his mother and his betrayal of her piety. The attempt of the heart to rid itself of its burden is thwarted by the power of feeling, a power beyond voluntary control. The passage apparently expressed for Mrs. Stowe a psychological truth of great significance, an essence of the inner life of one who had sought, as she knew Byron had, to fling aside the weight of the "glacial" Calvinistic creed. Nobody, she felt, spoke of this private struggle more accurately or profoundly than he did.

Further insight into the workings of the sensitive soul and its response to the created universe was to be had from *Manfred*. Mrs. Stowe's affinity with Byron in this respect is unmistakable in her description of Dred, the savage lord of the Great Dismal

Swamp. She is speaking of Dred's reading of the Bible and its inspiration of his errand of wrath, yet her language is far more Byronic than biblical.

As the mind, looking on the great volume of nature, sees there a reflection of its own internal passions, and seizes on that in it which sympathizes with itself,—as the fierce and savage soul delights in the roar of torrents, the thunder of avalanches, and the whirl of ocean storms,—so is it in the great answering volume of revelation. . . .

In the vast solitudes which he daily traversed, these things entered deep into his soul.[26]

The tempestuous soul that finds its elemental counterpart in the enormous forces and images of nature, the isolated spirit gratified by vast solitudes as it could never be by mortal comforts, is splendidly Byronic. Among writers of Mrs. Stowe's generation no aspect of Byron's work is more potent than the sublime recognition of the darkest inner self in the awful symbolism of nature.

The Byronic villain is a familiar figure in nineteenth-century literature, and he was especially significant for Mrs. Stowe. Beginning with Simon Legree, she created a long line of such characters in her fiction, the last and greatest of these being her portrait of Byron himself, the "moral monster" of Lady Byron's history.

Legree is an extremely crude and incomplete version of the type as Mrs. Stowe later developed him. He is ugly and bestial and drunkenly possessed by demons. Yet he anticipates the Byronic villain of the later fiction in that he is motivated in wickedness by an inner wound, the pain of a guilty conscience. Having been nurtured in childhood by the loving Christian faith of his mother, he commits himself to inexorable self-destruction by denying that within himself which he can never erase or forget. Mrs. Stowe's first novel also pictures one other

such character, Augustine St. Clare, who, although not an active
agent of evil, is yet helpless to resist it because he too suffers
from a divided soul. In describing this sensitive soul, estranged
from its own better nature, Mrs. Stowe explicitly compares St.
Clare to "Moore, Byron and Goethe."

In *The Minister's Wooing*, published only seven years later
than *Uncle Tom's Cabin*, we find the figure of the Byronic villain in full flower in the person of Aaron Burr. Here is the
worldly, sophisticate of fine sensibility and great charm who suffers from an exquisite secret guilt because he has denied the
religion of his grandfather Edwards. We remember Mrs. Stowe's
analysis of his private agony. "Nobody knew the true better
than Burr. He knew the godlike and the pure. He had felt its
beauty and its force to the very depths of his being." Mrs. Stowe
is totally in sympathy with his rejection of the cruel theology of
Edwardsean Calvinism, yet the consequences for Burr have been
disastrous. In rejecting that religion of his childhood he has rejected all Christian faith and has bound himself into one of
"those interior crises in which a man is convulsed with the
struggle of two natures, the godlike and the demoniac, and from
which he must pass out more wholly to the dominion of the one
or the other." [27] This analysis entirely concurs with Lyman
Beecher's twenty-five years earlier of the sources of Byron's
magnificent damnation.

Ellery Davenport in *Oldtown Folks* is cast in the same mold
and caught in exactly the same dilemma. Even more than Burr,
Davenport is a scoffer, and Mrs. Stowe explains his cunning
perversity by yet another story of passionate inner conflict: "He
had not been able entirely to rid himself of a belief in what he
hated." In consequence, "Ellery Davenport was at war with
himself, at war with the traditions of his ancestry . . . he took
a perverse pleasure in making his position good by brilliancy of
wit and grace of manner which few could resist." "Such men,"
observes Mrs. Stowe, "are not, of course, villains; but, if they

ever should happen to wish to become so, their nature gives them every facility." [28] Byron, she thought, did so wish.

Mrs. Stowe's lifelong belief that the poet was plagued by a divided soul was not fantastic. Marchand's recent biography documents such a struggle very clearly and shows too that Lady Byron was engaged on the side of the angels even before they were married. Marchand quotes a letter from Byron to Anne Isabella Milbanke, the future Lady Byron, in response to her accusation that he had been avoiding the subject of religion in his letters to her.

'I was bred in Scotland among Calvinists in the first part of my life which gave me a dislike to that persuasion. . . . I believe doubtless in God, and should be happy to be convinced of much more. If I do not at present place implicit faith in tradition and revelation of any human creed, I hope it is not from want of reverence for the Creator but the created. . . .' [29]

Speaking in more general terms, Sir Herbert Grierson states the view that "Byron is the only English romantic poet who has a sense of sin, and is, therefore, capable of a tragic view of life." [30] It is not, in fact, a controversial point that Byron was troubled by the Calvinism of his youth and that he rebelled against it. To this extent Mrs. Stowe is on firm and common ground.

Her notion about the psychological effects of this rebellion on Byron's conscience and his consequent guilty compulsion towards wickedness, although not particularly subtle or original, was a more personal perception. It came, I am certain, out of her own religious experience. Mrs. Stowe had been taught in her own childhood a catechism approximately the same as Byron's in its definitions of basic Calvinist dogma. I have said elsewhere that she never, as an adult, believed in the five tenets of Calvinism. She had, however, been taught them as a child, and she always was aware that she did not believe them. Mrs. Stowe did not reject Calvinism, if one means by that term that she disavowed a position which she had once professed. She did reject it in the sense of deliberately and explicitly stating her differences with it. Moreover, although there can be no question about her repudiation of Calvinist theology in favor of the liberalized, evangelical position, there is sufficient evidence in her admiration of Edwards's "poetic" appreciations of Sarah Pierpont and Phoebe Bartlett and in her picture of his sublimely wicked rationality to show, even without the further picture of the heroic generations of the seventeenth century, that Mrs. Stowe saw the thing she had rejected as potentially heroic. She did, without a doubt, feel within herself those promptings which she ascribes to her Byronic villains and those periods of distress when the heart secretly longs for that which the mind has rejected, when the religion of one's grandfathers steals upon the imagination with an unwelcome grandeur. Throughout the New England novels one notices this uneasy combination of anger at Edwards and of relief at having escaped the perils of the old "glacial" system, and, on the other hand, repeated insistence that the world in which she lived had never witnessed a nobility comparable to that of the colonial past. Thus the succession of villains whose wickedness is defined as a flight from the memory of goodness and the example of the past all owe a debt to Mrs. Stowe's private recognition of her own spiritual autobiography.

If we accept her analysis of the inner conflict of these characters as resulting in the need to escape into diabolic self-defense, we might picture Mrs. Stowe's response as proceeding exactly in the other direction. Where Burr and Davenport and most of all Byron himself in her analysis escape guilt by revelling in splendid wickedness, Mrs. Stowe makes her own escape into splendid goodness. She becomes an exhibitionist of virtue, a crusader for good causes, a public prophetess on the side of the angels. The hyperbole of her language of sacrifice and love and the intensity of her pronouncements on the value of everything from cheap jewelry to Unitarian theology express a moralistic preoccupation which was often just short of hysterical. Whether or not one could say that Victorian righteousness commonly had an element of compensation for religious doubt, it is demonstrable that Mrs. Stowe herself had a passion for self-vindication. In the article on Byron, she was to a large extent merely naive in thinking that the majority of her readers would respond with grateful horror to the truth she was responsible to bring before them, but, in the book itself, she was certainly engaged in her own vindication as much as in that of Lady Byron.

When Mrs. Stowe saw in the splendid Lord Byron a fabulous mirror of her own conflict (and in herself a kinship with that troubled spirit), she was looking at a drama of thought and of conscience that had been very private to her. And yet she probably also recognized that in various forms this same conflict had been going forward in the innermost thoughts and consciences of many, perhaps a majority, of her generation. Certainly it had profoundly affected Emerson. Hawthorne too, although he had as little sympathy with their theology as did Emerson, saw the old Puritans with an evident respect and not only admired them for subscribing to what Emerson had called "the high tragic school" but also chose to set much of his work in the colonial period where the moral 'lights and shadows' were of a sufficient intensity.

A further reason for Mrs. Stowe's long and intimate involvement with Byron's life and work lay in his reputation as a renowned champion of liberty. The hero of the Greek war for independence was never far from the mind of the Lord's chosen foe of Negro slavery. When Mrs. Stowe visited Europe in the eighteen-fifties and heard in some detail about the mid-century revolutions and libertarian movements there, she quickly concluded that the American struggle against slavery was part of a single manifestation of the Western conscience. Moreover, whereas for Wordsworth and many like him in England, the

failure of the French Revolution had produced a complete dis-
illusionment with all politics and a program of retreat from its
treacheries, Byron's active commitment to the Greek cause was
much more congenial to Americans, whose Revolution had not
failed and whose politics were still vastly optimistic. Not only
Mrs. Stowe but also a great many of her generation saw America
as the natural sympathizer with democratic causes throughout
Europe.

A final attraction in Mrs. Stowe's passionate involvement with
Byron was, quite simply, his romanticism. I have mentioned her
imitation of his dashing young hero, and her emulation of the
proud, tumultuous, solitary giant in her warrior of the Great
Dismal Swamp. And I have suggested that from the time of
*Uncle Tom's Cabin* onwards she found in Byron's words the
most perfect expression she knew of the power of feeling, "the
chain wherewith we're darkly bound." To a lesser extent the
angelic heroine herself was formed from an appreciation of Byron's
young women, among whom Aurora Raby was always a declared favorite of Mrs. Stowe. Beyond these particulars, however,
lies the whole world of drama and passion which Byron created
and within which Mrs. Stowe had privately dwelt all her life. He
seemed, especially to readers on whom his wit was very largely
lost, to have rendered life itself into a fabulous poem, and to
have rendered his own life, however monstrous, into a spectacle
of cosmic significance. Despite her sardonic asides about the
paltry make-believe of novels, her scorn for the "music of oars
and chiming waters" and her staunch allegiance to "the flat,
bare, oozy tide-mud" of reality in preference to what I have
called the false comforts of literature, Mrs. Stowe adored Byron's
romance. She saw in him a kindred spirit for whom novels and
even poems might serve up small pleasures but for whom life
itself, real life, was tragic drama and high romance.

In *The Minister's Wooing,* in a chapter entitled "In Defense
of Romance," Mrs. Stowe gives her own definition of the genre.

'This is the victory that overcometh the world,'—to learn to be fat and tranquil, to have warm fires and good dinners, to hang your hat on the same peg at the same hour every day, to sleep soundly all night, and never to trouble your head with a thought or imagining beyond. . . .

All prosaic, and all bitter, disenchanted people talk as if poets and novelists *made* romance. They do,—just as much as craters make volcanoes, no more. . . .

Let us look up in fear and reverence and say, 'GOD is the great maker of romance. . . . HE, who strung the great harp of Existence with all its wild and wonderful and manifold chords, and attuned them to one another,—HE is the great Poet of life.' Every impulse of beauty, of heroism, and every craving for purer love, fairer perfection, nobler type and style of being than that which closes like a prison-house around us, in the dim, daily walk of life, is God's breath, God's impulse. . . .

The scoffing spirit that laughs at romance is an apple of the Devil's own handing from the bitter tree of knowledge; it opens the eyes only to see eternal nakedness.[31]

When Byron scoffed she found him diabolic. Yet to her mind no one ever apprehended the romance of the created world itself with more brilliance. Her anathemas against him in *Lady Byron Vindicated* are the protests of a betrayed lover, not of a dispassionate critic. What she secretly wanted was, like her father, to "have got him out of his troubles." In 1870, she did not believe that it was too late. Privately she conceived her own role in writing the book to be identical to Lady Byron's wifely part, which she had once described to her friend.

. . . I often think that God called you to this beautiful and terrible ministry when He suffered you to link your destiny with one so strangely gifted, so fearfully tempted, and that the reward which is to meet you, when you enter within the veil, where you must soon pass, will be to see the angel, once chained and defiled within him, set free from sin and glorified, and so know that to you it has been given, by your life of love and faith, to accomplish this glorious change.[32]

The two women were so alike that they even had the same aspirations for the life hereafter. Thus when Mrs. Stowe conceived it to be her "duty" to write the book and to reveal to the deluded world that Byron had indeed been every bit as wicked as Lucifer himself—for so incest surely seemed to her—the rewards of telling the truth were not to be in this world alone but, even more gloriously, above, where it might be the giant still languished in chains, awaiting the last purgings of his earthly sins.

As in most lovers' quarrels, Mrs. Stowe's exposé rings with all the intensity of her original love. It was Byron himself who insisted upon the kinship between love and hate, and the two grew together in Mrs. Stowe's breast. Her final portrait is of a man who had fallen like Lucifer from the proud heights of his own genius, the best of God's creatures become the worst, become monstrous. Her image is, quite naturally, the sinful idol, the Golden Calf.

This Byron, whom they all knew to be obscene beyond what even their most drunken tolerance could at first endure; this man, whose foul license *spoke out* what most men conceal from mere respect to the decent instincts of humanity . . . turned out a perfected idol for a world longing for one, as the Israelites longed for the calf of Horeb.

The image was to be invested with deceitful glories and shifting haloes,—admitted faults spoken of as peculiarities of sacred origin,—and the world given to understand that no common rule or measure could apply to such an undoubtedly divine production; and so the hearts of men were to be wrung with pity for his sorrows as the yearning pain of a god, and with anger at his injuries as sacrilege on the sacredness of genius, till they were ready to cast themselves at his feet, and adore.[33]

Perhaps the world is always longing for gods and idols to adore, but Mrs. Stowe's world, divested of its traditional faith by the rationalists of the eighteenth century and subsequently

further shaken by inward doubts and melancholy, was excep-
tionally so moved. Mrs. Stowe is one conspicuous spokesman,
partly because of her clerical background, for the sense of loss
which Emerson too expressed of that "high tragic school" of
men who had once seen life, real life, in truly cosmic and heroic
proportions, and who, in the very recognition of their probable
eternal damnation, lived as giants and warriors in the struggle
between God and the devil. As the nineteenth century waned
and religious doubt and controversy grew ever more painful,
Byron's voice became more compelling, not because he gave an
answer to doubt but because he dramatically acknowledged it.
And because, following his rejection of Calvinism, he had created
for himself a relation to the universe as passionate and as dangerous as anything the old creed demanded. This was the chief
need and goal of the imaginative lives of sensitive American
readers and writers of Mrs. Stowe's time.

Speaking in a kind of literary shorthand, we could summarize
this way: Mrs. Stowe's generation in America was at first attracted to Wordsworthian Romanticism, a beatific substitute for
Christianity which offered a healing of man's soul and of his
relation to his world, to nature. Later many of them came to
express a Byronic defiance of Christian ideals, a sense of sickness, of secret wounds, of mutilation rather than healing and
health. They move from a vision of wholeness to images of
destruction; from praise of beneficial solitude and bountiful
freedom to a concern for isolation, Narcissism, megalomania.
Emerson shifts from the systematic wholeness and categorical
optimism of *Nature* (1836) to a doctrine of struggle between
the human will and the natural environment, "fate," circum-
stance. Melville's early novels abound in a playful, innocent
exultation in the natural world, and their satire is not bitter; in
a few years he had turned to the sufferings and blasphemies of
Ahab and to the disastrous experience of Pierre, his incest, his
vision of the mutilated Titan. Hawthorne's "short, quick prob-

ings at the very axis of reality," for which Melville so memorably
praised him, became almost inevitably and often in spite of himself, according to Hawthorne's testimony, researches into darkness, "positively a hell-fired story" as he said of *The Scarlet Letter*. The Byronic sense of sin and conflict and tragedy in real
life, and his ability to project his own magnificent damnation
not only into his poetry but onto the stage of European history
as well, were ultimately of vastly more importance for Americans
of the first half of the nineteenth century than were Wordsworth's consolations and pieties, issued from the remote tran-
quility of the English lakes.

From the tearful excesses of the sentimental heroines of popular melodrama—the little Evas and little Nells and their ilk—to
the grim destinies of Ahab, Ethan Brand, and Dred, the American reader was presented with a drama of sorrow and tragedy in
which, however, men were still heroic and life was still passionate and awesome. However glib Mrs. Stowe may often
become about home and mother and however tedious her lessons
on love and goodness, her recognition of that "moral monster,"
Lord Byron, as the creator of the most authentic record of the
soul in torment and as the heroic actor in one of the most noble
struggles of the history of their time, shows that her understanding of life, real life, was, like his, a perception of spiritual
tragedy. Her literary contemporaries mostly came to share this
view, if they did not hold it from the start. The history of her
country, as she foresaw, was to record national tragedy in civil
war. Mindful of a Calvinist past and not altogether despairing
of the promises of rationalist idealism embodied in the traditions
of the Revolution, Mrs. Stowe and her generation witnessed a
hellish civil war and its murderous aftermath. Whether one
thought back to the angry God of Edwards, or remembered the
hell-fire oratory of early nineteenth-century revivalism; whether
he thought of the fratricidal war or the assassination of Lincoln and the failure of Reconstruction,—whether, that is, he

was condemned by the standards of the past in which he might no longer believe or threatened by what might prove to be the greater evils of the future—an American of Mrs. Stowe's generation was likely to have experienced the "terror of damnation." Byron understood that experience.

When James Baldwin used the phrase in 1949 he meant to tell us how much he despised *Uncle Tom's Cabin.* He accuses Mrs. Stowe of hypocrisy, of disguising a "merciless doctrine" according to which black men are evil and diabolical by a pretense of virtuous concern for their welfare (somewhat the same complaint as was made against Lady Byron). According to Baldwin, Mrs. Stowe would really like to annihilate the blacks but cannot and so must "purify" them in order to "embrace" them. "Tom, therefore, her only black man, has been robbed of his humanity and divested of his sex," by which Baldwin means to show the true atrocity lurking beneath Mrs. Stowe's pretended benevolence. Although she is often offensively condescending toward the Negroes, Mrs. Stowe's concern for them is not insincere. The fact, for instance, that Uncle Tom is not sexually predatory, that he is full of "paternal" love, is certainly not regarded by Mrs. Stowe, as it is by Baldwin, as a sign of Tom's weakness, much less of his inhumanity.

We need not however accept Baldwin's analysis of Mrs. Stowe's hypocrisy in order to appreciate his description of the evangelical imagination populated by angels and devils.

*Uncle Tom's Cabin,* then, is activated by what might be called a theological terror, the terror of damnation; and the spirit that breathes in this book, hot, self-righteous, fearful, is not different from that spirit of medieval times which sought to exorcise evil by burning witches; and is not different from that terror which activates a lynch mob.[34]

What Baldwin, more keenly than most of Mrs. Stowe's twentieth-century readers, recognizes, is the evangelical temper of the novel, its emotional extravagance. Ironically, he attacks Mrs. Stowe in the same extravagant language as that he mistrusts.

If we need, as Baldwin argues, a new reality today (and our need is not less twenty years after the case was originally made), a reality which does not compel the black man to "redeem his humanity" or the white perpetually to expiate his "guilt," then we need a new clarity about our language. Words which once belonged to religious discourse and which Mrs. Stowe still understood in that sense—"redeem," "guilt," "damnation," "national sins"—have never been more widely used than they are today. These words and concepts, although they have surely been repeated to the point of abuse, have not lost their meaning but rather, having acquired too many loaded meanings, have settled like a miasma over the American mind, obscuring whatever new possibilities we might otherwise find or create. To see clearly our way, to understand truly our past, is always our endeavor. It is important that we should know what is the value to us today of the best work of Harriet Beecher Stowe.

# Notes

CHAPTER I

1. Harriet Beecher Stowe, *Uncle Tom's Cabin; or, Life Among the Lowly* (Garden City, n.d.), p. 507. All references to *Uncle Tom's Cabin* will be to this edition, which reprints the original text of 1852. The title of the novel will be abbreviated as *UTC*.

2. Stowe, *UTC*, p. 185.

3. *Ibid.*, p. 155.

4. *Ibid.*, p. 157.

5. *Ibid.*, p. 160.

6. *Ibid.*, p. 271.

7. *Ibid.*, pp. 136–37.

8. *Ibid.*, pp. 97–98.

9. *Ibid.*, p. 111.

10. Cf. Edmund Wilson, *Patriotic Gore* (New York, 1962), ch. XI.

11. Quoted in Lyman Beecher Stowe, *Saints Sinners and Beechers* (Indianapolis, 1934), p. 36.

12. Stowe, *UTC*, p. 304.

13. *Ibid.*, p. 255.

14. *Ibid.*, pp. 335–38.

15. *Ibid.*, p. 482.

16. Letter from Charles Kingsley to Harriet Beecher Stowe, 12 August, 1852. Beecher-Stowe Collection, Schlesinger Library, Radcliffe College. All letters from this collection are quoted by permission of Mr. David B. Stowe and the Schlesinger Library.

17. Charles H. Foster, *The Rungless Ladder* (Durham, N.C., 1954), p. 48.

18. If Kingsley appreciated her realism, George Gilfillan of "The Spasmodic School" sympathized with her piety. Gilfillan

described his meeting with Mrs. Stowe as "a moment of the Millennium sent before its time." Quoted by Jerome Hamilton Buckley, *The Victorian Temper* (Cambridge, Mass., 1951), p. 50.

19. Letter from Charles Kingsley to Harriet Beecher Stowe, 12 August, 1852. Beecher-Stowe Collection, Schlesinger Library, Radcliffe College.

20. Stowe, *UTC*, p. 23.

21. *Ibid.*, p. 93.

22. *Ibid.*, pp. 100–103.

23. *Ibid.*, p. 149.

24. *Ibid.*, pp. 353–54.

25. *Ibid.*, p. 365.

26. *Ibid.*, p. 368.

27. *Ibid.*, p. 370.

28. *Ibid.*, p. 423.

29. *Ibid.*, p. 430.

30. *Ibid.*, p. 430.

31. *Ibid.*, p. 431.

32. *Ibid.*, p. 455.

33. *Ibid.*, p. 487.

34. *Ibid.*, p. 488.

35. *Ibid.*, p. 488.

36. *Ibid.*, p. 485.

37. Cf. H. Richard Niebuhr, *The Kingdom of God in America* (Hamden, Conn., 1956).

CHAPTER 2

1. Harriet Beecher Stowe, *Dred: A Tale of the Great Dismal Swamp*, 2 vols. (Boston, 1896), I, 382–83.

2. *Ibid.*, p. 385.

3. *Ibid.*, p. 395.

4. *Ibid.*, pp. 247–48.

5. *Ibid.*, pp. 263–64.

6. *Ibid.*, p. 470.

7. Stowe, *Dred*, II, 12.

8. *Ibid.*, p. 12.

9. Stowe, *Dred*, I, 264.

10. Milly's story may be found in Stowe, *Dred*, I, 222–29 *passim*.

11. Mary Chesnut's great relief, recorded in her diary, over

Mrs. Stowe's omission of the subject of miscegenation in *Uncle Tom's Cabin* was premature.

12. Stowe, *Dred*, I, 42.

13. *Ibid.*, pp. 249–53 *passim.*

14. Stowe, *Dred*, II, 188.

15. Stowe, *Dred*, I, 250.

CHAPTER 3

1. Stowe, *UTC*, p. 79.

2. *Ibid.*, pp. 187–88.

3. *Ibid.*, pp. 186–87.

4. *Ibid.*, pp. 76–78.

5. *Ibid.*, p. 380.

6. Quoted in Forrest Wilson, *Crusader in Crinoline; The Life of Harriet Beecher Stowe* (Philadelphia, 1941), pp. 259–60.

7. Stowe, *UTC*, p. 510.

8. *Ibid.*, pp. 250–53.

9. *Ibid.*, pp. 253–54.

10. Stowe, *Dred*, I, xiii.

11. *Ibid.*, p. 39.

12. *Ibid.*, p. 4.

13. *Ibid.*, pp. 46–51 *passim.*

14. *Ibid.*, p. 209.

15. All quotations from the camp-meeting are taken from Stowe, *Dred*, I, 304–39.

16. *Ibid.*, p. 292.

CHAPTER 4

1. The four novels, in the order of their hard-cover publication, are: *The Minister's Wooing* (1859); *The Pearl of Orr's Island* (1862); *Oldtown Folks* (1869); *Poganuc People* (1878).

2. Harriet Beecher Stowe, *The Mayflower, and Miscellaneous Writings* (Boston, 1879), p. 40.

3. *Ibid.*, p. 97.

4. *Ibid.*, p. 185.

5. Harriet Beecher Stowe, *Agnes of Sorrento* (Boston, 1896), p. 75.

6. Stowe, *Mayflower*, p. 106.

7. Sarah Orne Jewett, *The Country of the Pointed Firs* (Garden City, 1954), p. 49.

8. Stowe, *Oldtown Folks* (Boston, 1896), II, 76.

9. Stowe, *The Minister's Wooing*, p. 19.

10. Cf. Niebuhr, *The Kingdom of God.*

11. Stowe, *The Minister's Wooing*, p. 66.

12. Harriet Beecher Stowe, *The Pearl of Orr's Island* (Boston, 1896), pp. 40–41.

13. Harriet Beecher Stowe, *Oldtown Folks*, I, 1.

14. Harriet Beecher Stowe, *The Minister's Wooing* (Boston, 1896), p. 1.

15. *Ibid.,* p. 1.

16. *Ibid.,* p. 13.

17. Stowe, *Oldtown Folks,* II, 41.

18. Stowe, *Oldtown Folks,* I, xxiv.

19. William Bradford, *Of Plymouth Plantation 1620–47,* S. E. Morison, ed. (New York, 1952), pp. 61–63 *passim.*

20. The slavery novels do also convey some of Mather's sense of declension from earlier greatness. By allusion to the example of the heroic Revolution and its language of liberty, Mrs. Stowe conducts a Matherish argument against the present falling off from the standards of a nobler past.

21. Stowe, *The Minister's Wooing*, pp. 177–78.

22. Stowe, *Oldtown Folks,* II, 35.

23. *Ibid.,* pp. 92–93.

24. Stowe, *Oldtown Folks,* I, xxiii.

25. Stowe, *The Minister's Wooing*, p. 62.

26. *Ibid.,* p. 18.

27. Stowe, *Oldtown Folks,* I, 428.

28. *Ibid.,* p. 3.

29. *Ibid.,* pp. 3–7 *passim.*

30. *Ibid.,* pp. 6–7.

31. *Ibid.,* pp. 433–34.

32. *Ibid.,* II, 58–61 *passim.*

33. *Ibid.,* I, xxiii–xxiv.

34. *Ibid.,* II, 61.

35. An interesting case in point is the matter of Horace Holyoke's visions. Appropriately enough, since the novel is set in Natick and includes many of Calvin Stowe's stories and reminiscences of his childhood there, the narrator of the novel is subject to visions to

the same remarkable degree as Mrs. Stowe's husband had been and remained all his life. Holyoke's account of his own visions relies entirely on Calvin Stowe's testimony.

36. Letter from Harriet Beecher Stowe to Charlie Stowe, 4 February (1881?). Beecher-Stowe Collection, Schlesinger Library, Radcliffe College.

37. Stowe, *The Minister's Wooing*, pp. 16–17.

38. *Ibid.*, p. 221.

39. *Ibid.*, p. 245.

40. *Ibid.*, p. 247.

41. *Ibid.*, p. 247.

42. *Ibid.*, p. 304.

43. *Ibid.*, pp. 346–47.

44. *Ibid.*, p. 347.

45. *Ibid.*, p. 193.

46. Stowe, *Oldtown Folks*, I, 344.

47. *Ibid.*, p. 344.

48. *Ibid.*, p. 416.

49. *Ibid.*, p. 416.

50. *Ibid.*, p. 417.

51. *Ibid.*, pp. 417–19 *passim.*

52. *Ibid.*, p. 263.

53. *Ibid.*, pp. 85–86 *passim.*

54. Perry Miller, *Errand into the Wilderness* (Cambridge, Mass., 1956), ch. VIII.

55. *Ibid.*, pp. 197–98.

56. Quoted in Miller, *Errand*, pp. 200–201.

57. Stowe, *The Pearl of Orr's Island*, pp. 366–67 *passim.*

58. Stowe, *UTC*, p. 304.

59. *Ibid.*, pp. 176–77.

60. Stowe, *Agnes*, pp. 104–05 *passim.*

61. Stowe, *The Minister's Wooing*, pp. 287–88 *passim.*

62. Stowe, *The Pearl of Orr's Island*, p. 186.

63. Stowe, *Oldtown Folks*, I, 296.

64. *Ibid.*, p. 105.

65. Stowe, *The Pearl of Orr's Island*, p. 193.

66. *Ibid.*, pp. 320–21 *passim.*

67. *Ibid.*, p. 341.

68. *Ibid.*, p. 351.

69. *Ibid.*, pp. 361–62.

70. Stowe, *Oldtown Folks,* I, 151.

71. *Ibid.,* p. 178.

72. *Ibid.,* p. 240.

73. *Ibid.,* pp. 246–47 *passim.*

74. *Ibid.,* p. 249.

75. *Ibid.,* p. 251.

76. Stowe, *Poganuc People* (Boston, 1896), p. 1.

77. *Ibid.,* p. 73.

78. *Ibid.,* p. 177.

79. *Ibid.,* p. 178.

80. The sensitive, secluded young girl, nurturing romantic fantasy from books such as *The Arabian Nights* and known to those around her by a certain idealistic naiveté, is recognizable in the portraiture of Henry James. James eliminates the religious message, and of course modifies her in other ways, but he does imagine Isabel Archer in a lonely office, a product of her own book-nourished fancy as much as of Albany—contrasted in this respect to her sisters—and distinguished by a pure imaginative innocence at once unrealistic and beautiful. James's heroines often fulfill their destinies by self-sacrifice; in this more than anything else they realize Mrs. Stowe's ideal.

81. Stowe, *Poganuc People,* p. 180.

82. *Ibid.,* pp. 204–05.

83. *Ibid.,* pp. 217–18.

84. *Ibid.,* p. 127.

85. *Ibid.,* p. 266.

86. *Ibid.,* p. 139.

CHAPTER 5

1. Harriet Beecher Stowe, *Household Papers and Stories* (Boston, 1896), pp. 436–37. This volume of the collected works includes the two series of articles Mrs. Stowe did for the *Atlantic,* "House and Home Papers" and "The Chimney-Corner." It also includes three additional short pieces, "Our Second Girl," "A Scholar's Adventures in the Country," and "Trials of a Housekeeper." References to all these articles and stories will cite the page numbers in this volume, volume eight, of the collected edition.

2. Stowe, *Household Papers,* pp. 443–45 *passim.*

3. *Ibid.,* pp. 296–97.

4. The stylistic impasse in which Hawthorne found himself during most of the decade before his death in 1864 is painfully clear in Edward H. Davidson's edition of Hawthorne's unfinished romance, *Doctor Grimshawe's Secret* (Cambridge, Mass., 1954). Davidson's text juxtaposes, in their chronological order, the fragments of narrative with the long critical notes Hawthorne stopped to write to himself, in which he expressed his impatience with elements in the story not in themselves very different from earlier successful stories and tales. Davidson has given us a dramatic document from which to study a major artist's imaginative collapse under the strain of the war years.

5. Quoted in Wilson, *Crusader in Crinoline*, p. 289.

6. Cf. Russell Lynes, *The Tastemakers* (New York, 1949) for an entertaining and informative discussion of the journalistic activity in this field, and especially for the relations between the manufacturer, the consumer and the helpful domestic pundit.

7. Letter from Harriet Beecher Stowe to Charlie Stowe, 4 February (1881?). Beecher-Stowe Collection, Schlesinger Library, Radcliffe College.

8. Mrs. Stowe refers to the purchase of the pew in a postscript. Letter from Harriet Beecher Stowe to Hattie and Eliza Stowe, 5 April, 1864. Beecher-Stowe Collection, Schlesinger Library, Radcliffe College.

9. Letter from Harriet Beecher Stowe to Hattie Stowe, Jan.–Feb., 1862. Beecher-Stowe Collection, Schlesinger Library, Radcliffe College.

10. Letter from Harriet Beecher Stowe to Catharine Beecher and Mary Perkins, 1867. Beecher-Stowe Collection, Schlesinger Library, Radcliffe College.

11. Note in Mrs. Stowe's handwriting, no addressee, no date. Beecher-Stowe Collection, Schlesinger Library, Radcliffe College.

12. Horace Bushnell, *Christian Nurture* (New Haven, 1967), pp. 4–7 *passim*.

13. *Ibid.*, p. 4.

14. Cf. Barbara M. Cross, *Horace Bushnell, Minister to a Changing America* (Cambridge, Mass., 1958).

15. Bushnell, *Christian Nurture*, p. 15.

16. Cf. Catharine Beecher, *Common Sense Applied to Religion; or, The Bible and the People* (New York, 1857) and *An Appeal to the People on Behalf of Their Rights as Authorized Interpreters of*

*the Bible* (New York, 1860). *An Appeal* was the second volume of *Common Sense* and was first published in 1859. Compared to the temerity of her older sister, Mrs. Stowe's habitual style of preaching is positively timid.

17. Letter from George Eliot to Harriet Beecher Stowe, 11 July, 1869. Beecher-Stowe Collection, Schlesinger Library, Radcliffe College.

18. Stowe, *Household Papers*, pp. 381–82 *passim.*

19. *Ibid.,* pp. 129–30.

20. *Ibid.,* p. 46.

21. *Ibid.,* p. 31.

22. *Ibid.,* p. 71.

23. *Ibid.,* p. 216.

24. Harriet Beecher Stowe to Calvin Stowe, 19 July, 1844. Beecher-Stowe Collection, Schlesinger Library, Radcliffe College.

25. John Ruskin, *The Crown of Wild Olive,* "Traffic," *The Works of John Ruskin,* eds. E. T. Cook and Alexander Wedderburn (London, 1905), XVIII, 436.

26. *Ibid.*

27. Stowe, *Household Papers,* p. 86.

28. *Ibid.,* pp. 52–53.

29. Stowe, *My Wife and I* (Boston, 1896), p. 36.

30. Stowe, *Household Papers,* p. 139.

31. Ruskin, "Traffic," p. 442.

32. Harriet Beecher Stowe, *My Wife and I* (Boston, 1896), p. 425.

33. *Ibid.,* pp. 194–95.

34. Stowe, *My Wife and I,* p. 396.

35. *Ibid.,* p. 185.

36. *Ibid.,* p. 448.

37. Cf. J. C. Furnas, *Goodbye to Uncle Tom* (New York, 1956) and others. James Baldwin, in his brilliant essay "Everybody's Protest Novel," *Partisan Review,* XVI (1949), 578–85, argues that over *Uncle Tom's Cabin* hangs "the terror of damnation" and that, terrified, Mrs. Stowe hates and fictionally destroys the Negroes whose sufferings she pretends to pity. The terror of damnation does hang over the book, but Baldwin misconstrues its source. He thinks Mrs. Stowe could not distinguish the Prince of Darkness from a human black man.

38. Stowe, *My Wife and I,* pp. 251–52.

39. *Ibid.,* pp. 215–16 *passim.*
40. *Ibid.,* p. 191.
41. Lionel Trilling, *The Liberal Imagination* (Garden City, 1953), pp. 65–96.

CHAPTER 6

1. Doris Langely Moore, in *The Late Lord Byron* (Philadelphia, 1961), p. 454, n. 4, states that "Her article was in the editor's hands before she had seen the book or the reviews." Forrest Wilson, in *Crusader in Crinoline* (Philadelphia, 1941), pp. 535–36, states that she read the Countess Guiccioli's *Recollections* in May, adding that "not more than six weeks elapsed from the time Harriet picked up the Guiccioli book until she had written her long article for the *Atlantic, The True Story of Lady Byron's Life."* Although Mrs. Moore lists Wilson's book in her bibliography, we may doubt that she has carefully studied his evidence. She incorrectly gives the publishing date of *Crusader in Crinoline* as 1902. Moreover, Mrs. Moore, although she contradicts Wilson's testimony by implication in her footnote, does not discuss it, much less refute it, in her own discussion of Mrs. Stowe's book.

2. Letter from Oliver Wendell Holmes to Harriet Beecher Stowe, 4 July, 1869. Beecher-Stowe Collection, Schlesinger Library, Radcliffe College.

3. Harriet Beecher Stowe, *Lady Byron Vindicated* (Boston, 1870), p. 2. For an exactly similar self-justification, see Catharine Beecher, *Truth Stranger Than Fiction* (New York, 1850) wherein the elder Miss Beecher not only publicly "defends" Delia Bacon against charges Miss Bacon wished silenced and forgotten but also prints letters to herself from Delia Bacon which most movingly implore her not to proceed with this public "vindication." Catharine's analysis of the controversy over McWhorter's trial is a melodramatic tale of villains and conspirators and the persecution of an innocent woman.

4. Quoted in Wilson, *Crusader in Crinoline,* p. 423.

5. *Ibid.*

6. Mrs. Follen, a common acquaintance, had also exercised her talents for gossip in telling each woman about the other in the interval between Mrs. Stowe's trips. The fact that she first heard

the story from someone else may have encouraged her to suppose, as she did in 1869, that other persons were keeping culpably silent.

7. Wilson, *Crusader in Crinoline*, p. 428.

8. Quoted in Wilson, *Crusader in Crinoline*, p. 429.

9. Wilson, *Crusader in Crinoline*, p. 535.

10. Stowe, *Lady Byron Vindicated*, pp. 100–01.

11. *Ibid.*, p. 102.

12. *Ibid.*, p. 103.

13. Quoted in Stowe, *Lady Byron Vindicated*, pp. 145–50 *passim.*

14. Stowe, *Lady Byron Vindicated*, p. 152.

15. Stowe, *Lady Byron Vindicated*, pp. 154–55.

16. *Ibid.*, p. 192.

17. Cf. Wilson, *Crusader in Crinoline*, p. 568.

18. See the satirical portraits of the suffragettes in *My Wife and I.*

19. Quoted in Wilson, *Crusader in Crinoline*, p. 428.

20. Stowe, *Lady Byron Vindicated*, p. 434.

21. Quoted in Wilson, *Crusader in Crinoline*, p. 62.

22. Quoted in Wilson, *Crusader in Crinoline*, p. 63.

23. George Gordon, Lord Byron, *Poetical Works* (London, 1967), p. 310.

24. Stowe, *The Minister's Wooing*, p. 25.

25. Stowe, *UTC*, p. 427.

26. Stowe, *Dred*, I, 263–64 *passim.*

27. Stowe, *The Minister's Wooing*, p. 304.

28. Stowe, *Oldtown Folks*, I, 417–19 *passim.*

29. Quoted in Leslie A. Marchand, *Byron, A Biography* (New York, 1957), I, 411.

30. Sir Herbert Grierson, *Essays and Addresses* (London, 1940), pp. 11–12.

31. Stowe, *The Minister's Wooing*, pp. 88–90 *passim.*

32. Harriet Beecher Stowe to Lady Byron, 30 June, 1857. Quoted in *Life and Letters of Harriet Beecher Stowe,* ed. Annie Fields (Boston, 1897), p. 247.

33. Stowe, *Lady Byron Vindicated*, pp. 99–100.

34. James Baldwin, "Everybody's Protest Novel," *Partisan Review*, XVI (1949), 581.

# Index